# the cult
## of the saints

7.95

The Haskell Lectures on History of Religions
New Series, No. 2

Joseph M. Kitagawa, General Editor

# PETER BROWN

# the cult
# of the saints

Its Rise and Function in Latin Christianity

The University of Chicago Press

The University of Chicago Press, Chicago 60637
S C M Press, Ltd., London, WC1B 3QX

**Library of Congress Cataloging in Publication Data**

Brown, Peter Robert Lamont.
  The cult of the saints.

  (Haskell lectures on history of religions; new ser., no. 2)
  Includes bibliographical references and index.
  1. Christian saints—Cult—History—Addresses, essays,
lectures.  I. Title.  II. Series.
BX2333.B74        270.2        80-11210
ISBN 0-226-07621-0 (cloth)
      0-226-07622-9 (paper)

To my parents

# Contents

# Foreword

As Peter Brown notes in the following pages, a sharp distinction between the religious experiences of the elite and the vulgar was a commonplace long before David Hume crystallized it in his *Natural History of Religion*. Such a "two-tiered model" has, in fact, survived to the present day. All too often the significant religious experience of a people is limited to that of its intellectual leadership, while much of the everyday religious activity of the people is relegated to the realm of popular superstition.

But the two-tiered model sounds far less persuasive to us than it did to Hume and his contemporaries. Increasingly scholars are turning their attention to the religious lives of women, the poor, and other groups often omitted by past scholarship. Although some of them bear the tell-tale marks of apologetic writing, many of these works have contributed significantly to our understanding of the wide range of human religious experience. They have helped make comprehensible what was often unknown or, where known, misunderstood. And the best of them have helped us to understand not only the religious phenomena themselves but the ways in

which they arose within and contributed to a particular economic, political, and social situation.

I know no better example of this kind of scholar than the 1978
Haskell Lecturer at the Divinity School of the University of
Chicago. Fortunately for us, this lecturer was Peter Brown. In
addition to his breadth of knowledge, he brought to bear the
careful craftsmanship and felicitous use of the language which
we have come to expect from the author of *Augustine of Hippo*.
The result was an unforgettable week for many of us—
undergraduates, graduate students, and faculty members alike.
As the following pages attest, it was a remarkable achievement
for a number of reasons.

First, he told a marvelous story of the rise of the cult of the
saints. Although he did not set out to prepare an exhaustive
history of this striking development in the late-antique world,
his account in fact told much of that fascinating story—and told
it with great understanding, sympathy, and skill. A number of
graduate students remarked to me that at the beginning of the
five lectures, they had no interest in the cult of the saints at all;
by their conclusion, they had more interest in that subject than
in their own area of research! As told by Peter Brown, it was
indeed a marvelous story.

Second, throughout the lectures, he placed the cult of the
saints artfully within its social, political, economic, and even
architectural context. As he noted, this was a dynamic context
which underwent fundamental alterations between the fourth
and the sixth centuries. The dynamics of the age partly reflected
and partly prepared the way for the increasingly important role
of the cult of the saints in the late antique world.

Finally, it is his picture of this late antique world that made
Brown's lectures so exciting. If not a totally closed book, the
period of late antiquity is for many of us at least very obscure.
But his account of what might appear to be (at least to the
advocate of the two-tiered model) a superstitious fragment provided us with a perspective from which to view in some detail
the rich complexity of the whole late antique world. For that we
remain in his debt.

As a Haskell Lecturer, Peter Brown continued what has been
a very distinguished tradition. Established in 1895, the Haskell

Lectureship on Comparative Religions has brought many leading scholars on the history of religions from abroad to the campus of the University of Chicago. The name of Peter Brown adds new honor to this lectureship. It is also an honor for the Committee on Haskell Lectures to make this volume available to a wider public.

Joseph M. Kitagawa

# Preface

The six chapters of this book are a slightly expanded version of the Haskell Lectures, which I had the honor to deliver in the School of Divinity at the University of Chicago in April 1978. As is only to be expected in that place, I ended up, yet again, by learning in the company of so many friends and colleagues how much I had still to learn, by sharing with them the quiet confidence of those who teach so as to learn. For that rare experience, my thanks go first and foremost to Dean Joseph Kitagawa, for his warmth and untiring, discreet solicitude, and to all his colleagues in the School of Divinity. Yet these lectures would not have been presented at Chicago as they were if, in the previous year, I had not benefited from the candor and energy with which their main themes were discussed and corrected in two seminars, the first organized by Professor Elizabeth Kennan at the Catholic University of America, as part of the Mellon Program on Early Christian Humanism, and the second by Professor Will Oxtoby, in the Program for Comparative Religion at the University of Toronto. It was the generous enthusiasm of those seminars that made me think that such a topic was xiii worth presenting as a series of formal lectures.

It is with some trepidation, however, that I now realize that I have attempted to tell in my own words, in the short compass of six lectures, a story on which great scholars of the early church and of its cultural and religious surroundings have lavished their attention for well over a century. I would not wish my treatment to be mistaken for what it is not.

It is not a complete treatment of the rise of the cult of saints in late antiquity. Being an essay in interpretation, it does not attempt to replicate the encyclopedic erudition on which it has drawn with admiration and gratitude. I have referred only to those works which have influenced, challenged and inspired me, in the hope that they may have a similar effect on others, and so that others may share with me the information on which I have drawn to form my own conclusions.

As I wrote, I found that the scope of my inquiry had insensibly narrowed. Within the wide world of late-antique Christianity, the Latin-speaking countries of the Mediterranean and their northern extension in Gaul imposed themselves on me as a distinctive region, forming a cultural and religious continuum of its own, and ideally suited, by reason of the abundance, accessibility and coherence of its evidence, for such a study.

Furthermore, I trust that I have made plain throughout this book, and especially at the end of the second chapter, that a reinterpretation of the rise and function of the cult of saints calls for a decision by scholars concerning what evidence and what areas of late-antique society and culture they should concentrate upon as likely to be most revealing of the religious situation of the time. My own decision forced itself in upon me. From Paulinus of Nola and Ambrose, in the late fourth century, to Gregory of Tours and Venantius Fortunatus, in the late sixth, I found myself to my delight in the company of highly articulate, indeed, of magnificently *visible* friends of the "invisible friends." The motives of such men, their expectations, the social and cultural world that colored their language and gave such an inimitable flavor to these men's warm capacity for love and loyalty to the invisible dead, are better known to us than is any other aspect of this subject. I confess that I have plucked down their evidence with both hands.

In so doing, I have left many books on the cult of saints in late antiquity yet to be written: there will be books that cover the Christianity of Byzantium and the Near East; books that will do more justice than I have done to the humble and inarticulate who gathered habitually around the shrines—the poor, the sick, the women, the pilgrims; above all, I trust, books that will redress the balance of this book, by looking beyond the dazzling creations by which a distinctive and influential clerical elite strove, in architecture, poetry, historical narrative, and ceremonial, to do justice to their own interpretation of the meaning and benefits of the worship of the saints, to other groups within the Christian community for whom the same cult fulfilled different needs and among whom the love of the saints erupted, at times, in very different but no less meaningful forms of expression; and even books on how the cult of the saints, viewed by different groups in different regions (and even by the Christian community in different moods) could mean very little. It is sufficient that this book should open a way to some of these approaches, and essential that it should not be held to have excluded any one of them.

For I cannot resist the impression that, for all the patient erudition that has piled up behind him, the student of the cult of saints now finds himself in the most pleasurable of all positions—back at the beginning, with a once-familiar territory calling, yet again, for exploration. In the words of an old master of medieval history: "Above all, by slow degrees the thoughts of our forefathers, their common thoughts about common things, will have become thinkable once more. There are discoveries to be made; but also there are habits to be formed."[1]

# Chapter One

## The Holy and the Grave

This book is about the joining of Heaven and Earth, and the role, in this joining, of dead human beings. It will deal with the emergence, orchestration, and function in late antiquity of what is generally known as the Christian "cult of saints." This involves considering the role in the religious life and organization of the Christian church in the western Mediterranean, between the third and sixth centuries A.D., of whole tombs, of relic fragments and of objects closely connected with the dead bodies of holy men and women, confessors and martyrs.

The cult of saints, as it emerged in late antiquity, became part and parcel of the succeeding millennium of Christian history to such an extent that we tend to take its elaboration for granted. Its origin has received a certain amount of attention and, given the tantalizing state of the evidence, both literary and archaeological, it is likely to continue to do so. But the full implications of what it meant to contemporaries to join Heaven and Earth at the grave of a dead human being has not been explored as fully as it deserves. For to do that was to break barriers that had existed in the back of the minds of

1

Mediterranean men for a thousand years, and to join categories and places that had been usually meticulously contrasted.

One thing can be said with certainty about the religion of the late-antique Mediterranean: while it may not have become markedly more "otherworldly," it was most emphatically "upperworldly."[1] Its starting point was belief in a fault that ran across the face of the universe. Above the moon, the divine quality of the universe was shown in the untarnished stability of the stars. The earth lay beneath the moon, *in sentina mundi*—so many dregs at the bottom of a clear glass.[2] Death could mean the crossing of that fault. At death, the soul would separate from a body compounded of earthly dregs, and would gain, or regain, a place intimately congruent with its true nature in the palpable, clear light that hung so tantalizingly close above the earth in the heavy clusters of the Milky Way.[3] Whether this was forever, or, as Jews and Christians hoped, only for the long hiatus before the resurrection of the dead, the dead body joined in the instability and opacity of the world beneath the moon, while the soul enjoyed the unmovable clarity of the remainder of the universe.[4]

Writing in the second century A.D., Plutarch had made the matter plain. Popular belief in the bodily *apotheosis* of Romulus—the disappearance of his corpse into Heaven—struck him as a sad example of the workings of the "primitive mind." For the known structure of the universe was against it. The virtuous soul could have its share in the divinity of the stars; but this could happen only after the body had been discarded, and the soul had regained its rightful place, passing to the sky, as quick and dry as a lightning flash leaving the lowering, damp cloud of the flesh.[5] In believing in the resurrection of the dead, Jews and Christians could envisage that one day the barriers of the universe would be broken: both Elijah and Christ had already done what Plutarch said Romulus could not have done. But, for the time being, the barrier between earth and the stars remained as firmly established for the average Christian as for any other late-antique men. Thus, when he came to write on the subject of the resurrection, Prudentius, a Christian of the late fourth century, could express his belief only in language which is so faithful a reversal of the traditional world view as to amount to a tacit recognition of its resilience:

But should the fiery essence of the soul think on its high origin, and cast aside the numbing stain of life: then will it carry with it, too, the flesh in which it lodged and bear it also back among the stars.[6]

But the resurrection was unimaginably distant, and Prudentius was a singularly enterprising poet. The average Christian monumental mason, and his patrons, continued through the fifth and sixth centuries to cover tombs with verse that took the old world view for granted.[7] An early-sixth-century bishop of Lyons, for instance, was quite content not to linger among dizzying paradoxes: the immemorial antithesis was enough for him—Astra fovent animam corpus natura recepit.[8]

Yet a near-contemporary of the emperor Julian the Apostate, the rabbi Pinḥas ben Ḥama, could point to a paradox involved in the graves of saints. He used to say:

If the fathers of the world (the patriarchs) had wished that their resting place should be in the Above, they would have been able to have it there: but it is when they died and the rock closed on their tombs here below that they deserved to be called "saints."[9]

For the rabbi was speaking of the tombs of the patriarchs in the Holy Land. Their occupants were "holy" because they made available to the faithful around their tombs on earth a measure of the power and mercy in which they might have taken their rest in the Above. The graves of the saints—whether these were the solemn rock tombs of the Jewish patriarchs in the Holy Land or, in Christian circles, tombs, fragments of bodies or, even, physical objects that had made contact with these bodies—were privileged places, where the contrasted poles of Heaven and Earth met. Late-antique Christian piety, as we shall see through these chapters, concentrated obsessively on the strange flash that could occur when the two hitherto distinct categories joined in the back of men's minds.

By the end of the sixth century, the graves of the saints, which lay in the cemetery areas outside the walls of most of the cities of the former Western Empire, had become centers of the ecclesiastical life of their region.[10] This was because the saint in Heaven was believed to be "present" at his tomb on earth. The soul of Saint Martin, for instance, might go "marching on"; but his body, at Tours, was very definitely not expected to "lie a-mouldering in the grave." The local Jewish doctor might have his doubts: "Martin will do you no good, whom the earth now rests, turning him to earth. . . . A dead man can give no healing to the living."[11] They are not doubts shared by the inscription on the tomb:

> Hic conditus est sanctae memoriae Martinus episcopus
> Cuius anima in manu Dei est, sed hic totus est Praesens manifestus omni gratia virtutum.
>
> [Here lies Martin the bishop, of holy memory, whose soul is in the hand of God; but he is fully here, present and made plain in miracles of every kind.][12]

The joining of Heaven and Earth was made plain even by the manner in which contemporaries designed and described the shrines of the saints. Filled with great candelabra, their dense clusters of light mirrored in shimmering mosaic and caught in the gilded roof, late Roman *memoriae* brought the still light of the Milky Way to within a few feet of the grave.[13]

To a Mediterranean man of traditional background, much of this would have been peripheral, and some of it, downright disgusting. As Artemidorus of Daldis wrote in the second century A.D., to dream that you are a tanner is a bad dream, "for the tanner handles dead bodies and lives outside the city."[14] The rise of the Christian cult of saints took place in the great cemeteries that lay outside the cities of the Roman world: and, as for the handling of dead bodies, the Christian cult of saints rapidly came to involve the digging up, the moving, the dismemberment—quite apart from much avid touching and kissing—of the bones of the dead, and, frequently, the placing of these in areas from which the dead had once been excluded. An element of paradox always surrounded the Christian breaching of the established map of the universe. But the impact of the cult of saints on the topography of the Roman city was unambiguous: it gave greater prominence to areas that had been treated as antithetical to the public life of the living city;[15] by the end of the period, the immemorial boundary between the city of the living and the dead came to be breached by the entry of relics and their housing within the walls of many late-antique towns, and the clustering of ordinary graves around them.[16] Even when confined to their proper place, the areas of the dead, normative public worship and the tombs of the dead were made to coincide in a manner and with a frequency for which the pagan and Jewish imagination had made little provision.[17]

The breaking down and the occasional inversion of ancient barriers implied in the late-antique cult of saints seems to mark the end of a way of seeing the relation between the human dead and the universe, and, as an immediate consequence, a shifting of the barriers by which Mediterranean men had sought to circumscribe the role of the dead, and especially of those dead to whom one had to strong links of kinship or place.[18] Pagan parallels and antecedents can only take us so far in understanding the Christian cult of saints, very largely because the pagan found himself in a world where his familiar map of the relations between the human and the divine, the dead and the living, had been subtly redrawn.

Let us take one well-known example: the relation between the ancient cult of the heroes and the Christian cult of the martyrs.[19] To idealize the dead seemed natural enough to men in Hellenistic and Roman times. Even to offer some form of worship to the deceased, whether as a family or as part of a public cult in the case of exceptional dead persons, such as heroes or emperors, was common, if kept within strictly defined limits. Thus, the practice of "heroization," especially of private cult offered by the family to the deceased as a "hero" in a specially constructed grave house, has been invoked to explain some of the architectural and artistic problems of the early Christian *memoria*.[20] But after that, even the analogy of the cult of the hero breaks down. For the position of the hero had been delimited by a very ancient map of the boundaries between those beings who had been touched by the taint of human death and those who had not: the forms of cult for heroes and for the immortal gods tended to be kept apart.[21] Above all, what appears to be almost totally absent from pagan belief about the role of the heroes is the insistence of all Christian writers that the martyrs, precisely because they had died as human beings, enjoyed close intimacy with God. Their intimacy with God was the *sine qua non* of their ability to intercede for and, so, to protect their fellow mortals. The martyr was the "friend of God." He was an intercessor in a way which the hero could never have been.[22]

Thus, in Christian belief, the grave, the memory of the dead, and the religious ceremonial that might surround this memory were placed within a totally different structure of relations between God, the dead, and the living. To explain the Christian cult of the martyrs as a continuation of the pagan cult of heroes[23] helps as little as to reconstruct the form and function of a late-antique Christian basilica from the few columns and capitals taken from classical buildings that are occasionally incorporated in its arcades.[24]

Indeed, Christian late antiquity could well be presented as a reversal of the *Hippolytus* of Euripides. The hard-bitten message of that play had been that the boundaries between gods and humans should remain firm. Whatever intimacy Hippolytus may have enjoyed with the goddess Artemis, when he was alive, the touch of death opened a chasm between Artemis, the immortal, and Hippolytus, the dying human being. She could no longer look at him:

> ἐμοὶ γὰρ οὐ θέμις φθιτοὺς ὁρᾶν
> οὐδ᾽ ὄμμα χραίνειν θανασίμοισιν ἐκπνοιαῖς
>
> [It is not right for me to look upon the dead,
> And stain my eyesight with the mists of dying
> men.][25]

We need only compare this with the verse of the Psalms that is frequently applied by Latin writers to the role of the martyrs, "Oculi Domini super iustos, et aures eius ad preces eorum" (33:16)[26] to measure the distance between the two worlds.

Nothing could be more misleading than to assume that, by the middle of the fourth century, some insensible tide of religious sentiment had washed away the barriers by which Mediterranean pagans had sought for so long to mark off the human dead from the living. Far from it: on this point, the rise of Christianity in the pagan world was met by deep religious anger. We can chart the rise to prominence of the Christian church most faithfully by listening to pagan reactions to the cult of martyrs. For the progress of this cult spelled out for the pagans a slow and horrid crumbling of ancient barriers which presaged the final spreading again over the earth of that "darkness spoken of in the old myths" in which all ancient landmarks would be blotted out.[27] In attacking the cult of saints, Julian the Apostate mentions the cult as a novelty for which there was no warrant in the gospels; but the full weight of his religious abhorrence comes to bear on the relation between the living and the corpses of the dead that was implied in the Christian practice: "You keep adding many corpses newly dead to the corpse of long ago. You have filled the whole world with tombs and sepulchres."[28] He turned against the cult practiced at the tombs of the saints all the repugnance expressed by the Old Testament prophets for those who haunted tombs and burial caves for sinister purposes of sorcery and divination.[29] As an emperor, Julian could give voice to his own profound distaste by reiterating the traditional Roman legislation that kept the dead in their proper place. How could men tolerate such things as Christian processions with relics?

> ... The carrying of the corpses of the dead through a great assembly of people, in the midst of dense crowds, staining the eyesight of all with ill-omened sights of the dead. What day so touched with death could be lucky? How, after being present at such ceremonies, could anyone approach the gods and their temples?[30]

In an account of the end of paganism in Egypt, by Eunapius of Sardis, we catch the full charnel horror of the rise of Christianity:

> For they collected the bones and skulls of criminals who had been put to death for numerous crimes ... made them out to be gods, and thought that they became better by defiling themselves at their graves. "Martyrs" the dead men were called, and ministers of a sort, and ambassadors with the gods to carry men's prayers.[31]

In the course of the late fourth and fifth centuries, the growth of the cult of martyrs caused a visible shift in the balance of importance accorded to the areas of the living and the areas of

the dead in most late-antique towns. Great architecture mush-
roomed in the cemeteries. To take only one example: at the
beginning of the fifth century, the north African city of Tebessa
came to be flanked by an enormous pilgrimage site, built in the
cemetery area, presumably around the grave of Saint Crispina.
The shrine was in the full-blooded, public style associated with
the Theodosian renaissance. Its pilgrim's way, 150 meters long,
passed under great triumphal arches and along arcaded courtyards, echoing, among the tombs outside Tebessa, the por-
ticoes and streets of a classical city.[32] In the same years Paulinus
of Nola could congratulate himself on having built around the
grave of Saint Felix, in a peripheral cemetery area still called
Cimitile, "the cemetery," a complex so impressive that the
traveler might take it for another town.[33]

Indeed, when it came to shifting the balance between places
and non-places in the ancient man's map of civilization, Christianity had a genius for impinging with gusto on the late-
Roman landscape. In the course of the fourth century, the
growth of monasticism had revealed how wholeheartedly
Christians wished to patronize communities which had opted
pointedly for the antithesis of settled urban life. In the proud
words of Athanasius, writing of Saint Anthony and his monks,
the monks had "founded a city in the desert," that is, in a place
where no city should be.[34] In the late fourth and fifth centuries,
the Christian bishops brought the shift in the balance between
the town and the non-town out of the desert and right up to the
walls of the city: they now founded cities in the cemetery.[35]

What is even more remarkable is the outcome of this shift.
The bishops of western Europe came to orchestrate the cult of
the saints in such a way as to base their power within the old
Roman cities on these new "towns outside the town." The
bishop's residence and his main basilica still lay within the city
walls. Yet it was through a studiously articulated relationship
with great shrines that lay at some distance from the city—Saint
Peter's, on the Vatican Hill outside Rome, Saint Martin's, a little
beyond the walls of Tours—that the bishops of the former cities
of the Roman Empire rose to prominence in early medieval
Europe.

We shall frequently have occasion to observe that the bishops' control of these shrines should not be taken for granted: as the Duke of Wellington said of the battle of Waterloo, the victory was "a dam' close-run thing." But the victory, once won, was decisive for the history of the church in western Europe. In a characteristically rhetorical flourish, Jerome had challenged a critic of the cult relics:

> [So you think,] therefore, that the bishop of Rome does wrong when, over the dead men Peter and Paul, venerable bones to us, but to you a heap of common dust, he offers up sacrifices to the Lord, and their graves are held to be altars of Christ.[36]

The subsequent success of the papacy could only prove that the bishop of Rome had *not* done wrong.

To gain this advantage, further ancient barriers had to be broken. Tomb and altar were joined. The bishop and his clergy performed public worship in a proximity to the human dead that would have been profoundly disturbing to pagan and Jewish feeling. Furthermore, an ancient barrier between the private and the public, that had been shared as deeply by a former generation of Christians as by any other late-antique men, came to be eroded. The tomb of the saint was declared public property as the tomb of no other Christian was: it was made accessible to all, and became the focus of forms of ritual common to the whole community. Every device of architecture, art, ceremony, and literature was mobilized to ensure that holy graves and relics were made both more eminent and more available than were the family graves that filled the cemeteries. Indeed, if for all late-antique men the grave was "a fine and private place," owned and cared for by the family, the graves and relics of the saints stood out in high relief: they were "non-graves."

The joining of the ecclesiastical hierarchy of western Europe to the tombs of the dead set the medieval Catholic church apart from its Byzantine and Near Eastern neighbors—Christian, Jewish, and Muslim. In western Europe, the power of the bishop tended to coalesce with the power of the shrine.

Elsewhere, the shrine tended to go its own way.[37] The great Christian shrines and pilgrimage sites of the eastern Mediterranean and the Near East—even Jerusalem—were never mobilized, as they came to be in the West, to form the basis of lasting ecclesiastical power structures.[38]

In Judaism the holy graves and the rabbinate drifted apart. The *loci* where Heaven and Earth had met, in the opinion of the rabbi Pinḥas ben Ḥama, still lacked their *impresarios*. There was no denying the existence of so many tombs of the saints nor of their importance for the Jewish communities. But the leaders of Jewish learning and spirituality did not choose to lean upon tombs, as Christian bishops did, with the result that these maintained a low profile. It is hardly surprising, given the manner in which they were taken for granted, that we have had to wait until 1958 for Joachim Jeremias to recover for us the full significance of Jewish holy graves in late antiquity.[39] In Islam, the situation is more tantalizing. The holy tomb, though of inestimable importance throughout all regions of the Islamic world, existed always a little to one side of Muslim orthodoxy.[40] Vivid ethnographic material on the function of modern Muslim shrines, which seems to carry us back directly in time into the western Europe of the early middle ages, comes not from the dry center of the Islamic tradition, but from its ever-fertile peripheries—from the mountains of Morocco and from Sufi lodges scattered between Indonesia and the Atlas.[41] Thus, holy graves existed both in Judaism and in Islam. But to exist was never enough. Public and private, traditional religious leadership and the power of the holy dead never coincided to the degree to which they did in western Europe. The state of our evidence reflects something of the evolution that we have described: we can trace the rise of the holy dead in western Europe with such clarity largely because, as in a pair of binoculars, the two sets of images, from the two lenses, the shrine and the official religious leadership, slide so easily together.

Whatever their relation with the ecclesiastical hierarchy, the Christian Mediterranean and its extensions to the east and northwest came to be dotted with clearly indicated *loci* where Heaven and Earth met. The shrine containing a grave or, more frequently, a fragmentary relic, was very often called quite simply, "the place": *loca sanctorum,* ὁ τόπος.[42] It was a place where the normal laws of the grave were held to be suspended. In a relic, the chilling anonymity of human remains could be thought to be still heavy with the fullness of a beloved person. As Gregory of Nyssa said,

> Those who behold them embrace, as it were, the living body in full flower: they bring eye, mouth, ear, all the senses into play, and then, shedding tears of reverence and passion, they address to the martyr their prayers of intercession as though he were present.[43]

It could be a threatening presence. Jerome wrote:

> Whenever I have been angry or had some bad thought upon my mind, or some evil fantasy has disturbed my sleep, I do not dare to enter the shrines of the martyrs. I quake with body and soul.[44]

A sixth-century layman wrote to his spiritual father in Gaza:

> When I find that I am in a place where there are relics of the holy martyrs, I am obsessed by the need to go in and venerate them. Every time I pass in front of them, I feel I should bow my head.

The old man replied that one prostration should be enough, or, if the urge is very strong, three. Should he go in, then the layman continued, whenever the fear of God strikes him?

> No: do not go in out of fear. Only enter at fitting times for prayer.

> But when I am just about to go in, then the fear of God really does come on me![45]

The activities of less squeamish souls reveal to us a Mediterranean landscape covered, in its most settled parts, with a grid of shrines. Around A.D. 600, a gang of burglars operating in Upper Egypt could make a start at the Place of Apa Collouthos, outside Antinoë, go south a few miles to Saint Victor the General, cross the Nile to Apa Timothy, and head downstream again at nightfall to the Place of Apa Claudius, reaping a swag of silver altar tablets, silk and linen hangings, even the silver

necklaces and the crosses from around the necks of the mum-
mified saints.[46]

Wherever Christianity went in the early Middle Ages, it
brought with it the "presence" of the saints. Whether this was
unimaginably far to the north, in Scotland, where local
craftsmen attempted to copy, in their "altar tombs," the shape
of the high-ridged sarcophagi of late-Roman Gaul;[47] or on the
edge of the desert, where Rome, Persia, and the Arab world met
at the shrine of Saint Sergius at Resafa—a shrine in whose trea-
sury even the pagan king of kings of Persia, Khusro II Aparwez,
had placed a great silver dish recounting his gratitude to the
saint is a style which makes this *ex voto* the last address of a
Near Eastern monarch to a supernatural figure (of which one of
the first was carved by the Achaemenian predecessor of Khusro,
Cyrus, high on the rock face of Bisutun);[48] or even further to the
east, among the Nestorian Christians of Iraq, Iran, and central
Asia,[49] late-antique Christianity, as it impinged on the outside
world, *was* shrines and relics.[50]

This is a fact of life which has suffered the fate of many facts
of life. Its existence is admitted with a slight note of embar-
rassment; and, even when admitted to, it is usual to treat it as
"only too natural," and not a subject to linger over for prolonged and circumstantial investigation. I would like to end this
chapter by suggesting why this should have been so, and to
point out the disadvantages to the religious and social historian
of late antiquity of so dismissive an approach to a form of religious life that was plainly central to the position of the Christian church in late-antique society.

For it seems to me that our curiosity has been blunted by a
particular model of the nature of religious sentiment and a consequent definition of the nature of "popular religion." We have
inherited from our own learned tradition attitudes that are not
sensitive enough to help us enter into the thought processes
and the needs that led to the rise and expansion of the cult of
saints in late antiquity. That such models have entered our
cultural bloodstream is shown by one fact: long after the issue
of the rise of the cult of saints has been removed from its confessional setting in post-Reformation polemics, scholars of
every and of no denomination still find themselves united in a

common reticence and incomprehension when faced with this phenomenon. Plainly, some solid and seemingly unmovable cultural furniture has piled up somewhere in that capacious lumber room, the back of our mind. If we can identify and shift some of it, we may find ourselves able to approach the Christian cult of saints from a different direction.

The religious history of late antiquity and the early middle ages still owes more than we realize to attitudes summed up so persuasively, in the 1750s, by David Hume, in his essay *The Natural History of Religion*. The *Encyclopedia of Philosophy* describes this essay, somewhat loftily, as "an entertaining exercise in armchair anthropology from secondary sources."[51] Yet, like weightier successors in that genre, it was precisely the "armchair" quality of Hume's essay that accounts for the continued subliminal presence of its leading ideas in all later scholarship. For Hume drew on evidence that lay to hand in classical authors, which all men of culture read and would read up to our own times. He placed this evidence together with such deftness and good sense that the *Natural History of Religion* seems to carry the irresistible weight of a clear and judicious statement of the obvious. It was difficult to doubt the soundness of Hume's presentation of the working of the religious mind in general, and impossible to challenge, in particular, the accuracy of his portrayal of the nature and causes of superstition in the ancient world, drawn as it was from well-known classical authors.

Hume faced squarely the problem of the origins and variety of religious thought. Men, he insisted, against his orthodox contemporaries, were not natural monotheists, and never had been. They had not lost, through sin, the original simplicity of faith in the Supreme Being that had been granted to Adam and the patriarchs. Though theism remained an ideal, it was at all times a precarious ideal. And this was not because of human sinfulness, but because of the intellectual limitations of the average human mind. The intellectual and, by implication, the cultural and social preconditions for theism were difficult to achieve. For theism, in Hume's view, depended on attaining a coherent—and so, rational—view of the universe, such as might, in turn, enable the enlightened mind to deduce from the order of the visible world the existence of, and the forms of worship due to, a Supreme Being. Hence, Hume concludes, the extreme rarity of true monotheism, and its virtual impossibility in the distant, unrefined ages of the past.

Furthermore, the failure to think in theistic terms could be given a precise social *locus*—"the vulgar":

> The vulgar, that is, indeed, all mankind a few excepted, being ignorant and uninstructed, never elevate their contemplation to the heavens . . . so far as to discern a supreme mind or original providence.[52]

Hume was emphatic that this failure was not due solely to the intellectual limitations of "the vulgar." These limitations reflected an entire cultural and social environment, hostile to rationality. "The vulgar . . . being ignorant and uninstructed" tended to fragment those experiences of abstract order on which any coherent view of the universe could be based. For the average man was both notoriously ill-equipped through lack of instruction to abstract general principles from his immediate environment: and, in any case, in all but the most privileged ages, and among the most sheltered elites, the natural inability of the uninstructed intellect to think in abstract terms was heightened by fears and anxieties, which led men to personalize yet further the working of causes beyond their control, and so to slip ever deeper into polytheistic ways of thought. As a result, the religious history of mankind, for Hume, is not a simple history of decline from an original monotheism; it is marked by a constant tension between theistic and polytheistic ways of thinking:

> It is remarkable that the principles of religion have had a flux and reflux in the human mind, and that men have a natural tendency to rise from idolatry to theism, and to sink again from theism to idolatry.[53]

This characteristically sad and measured assessment of the limitations of average human thinking, and the manner in which these limitations were reflected in a constant "flux and reflux" of religious thought, provided Hume and his successors with a model for the cultural and social preconditions for religious change. For the "flux and reflux in the human mind" had a historical dimension. Some ages had it in them to be, at least marginally, less polytheistic than others: They were more secure, their elites were more cultivated, possibly more effective in controlling "the vulgar" or, at least, less permeable to their irrational ideas. Other ages could do nothing but relapse into idolatry of some form or other. And so the respective rise and fall of rationality could be assessed in terms of the relative strength, in any given society, of the "vulgar" and of the potentially enlightened few, and in terms of the relative pressure which the views of one side could exert upon those of the other.

The greatest immediate legacy of the *Natural History of Religion*, however, was not a sense of change: it was a sober respect for the force of inertia behind the religious practices of "the vulgar." Hume had made polytheistic ways of thinking appear plausible, almost universal, and, seemingly, ineradicable. Gibbon seized at once on this aspect of the essay. It lies behind the magisterial coherence of the twenty-eighth chapter of the *Decline and Fall*, which flows from a description of the nature and abolition of the pagan religion of the Roman Empire to the rise of the Christian cult of the saints without so much as an eddy marking the transition from one form of religion to the other: "Mr. Hume . . . observes, like a philosopher, the natural flux and reflux of polytheism and theism."[54] For Gibbon, Hume the philosopher had made the transition from polytheism to the cult of the saints obvious:

> The imagination, which had been raised by a painful effort to the contemplation and worship of the Universal Cause, eagerly embraced such inferior objects of adoration as were more proportioned to its gross conceptions and imperfect faculties. The sublime and simple theology of the primitive Christians was gradually corrupted; and the MONARCHY of heaven, already clouded by metaphysical subtleties, was degraded by the introduction of a popular mythology which tended to restore the reign of polytheism.[55]

What is more surprising is that it was, if anything, the religious revival of the nineteenth century that hardened the outlines of Hume's model, and made a variant of it part of many modern interpretations of early medieval Christianity. We need only turn to Dean Milman's *History of Latin Christianity*, to see

how this could happen. Milman presented the spread of the cult
of saints in Europe during the Dark Ages in a manner touched
with Romantic enthusiasm. Yet Hume's model was very much
part of his mental furniture.[56] For he identified the theism of
the enlightened few with the elevated message of the Christian
church; while the barbarian settlers of Europe, although their
mental processes might be described by Milman, the post-
Romantic reader of Vico, as "poetic" (and not, as Gibbon had
said more bluntly of them, as "fierce and illiterate")[57] retained
to the full the qualities of Hume's "vulgar." They represented
modes of thinking that fell far below those of the enlightened
leaders of the church. Milman merely added the whole span of
the barbarian West to Gibbon's Roman canvas:

> Now had commenced what may be called, neither un-
> reasonably nor unwarrantably, the mythic age of Chris-
> tianity. As Christianity worked downwards into the lower
> classes of society, as it received the crude and ignorant bar-
> barians within its pale, the general effect could not but be
> that the age would drag down the religion to its level, rather
> than the religion elevate the age to its own lofty standards.[58]

Indeed, the renewed loyalty of sensitive and learned minds to
the religious traditions of the past, in Anglicanism and Catholicism alike, heightened the lack of sympathy for the thought
processes of the average man. For those who wished to maintain the elevated truths of traditional Christianity had to draw
with even greater harshness the boundaries between their own
versions of "true religion" and the habitual misconception of
these by the "vulgar."

> In the next place what has power to stir holy and refined
> souls is potent also with the multitude; and the religion of
> the multitude is ever vulgar and abnormal; it will ever be
> tinctured with fanaticism and superstition, while men are
> what they are.[59]

Not Hume this time—but John Henry, Cardinal Newman. It is
by such stages that a particular model of the nature and origin
of the religious sentiment and, especially, of the forms that this
sentiment takes among "the vulgar" as "popular religion" has

come to permeate those great traditions of Protestant and Catholic scholarship on which we still depend for so much of our erudition on the religious and ecclesiastical history of late antiquity and the early middle ages.

In modern scholarship, these attitudes take the form of a "two-tiered" model. The views of the potentially enlightened few are thought of as being subject to continuous upward pressure from habitual ways of thinking current among "the vulgar." Hume was far more pessimistic than were those robust Victorian churchmen we have just described about the intellectual and religious resources of the few; but he had no doubts about who constituted "the vulgar." He was brutally plain about what he considered to be the intellectual and cultural limitations of the masses. Hume's "vulgar" have remained with us. To take only one example: the patient work of Hippolyte Delehaye in recovering the historical kernel of the *Acts of the Martyrs* is marked by a pessimism similar to that of Hume. To pass from the historical documents of the early church to their later legendary accretions was, for that sober Bollandist, to note the ease with which the truthful record of a "few enlightened minds" became swallowed up in the crowd:

> En effet, l'intelligence de la multitude se manifeste partout comme extrêmement bornée et ce serait une erreur de croire qu'elle subisse, en général, l'influence de l'élite. . . . Le meilleur point de comparaison pour en démontrer le niveau est l'intelligence de l'enfant.[60]

When applied to the nature of religious change in late antiquity, the "two-tiered" model encourages the historian to assume that a change in the piety of late-antique men, of the kind associated with the rise of the cult of saints, must have been the result of the capitulation by the enlightened elites of the Christian church to modes of thought previously current only among the "vulgar." The result has been a tendency to explain much of the cultural and religious history of late antiquity in terms of drastic "landslips" in the relation between the elites and the masses. Dramatic moments of "democratization of culture" or of capitulation to popular needs are held to have brought about a series of "mutations" of late-antique and early medieval

Christianity.[61] The elites of the Roman world are supposed to
have been eroded by the crisis of the third century, thus open-
ing the way to a flood of superstitious fears and practices introduced by the new governing classes of the Christian Empire;[62] "mass conversions" to Christianity, which are assumed
to have taken place as a result of the conversion of Constantine
and the establishment of Christianity as the state religion, are
said to have forced the hands of the leaders of the church into
accepting a wide variety of pagan practices, especially in relation to the cult of the saints; a further capitulation of the elites of
the Byzantine world to "the naive animistic ideas of the masses"
is supposed to have brought about the rise of the cult of icons
in the later sixth century A.D.[63]

Of each of these moments of "democratization" it is now
possible to say:

> Oh, let us never, never doubt,
> What nobody is sure about.

Applied in this manner, the "two-tiered" model appears to
have invented more dramatic turning points in the history of
the early church than it has ever explained.

Let us see what can be gained by abandoning this model. I
suggest that the greatest immediate advantage would be to
make what has been called "popular religion" in late antiquity
and the early middle ages more available to historical interpretation, by treating it as more dynamic. For the basic weakness of the "two-tiered" model is that it is rarely, if ever, concerned to explain religious change other than among the elite.
The religion of "the vulgar" is assumed to be uniform. It is
timeless and faceless. It can cause changes by imposing its
modes of thought on the elite; but in itself it does not change.

Now it is hardly necessary to labor the point that even in
relatively simple societies, shared beliefs can be experienced
and put to use in widely differing ways among differing sec-
tions of a society, and that it is quite possible for one section to
regard the religious behavior of the others as defective or
threatening.[64] Christianity, in particular, found itself committed to complex beliefs, whose full understanding and accurate
formulation had always assumed a level of culture which the

majority of the members of the Christian congregations were known not to share with their leaders.[65] Yet it is remarkable that men who were acutely aware of elaborating *dogmas*, such as the nature of the Trinity, whose contents were difficult of access to the "unlettered," felt themselves so little isolated for so much of the time from these same "unlettered" when it came to the shared religious *practices* of their community and to the assumptions about the relation of man to supernatural beings which these practices condensed.[66] In the area of life covered by religious practice—an area immeasurably wider and more intimately felt by ancient men than by their modern counterparts[67]—differences of class and education play no significant role. As Arnaldo Momigliano has put it, with characteristic wisdom and firmness,

> Thus my inquest into popular beliefs in the Late Roman historians ends in reporting that there were no such beliefs. In the fourth and fifth centuries there were of course plenty of beliefs which we historians of the twentieth century would gladly call popular, but the historians of the fourth and fifth centuries never treated any belief as characteristic of the masses and consequently discredited among the elite. Lectures on popular beliefs and Late Roman historians should be severely discouraged.[68]

The model of "popular religion" that is usually presented by scholars of late antiquity has the disadvantage that it assumes that "popular religion" can be understood only from the viewpoint of the elite. "Popular religion" is presented as in some ways a diminution, a misconception or a contamination of "*un*popular religion."[69] Whether it is presented, bluntly, as "popular superstition" or categorized as "lower forms of belief,"[70] it is assumed that "popular religion" exhibits modes of thinking and worshiping that are best intelligible in terms of a failure to be something else. For failure to accept the guidance of the elite is invariably presented as having nothing to do with any particular appropriateness or meaningful quality in "popular" belief: it is always ascribed to the abiding limitations of "the vulgar." Popular belief, therefore, can only show itself as a monotonous continuity. It represents an untransformed, unelevated residue of beliefs current among "the ignorant and uninstructed," that is, "all mankind, a few excepted."

Gibbon saw this implication, and exploited it with consummate literary skill, so as to introduce the still-explosive controversial issue as to whether or not the Catholic cult of saints has been a direct copy of pagan practice:

> The same uniform original spirit of superstition might suggest, in the most distant ages, the same methods of deceiving the credulity and affecting the senses of mankind.[71]

Up to the present, it is still normal to assume that the average *homo religiosus* of the Mediterranean, and more especially, the average woman, is, like Winnie the Pooh, "a bear of very little brain."[72] His or her religious ideas are assumed to be unsophisticated and tenacious of age-old practices and misconceptions.[73] We have at least added a few softening touches to the outright contempt of the Enlightenment for "the vulgar." We have developed a romantic nostalgia for what we fondly wish to regard as the immemorial habits of the Mediterranean countryman, by which every "popular" religious practice is viewed as an avatar of classical paganism.[74] We have become concerned to trace in paganism and Christianity alike a common response to the human condition.[75] These modern concerns have added genuine human warmth, precision, and vast erudition to the study of the pagan background of "popular" Christianity in the late-antique world. The concept of *Antike und Christentum* associated with the work of Franz Dölger has come to stay.[76] Nowhere has this erudition been mobilized more abundantly than in studies of the rise and articulation of the Christian cult of saints.[77] Yet it is still assumed that, however novel the views of the leaders of the church might be, the study of "popular religion" in late antiquity must be the study of continuity and not of change: for it is assumed to be a study of the unmoving subsoil from which Christianity sprang. As long as this is so, we have not moved far from the labor-saving formulas to which Gibbon once turned, with such studied detachment, to imply that there was, after all, nothing very surprising in the rise of the cult of saints.

It seems time to ask whether the late-antique historian can remain satisfied for much longer with so static and potentially undifferentiated a model. For it has left him in a quandary. He knows that the political, social, and economic trends of late antiquity led to profound and irreversible changes in the relations between men and men in their daily secular life. In western Europe, an empire fell, and throughout the Mediterranean enduring new structures of social relations replaced those current in the classical period. These changes manifested themselves differently in different regions; but they worked slowly and deeply into the lives of Mediterranean men of all classes and levels of culture, and not merely the elites. Yet the religious historian of late antiquity offers for the majority of the population of the late-antique world a vista of seemingly unbroken continuity: "plus ça change, plus c'est la même chose" still appears to be the guiding principle of a long and distinguished tradition of studies on late-antique "popular religion."

Yet we have seen in the beginning of this chapter that the rise of the cult of saints was sensed by contemporaries, in no uncertain manner, to have broken most of the imaginative boundaries which ancient men had placed between heaven and earth, the divine and the human, the living and the dead, the town and its antithesis. I wonder whether it is any longer possible to treat the explicit breaking of barriers associated with the rise and the public articulation of the cult of saints as no more than foam on the surface of the lazy ocean of "popular belief." For the cult of saints involved imaginative changes that seem, at least, congruent to changing patterns of human relations in late-Roman society at large. It designated dead human beings as the recipients of unalloyed reverence, and it linked these dead and invisible figures in no uncertain manner to precise visible places and, in many areas, to precise living representatives. Such congruence hints at no small change. But in order to understand such a change, in all its ramifications, we must set aside the "two-tiered" model. Rather than present the rise of the cult of saints in terms of a dialogue between two parties, the few and the many, let us attempt to see it as part of a greater whole—the lurching forward of an increasing proportion of late-antique society toward radically new forms of reverence, shown to new objects in new places, orchestrated by new leaders, and deriving its momentum from the need to play out the common preoccupation of all, the few and the "vulgar" alike, with new forms of the exercise of power, new bonds of human dependence, new, intimate, hopes for protection and justice in a changing world.

# Chapter Two

## "A Fine and Private Place"

We all set out the furnishings suited to a worthy
    grave,
And on the altar that marks the tomb of our mother,
    Secundula,
It pleased us to place a stone tabletop,
Where we could sit around, bringing to memory her
    many good deeds,
As the food and the drinking cups were set out, and
    cushions piled around,
So that the bitter wound that gnawed our hearts
    might be healed.
And in this way we passed the evening hours in
    pleasant talk,
And in the praise of our good mother.
The old lady sleeps: she who fed us all
Lies silent now, and sober as ever.

At Saint Peter the Apostle, before the main entrance,
at the second column in the porch, as you enter from
the left, on the men's side, Lucillus and his wife,
Januaria, a gentlewoman.

As you enter under the vaults, pass through an exit
door and go into a cemetery in the form of a hall, and,
on the right side as you come through the door, alongside the wall, you will find the grave. I have wished
to make that perfectly plain because, seeing her tomb,
we should remember all the good she has done us, and
that this is the plce where her bones lie in the sweet
perfume of sanctity. And I especially entreat each descendant that, at least on the day of her death, they go
where she lies, . . . as is the custom of many.

Three passages on graves: the first, a pagan inscription from Mauretania of the late third century A.D.;[1] the second, Christian, from Saint Peter's at Rome, in the fifth century A.D.;[2] the third, from Florence of the early fifteenth century A.D.—an extract from the *Ricordi*, the family memoirs, of Giovanni di Pagolo Morelli.[3]

They serve as reminders of the massive stability of the Mediterranean care of the dead. Burial customs are among the most notoriously stable aspects of most cultures. They are also an element in the religious life of a society that is splendidly indifferent to the labels usually placed upon forms of religious behavior by the tradition of religious history to which I referred in my last chapter. They cannot be neatly categorized as "pagan" or "Christian," "popular" or "superstitious." This is because, whatever their origins may appear to have been to a modern scholar, the customs surrounding the care of the dead were experienced by those who practiced them to be no more than part and parcel of being human. As a sixth-century Egyptian lady declared, such arrangements were duties which she had to discharge as a human being: τὰ ἀνθρωποπρεπῆ μου νόμιμα.[4]

What is as constant as the practices themselves is the overwhelming role of the family in the care of the dead. Yet here an element of conflict can arise. For the kin can express concern for the dead to a degree, or in a manner, that might conflict with the needs of the community as a whole. Excessive celebration of funerary rites, undue expressions of loyalty to the memory or to the tombs of the dead, could become a lever by which one group might hope to assert themselves, in the name of the departed, among their living fellows. The grave, precisely because it was "a fine and private place," could be a point of tension between the family and the community. Hence a fluctuation, at all periods of the history of the Mediterranean, in the treatment of the memory of the dead as this might be expressed in any tangible forms that reached beyond the immediate circle of bereaved kin and friends—in funeral rites, in burial customs, and in the form taken by periodic celebrations. The fluctuation betrays the determination of some societies to cut down to size the memory of those who, in being dead, had ceased to be active participants in social and political life, and the willingness of other societies to allow some of the dead, at least, to retain a high profile among the living, and, usually, to allow this high profile to be maintained, in the first instance, by the family of the deceased.

Hence, while Athenian democracy showed itself at its most unrelenting in the strict control of displays of family feeling at funerals, the Roman patriciate positively encouraged such funerals as demonstrations of family pride and continuity.[5] Later, in the Islamic world, the tension between family and community is betrayed in the wide variety of Muslim burial practices. The bleak self-effacement of orthodox burial, where the funeral is performed rapidly, in dry, unirrigated land, and the dead lie under a "stone of witness," ideally without so much as an epitaph, is the last, most trenchant recognition by the Muslim and his bereaved kin that they are members of a community in which all believers are equal under God, and among whom all social differences will be brought to nothing before the day of resurrection. Yet, by contrast, the Old Adam of social differentiation within the community of believers vigorously survives the grave in the walled garden houses of the mausolea of Cairo's "City of the Dead," where the families of a great Muslim town have long defied strict orthodox opinion by creating, among the tombs, faithful replicas of social distinctions among the living.[6] In a very different environment, again, no more impressive testimony to the origins of American democracy can be found than the contrast between the flamboyant tombs of the gentry in English churches and the blunt, reticent stubs of stone that fill the eighteenth-century cemetery in Cambridge, Massachusetts.[7]

In all these cases, we have moved from overt religious issues, such as the content of belief in the afterlife and the possible relation of the living to the dead, as these may be expressed in burial and memorial customs, to the less easily articulated issue of the relationship between the family and the community. For, in times of change, the grave and what the living consider they can do around the grave can emerge as an apposite arena in which conflicting views on this relationship may be fought out.[8] In Christian, as later in Muslim circles, tensions on this issue are articulated in terms of a conflict between correct teaching on the fate of the dead, on the one hand, and, on the other, beliefs and practices which are thought to represent misconceptions of "true" teaching, and are frequently branded as "superstitious" contaminations, from pre-Christian or pre-Muslim sources, of "true" practice. Yet, I would suggest that the genesis and resolution of such moments of conflict is better understood if the less explicit area of tension—the tension between the family and the community—is borne in mind.

This seems particularly true in the case of the Christian church in the Latin-speaking world of the late fourth and early fifth centuries. For one generation, a lively debate on "superstition" within the Christian church flickered around the cemeteries of the Mediterranean. In the 380s, Ambrose at Milan,[9] and, in the 390s, Augustine in Hippo, attempted to restrict among their Christian congregations certain funerary customs, most notably the habit of feasting at the graves of the dead, either at the family tombs or in the *memoriae* of the martyrs. In Augustine's explicit opinion, these practices were a contaminating legacy of pagan beliefs:

> When peace came to the church, a mass of pagans who wished to come to Christianity were held back because their feast days with their idols used to be spent in an abundance of eating and drinking.[10]

These pagans had now entered the church, and had brought their evil habits with them.[11]

A decade later, Jerome found himself forced to write, from the Holy Land, a defense of the Christian cult of relics against Vigilantius, a priest from Calagurris, in the upper Ebro valley. Behind the studied outrage of "this unpleasant fly-sheet"[12] we can glimpse circles in southern Gaul and northern Spain who had been genuinely disturbed by the forms taken by the cult of relics and of the martyrs: "We see the ceremonial of pagan worship introduced into the churches under the pretext of religious observance."[13]

Later still, in 421, Paulinus of Nola elicited from Augustine a careful statement of the theological pros and cons of a practice which Paulinus had allowed: the burial of a Christian nobleman, Cynegius, at the request of his mother, Flora, in close proximity to the grave of Saint Felix at Nola. This case of *depositio ad sanctos* was by no means uncommon at the time. Paulinus had buried his own little son beside the saints at Alcalá.[14] Yet he evidently thought it worthwhile to present Augustine with it as a problem; and Augustine considered the problem to have raised sufficiently profound issues on the nature of Christian burial in general and the cult of the saints in particular to merit a long and clear answer, the *De cura gerenda pro mortuis*.[15]

There was, therefore, a debate around the grave in these years; and it is a debate that was explicitly handled in terms that appear to lend weight to the "two-tiered" model of religious history that I discussed in the last chapter. For in this case it appears that articulate and cultivated leaders of the Christian church attempted to take a stand against "pre-Christian" practices among their congregations; that the weight of these practices had apparently increased with the conversion of the pagan masses to Christianity; and that the pressure of pagan ways of thinking and worshiping had made itself felt, also, in the ceremonial trappings and in the beliefs surrounding the new cult of martyrs. Seen in this way, the end of the generation saw a Pyrrhic victory for the leaders of the church. Pre-Christian practices were controlled among the laity at their own private graves, and the more rambunctious of these were totally excluded from festivals at the graves of the martyrs. Nevertheless, popular opinion had forced on all but a discontented few the frank acceptance of pagan forms of ceremonial and of potentially "superstitious" views on the localization of the soul at the grave in the case of the cult of relics and of the tombs of the saints. Thus, a clearly documented victory of the "vulgar" can be thought to lie at the roots of the sudden prominence achieved, in the late fourth and early fifth centuries, by the cult of the saints. The extent of the victory can be measured by the astonishing last book of Augustine's *City of God*. In this book, an elevated confrontation with the opinions of Plato, Cicero, and Porphyry on the relation of body and soul and the possibility of the resurrection of the body suddenly runs into a long catalog of the miracles recently performed at the local shrines of Saint Stephen at Hippo and Uzalis.[16] The change of tone has almost invariably upset modern scholars. It appears to confirm their worst suspicions about the extent to which the beliefs of the "vulgar" had come to exert, within a few decades, their upward pressure on the most refined mind in Christendom:

> Such silly stories had no doubt always been believed by the common herd [writes A. H. M. Jones in his *Later Roman Empire*] but it is a sign of the times that a man of the intellectual eminence of Augustine should attach importance to them.[17]

It is one of the strengths of the "two-tiered" model that, throughout ancient times, elites were formed who experienced the religious variations in their own society in a manner not perceptibly different from those outlined by Hume and subsequent scholars: for such elites, "superstition" was primarily a question of incorrect belief, and incorrect belief had a clear social *locus* among the "vulgar"—a "vulgar" to which all women were treated as automatically belonging, as members of "that timorous and pious sex."[18] Thus, Jerome simply disclaimed responsibility for the "superstitious" overtones of the cult of the martyrs by saying that such excesses must have been due to "the simplicity of laymen, and certainly, of religious women."[19] Jerome and his clerical colleagues were members of a singularly self-conscious and "uptight" generation. They formed the new clerical elite of the late-fourth-century Christian church. Clergymen of ascetic background and of austerely spiritualist intellectual bent, Ambrose, Augustine, and Jerome reacted to the religious habits of the majority of their fellows in a *de haut en bas* manner which appears reassuringly similar to the manner in which a modern scholar, working in the tradition of the "two-tiered" model, would expect them to have reacted to all manifestations of "popular religion."[20] The explanation offered explicitly by Augustine and implied by Jerome's somewhat offhand answer to the criticisms of Vigilantius, appears so satisfactory to the modern scholar that it would seem almost a denial of the obvious to look for any other.

Yet what is not realized, in the first place, is that Augustine's explicit reference to the increase in pagan practices within the Christian congregation as having been brought about by mass conversions, was apparently made on the spur of the moment. It was a plausible piece of clerical euhemerism. Yet it referred to practices which, whatever their long-term origin may have been, had been accepted as authentically Christian in all previous generations.[21] Those who practiced feasting at the graves need not have been semipagan converts. They are as likely to have been respectable Christian families, whom Augustine sought to shame into compliance with his reforms by offering this unflattering explanation of their practices. Furthermore, the seeming obviousness of the remark has led us to take its central assertion for granted. We should not do so: the evidence for "mass conversions" in the course of the fourth century and, indeed, in any time in late antiquity, is far less convincing than might be thought.[22] The archaeology of Hippo, in particular, seems, at present, to offer no support for Augustine's picture of the expansion of the Christian congregations. The churches hitherto excavated do not give the impression that at any time in the fourth century the Christian congregations had been swelled by a "landslide" of recent converts.[23] Those forms of accommodation which would later be forced upon the Catholic hierarchy in the New World and on European missionaries in Africa and Asia are irrelevant to late-antique conditions: neither "evangelization" nor "conversion" raised problems as massive as those which came to confront Christian missions in later times. Instead, we are dealing with surprisingly stable and inward-looking Christian communities. Rituals associated with the early-Christian discipline of prebaptismal catechesis and the solemn reading of the list of the names of the catechumens at the Sunday liturgy were practices from a more slow-moving age that were still taken for granted, despite the supposedly overwhelming pressure of numbers, in Mediterranean cities as far apart as sixth-century Arles and Antioch.[24] The "two-tiered" model has created a landslide that may never have happened;

and it has done so because only a landslide of the "vulgar" into the Christian church could satisfy the demands of its system of explanation when faced with the rise within the church of new forms of, apparently, "popular" religious feeling.

It is time, therefore, to step aside from this form of explanation and to set the conflicts in religious practice to which the late-fourth-century debate on "superstition" pointed against a wider background. We need to invoke evidence from a wider range of Christian communities; to take into account a wider range of Christian attitudes to the care of the dead and the cult of the martyrs; and to follow the story beyond that single, highly articulate generation, into the final rise to eminence among the Christian communities of the Latin West of the shrines of the saints. In so doing, we may touch on the deeper roots of the cult of saints in late-Roman society, and come a little closer to the energies that were unleashed in the remarkable generation of Christian leaders who acted as the *impresarios* of this cult.

In his fine book on *Household and Lineage in Renaissance Florence*, Francis Kent has referred to "the significance of the tendency, ubiquitous in medieval society, to see areas of feeling and experience through kinship colored glasses."[25] Let us pause for a moment to view the Christian church in late antiquity through "kinship colored glasses." The historian of the period seldom meets an isolated individual. Religious practice took place with the family and for the family:

> Then we came to Cana, where our Lord attended the wedding feast [wrote a pilgrim] and we lay down on that self-same feasting bench, where I, unworthy as I am, wrote all the names of my kinfolk.[26]

The progress of the Christian community, which can seem so homogeneous at first sight, rapidly dissolves into a loose bundle of family histories. For the historian Sozomen, the story of Christianity in Ascalon and Gaza was the story of his own and of a neighboring family:

> The first churches and monasteries created in that country were founded by members of this family and supported by their power and beneficence toward strangers and the

needy. Some good men belonging to this family have
flourished even in my own days; and in my youth I saw
some of them, but they were then very aged.[27]

At the same time, we must remember that the Christian
church had risen to prominence largely because its central ritual
practices and its increasingly centralized organization and financial administration presented the pagan world with an ideal
community that had claimed to modify, to redirect, and even to
delimit the bonds of the kin.[28] The church was an artificial kin
group. Its members were expected to project onto the new
community a fair measure of the sense of solidarity, of the
loyalties, and of the obligations that had previously been directed to the physical family. Nowhere was this made more
plain than in the care of the dead. By the early third century, the
Roman community had its own cemetery; and this cemetery
was sufficiently important for the deacon in charge, Callistus, to
gain considerable influence in the Roman church.[29] Occasionally, the burial of the poor and, even, of non-Christians emphasized the breaking of the barriers of the kin.[30] More often, the
boundaries of concern between the new kin group and those
outside it were drawn frequently and strictly: the community
would remember only its own members, while infidels, back-
sliders, and the excommunicate were excluded.[31] The careful
noting of the anniversaries of the deaths of martyrs and bishops
gave the Christian community a perpetual responsibility for
maintaining the memory of its heroes and leaders.[32]

Thus, the bishops of the fourth century inherited a situation
fraught with potential conflict. They had emerged as the single
leaders of communities placed in sprawling cities.[33] The liturgical practices of their church and the special position within
these of a privileged category of the dead condensed strong
centripetal drives within the Christian community. Yet, these
had been largely ritual solutions: Christianity did not attempt
to touch the average grave. For the overwhelming majority of
the Christian congregation, the family grave had remained "a
fine and private place"; and the Christian clergy, whatever they
may have wished, remained dependent for support on the laity
who owned such graves. Thus, the strong sense of community,
preserved by Christian ritual, was only so much icing on the

top of a rich and increasingly crumbly cake of well-to-do Christian families.[34] What became plain throughout the century was that the family grave, and *a fortiori* the martyr's grave, could become a zone of conflict between the centripetal elements, which had found convincing ritual expression for the ideal of the community of the believers, and strong centrifugal pulls. Family piety could lead to a "privatization" of religious practice, whether through ostentatious forms of celebration at the family grave, or by the extension to the graves of the martyrs of practices associated with strong private family loyalties.

In many ways, it was the tension between private and communal which led to the flaring up of the debate on "superstition" which I have described for the late fourth and early fifth centuries. Augustine deals with it explicitly; first with his congregation at Hippo and later when faced with the practice of *depositio ad sanctos*. Even the manner in which Vigilantius attacked the cult of relics shows that he was facing a similar tension. He was spokesman for the views of men who were concerned at the way in which ostentatious and particularized loyalties to the holy dead disrupted the ideal community of the believers.[35] The practices localized the saints at tombs that could not be accessible to all, creating thereby a privileged religious topography of the Roman world from which peripheral Christian communities would feel excluded.[36] Neglect of the local church in favor of Jerusalem and the holy places,[37] and the danger that the new feast days of the martyrs might devalue the common high day of Easter[38] were real, and understandable, objects of concern among the local clergy of southern Gaul and Spain.[39]

Such tensions come from a very different direction from that posited by the "two-tiered" model. As we have seen, the evidence of the pressure from "mass conversions" has been exaggerated. Nor is there any evidence that the *locus* of superstitious practice lay among the "vulgar." Indeed, it is the other way round: what is clearly documented is the tension caused by the way in which the demands of a new elite of well-to-do Christian laywomen and laymen were met by the determination of an equally new elite of bishops, who often came from the same class, that they and they alone should be the *patroni* of the publicly established Christian communities. Instead of a dialogue on "superstition" conducted between the disapproving "few" and the "common herd," we must begin with a conflict more plausible to late-Roman men—a conflict between rival systems of patronage.

Such considerations may help to put the rise of the cult of martyrs into a wider perspective. Its stages may become more clear as a result. For it is far from certain that what we have been calling, for the sake of convenience, the "rise of the cult of saints" in the late fourth century was any more than the vigorous appropriation of this cult by the bishops and the ruling classes of the Roman Empire. The cult itself has far deeper roots. Intense feelings for holy figures and the martyred dead reach back into late Judaism: they are part of an impressive continuum of beliefs.[40] What was far from certain, however, was who, within the Christian community, should have the monopoly of expressing and orchestrating such belief. At the beginning of the fourth century, this was unclear. For the influential patron had great advantages. He or she could obtain the body of the martyr with least resistance and could house it most fittingly. Hence in 295, the gentlewoman Pompeiana could appropriate the body of the young martyr Maximilianus: she

> obtained the body from the magistrate and, after placing it in her own chamber, later brought it to Carthage. There she buried it at the foot of a hill near the governor's palace next to the body of the martyr Cyprian. Thirteen days later, the woman herself passed away and was buried in the same spot. But Victor, the boy's father, returned to his home in great joy.[41]

Pompeiana had been able to obtain the body from the authorities to the apparent exclusion of the kin, and could place it in a group of special tombs surrounding that of Saint Cyprian, among which her own grave lay. At Salona, the first known Christian *memoria* was created in 304 by a well-to-do lady, Asclepia, above the grave of a martyr, Anastasius, in a building that had been designed to house also her own tomb and those of her family.[42] Thus, for the influential layman, the grave, always "a fine and private place," could reach out to appropriate the martyr, and so bring a holy grave, either directly or by implication, out of the Christian community as a whole into the orbit of a single family.[43]

Thus, a "privatization of the holy" by well-to-do Christian families was a very real prospect for the future development of the Christian church at the turn of the third and fourth centuries. Often the issue was made only too plain. A Spanish noblewoman resident in Carthage, Lucilla, was in a position to "fix" the election of her own dependent to the great see of Carthage, in 311–12, by judicious almsgiving.[44] She had owned a bone of a martyr, and had been in the habit of kissing it before she took the Eucharist: the conflict between "privatized" access to the holy and participation in forms of the holy shared by the community at large was given stark ritual expression by Lucilla's gesture. Lucilla, *potens et factiosa femina*, never forgave the rebuke she had received from the deacon on one such occasion.[45] Yet Lucilla was a sign of the times: the establishment of Christianity under Constantine made plain that, from the emperor downwards, the overmighty patron had come to stay.

It is with such incidents in mind that we can best approach the flicker of concern that played around the graves in the late fourth and early fifth centuries. The practice of *depositio ad sanctos*, for instance, threatened to make only too plain the play of family influence around the holy graves. It was a privilege which, as one inscription put it, "many desire and few obtain."[46] Once obtained, it mapped out in a peculiarly blatant manner, in terms of proximity to the saint, the balance of social power within the Christian community. The tension between the community of the dead and the demands of private status has always presented paradoxes to toy with:

> Here lie I at the chapel door,
> Here lie I because I'm poor.
> The further in the more you pay.
> Here lie I as warm as they.[47]

But it also raised a deeper issue: the relation between communal and private care of the souls of the dead. When Augustine wrote the *De cura gerenda pro mortuis,* this was at the forefront of his concerns. The private initiative of Flora in placing her son closer than anybody else to Saint Felix would seem to weaken the strength of the communal concern of the church, *pia mater communis,* "the loyal and common mother," that *all* Christians should, at the last day, enjoy the proximity of the saints.[48] Flora might seem to have taken upon herself to obtain a privilege for her son, which only the church could gain by its prayers for all Christians without discrimination. On the issue of *depositio ad sanctos* Augustine the bishop, the eloquent exponent of the ideal unity of the Catholic church and, one may suspect, the man of talent and son of a *tenuis municeps* whose education and later clerical career had enabled him to step aside a little from the aristocratic structures of the Latin West, was lukewarm. He accepted the practice; but he paints in distinctly pastel shades the associations of the *memoria* of Saint Felix, which Paulinus and his aristocratic friends had been painting with so rich a palette for over a generation.[49]

It is the same with Augustine's reaction to the practice of feasting at the family grave. Ultimately, "privatization" struck him as a more grave danger than "superstition." Whatever his explanation of the origin of such feasting might be, when it came to deciding what to do about it, Augustine was more alert to its immediate social function. Ostentatious feasting could be socially divisive,[50] and especially in a community where the upper class was evenly divided between Catholic and Donatist. The centrifugal pulls of family loyalties in a notoriously fissile congregation greatly preoccupied Augustine in those years.[51] He was, therefore, prepared to accept some form of feasting as long as it did not become competitive, exclusive, or an occasion for a family to flaunt the extent of its own dependents.

Yet we only need turn to other regions of the Christian world to realize that the balance between communal control and family feeling might be different and could lead to very different attitudes. In Rome, for instance, the Christian church rose to prominence on a slow tide of well-to-do lay patronage. With loving detail and great historical finesse, Charles Pietri has brought together the evidence for the late fourth and early fifth centuries: this was *"la grande époque de l'évergétisme chrétien."* [52]

It was a *grande époque* untroubled at any time by the mention of "superstition." When the senator Pammachius gave a feast to the poor on the anniversary of the death of his wife, he did it in the basilica of Saint Peter himself. Paulinus was delighted. If all senators gave displays of that kind, he wrote, Rome would not need to fear the threats of the Apocalypse.[53] Such practices and the applause they aroused take us into a very different milieu from that of Augustine.[54] They point to the most silent and decisive diplomatic triumph ever won by the bishops of Rome in the late antique period. Faced by vast cemeteries that could so easily have slipped irrevocably out of their control (and in which some strange things happened throughout the fourth century);[55] dependent on a laity whose leading members had been accustomed to maintaining the prestige of their families by lavish spending, the popes nonetheless managed to harmonize their own patronage system with that of their influential laity. Damasus, great patron of the catacombs, has every reason to be proud of the nickname bestowed on him by his enemies, *auriscalpius matronarum:* "The Ear Tickler of Noble Ladies."[56] For without constant discreet efforts by the bishops and their oligarchy of deacons, whose performances in the *conversazioni* of Roman noble houses were etched so bitterly by Jerome,[57] the Christian cult of saints in Rome would not have risen with such seemingly effortless exuberance to dazzle contemporaries throughout the Latin West.

We should now look more closely at the types of initiative which certain bishops took in patronizing the cult of the saints. For plainly we are dealing with a situation different from what we had been led to expect. We are neither faced with grudging or politic accommodation to a growing "popular" form of religiosity nor with measures designed to absorb leaderless pagan "masses" by a homeopathic dose of "superstition." Rather, we are dealing with changes in the cult of saints that articulate clearly changes in the quality of leadership within the Christian community itself.

The case of Ambrose, as it has recently been studied by Ernst Dassmann, makes this plain.[58] In Milan, the discovery of the relics of Saints Gervasius and Protasius, in 385, was an exciting event. But it was not the first time that relics had been discovered or received in Milan. The Christian cemetery areas were already dotted with quite sizeable martyr's *memoriae*. What was new was the speed and the certainty of touch with which Ambrose appropriated the relics. He moved them after only two days from the shrine of Saints Felix and Nabor, where they had been unearthed, into the new basilica which he had built for himself; and he placed them under the altar, where his own sarcophagus was to have stood. By this move, Gervasius and Protasius were inseparably linked to the communal liturgy, in a church built by the bishop, in which the bishop would frequently preside. In that way, they would be available to the community as a whole. Ambrose had made a discovery "of use to all"—*qui prosint omnibus*.[59]

Ambrose's aim was the *resurrectio martyrum*: a few graves studiously linked to the episcopal eucharistic liturgy should "begin to stand out" in a graveyard where, previously, holy graves had existed, but had lacked that clear focus.[60] At the same time, Ambrose restricted the random feasting which had been common at other *memoriae*, as too closely resembling pagan family anniversaries.[61] Within a few years, the acquiescence of a flourishing Milanese laity made itself plain in the exquisite and highly ceremonious sarcophagi that had edged into the bishop's new holy place. One of these contained Manlia Daedalia, "of famous family, of outstanding wealth, mother of the needy," the sister of none other than Manlius Theodorus, nobleman, courtier, man of letters, patron of Augustine and future praetorian prefect of Italy.[62]

Ambrose had not "introduced" the cult of the martyrs into Milan, still less had he merely acquiesced passively to previous practices. His initiatives had been firm and in many ways unusual: he had been prepared both to move bodies and to link them decisively to the altar of a new church. Rather, he was like an electrician who rewires an antiquated wiring system: more power could pass through stronger, better-insulated wires toward the bishop as leader of the community. Bishops took similar initiatives elsewhere. At Tebessa, in the heart of the new shrine built by Bishop Alexander, the "righteous ones of old" now enjoyed "a beautiful seat":

Where once long rest had robbed them from our gaze, they
blaze with light on a fitting pedestal, and their gathered

crown now blooms with joy.... From all around the Christian people, young and old, flow in to see them, happy to tread the holy threshold, singing their praises and hailing with outstretched hands the Christian faith.[63]

The miracle stories at the shrines of Saint Stephen at Hippo and Uzalis show a similar determination on the part of Augustine and his colleagues. Miraculous healings at the shrines, which had previously been treated by the recipients with a certain reticence as private events, the possession of the individual, are now deliberately made public:[64] files are kept,[65] the healed stand up and show themselves to the congregation, at Uzalis the hot, tired crowds are regaled with an anthology of the more dramatic cures.[66]

In this process of "rewiring" the figure of the martyr himself changes. We shall see, in the next chapter, the intense personal links which those who acted as *impresarios* of the cult established with their invisible friends and protectors. It is a complex and poignant story; but the outcome was plain—the martyr took on a distinctive late-Roman face. He was the *patronus*, the invisible, heavenly concomitant of the patronage exercised palpably on earth by the bishop. Hence the changes in the manner of celebrating his feast. The feastings, the *laetitiae*, which Augustine and Ambrose were concerned to exclude from the martyr's shrine, still appear, for all the disruptive ostentation and competitiveness that might accompany family grave practices, to have retained something of the face-to-face familiarity of an ideal kin group. In early Christian art, the meal of the dead is almost invariably presented as an eye-to-eye affair. No one is shown presiding, except in one case—and that is the aristocrat Junius Bassus, urban prefect of Rome.[67] Nothing is more impressive than the spate of eloquence, from all over the empire, with which a new generation of bishops now presented the festivals of the martyrs, no longer as family *laetitiae*, but as full-dress public banquets given by the invisible *patroni* to their earthly clients. The vast ceremoniousness of late-Roman relationships of dependence and munificence makes their language heavy with reverence.[68]

Not every biship felt that he had to stop at words. Paulinus of Nola knew that the solemn drinking at the festival of Saint Felix

was likely to be one passing fleck of unalloyed joy in the grim
lives of the peasants and drovers of the Abruzzi: so, in a hall
blazing with expensive new paintings that showed God's great
acts of power in distant times,[69] he allowed these exhausted
men, who had trudged there in the winter's cold, to settle down
in the warmth with their *gaudia*.[70] The habit continued. Gregory of Tours will devote twenty lines of rhapsodic prose to the
miraculous bouquet of a wine passed around at one martyr's
vigil.[71] This is not because he and his congregation had become
more lax. It is rather that the bishop has entered with greater
certainty into his role as the visible *patronus* beneath the invisible *patronus*. Once the lines of patronage are clearly drawn
to that one center, the feasting can begin again:

> This word have we spoken concerning the poor; God hath
> established the bishop because of the feasts, that he may
> refresh them at the feasts.[72]

What might have caused this shift? In the first place, a different kind of bishop, from families more accustomed to play the
role of the *grand seigneur*, was taking over the leadership of the
Christian communities.[73] At an age when Augustine was fer-
vently praying not to be thrashed by the small-town school-
teacher, Ambrose was playing at being a bishop, welcoming
even his mother by extending his hand to be kissed: here was a
man who would know how to face the world *satis episcopaliter*.[74]
In the small world of the Latin clergy, Ambrose could set the
tone throughout northern Italy, and his personal influence
reached to places as far apart as Hippo and Rouen.[75] His "style"
for the discovery and incorporation of relics rapidly became a
model for the Latin West.[76]

But why should so many other bishops, of very different
backgrounds and in many different areas, wish to follow Ambrose's example? Here we should not forget one factor: the growing wealth of the church.[77] In a society where wealth slipped
ponderously from hand to hand through inheritance more
than through any other means, a century of undisturbed accumulation of endowments left the bishops of the Latin church
with a wealth undreamed of in previous generations.[78] It was
the mass of new wealth, not the mass of new converts, that

rested most heavily on the bishops. By 412, Augustine, as bishop, had control of property twenty times greater than he had ever owned for himself;[79] by 426, his community of technically propertyless clergymen was suffering from the strain of not having enough objects on which to spend the money they had given over to the church.[80] Exempt from many forms of taxation,[81] and not subject to the periodic financial bloodlettings that accompanied a secular career, the leaders of the Christian community found themselves in a difficult position. They had all the means of social dominance, and none of the means of showing it in acceptable form. For bitter envy always fell on undistributed wealth in the ancient world, and the bishops could be made to feel this as much as any secular *potentes*. Yet they lacked the normal outlets by which the layman could buy off envy by ostentatiously flirting with bankruptcy in bouts of public giving.[82] For the traditional categories of Christian giving could no longer absorb so much accumulated wealth. Though remaining important as symbolic categories, the poor, the stranger, the sick, and other unprotected categories had reached their limits in the Latin West as consumers of surplus wealth. The dangerous weight of rising population pressing against limited resources, which Evelyne Patlagean has now so brilliantly shown to lie at the root of the *misère* of many provinces of the eastern Mediterranean, does not appear to have affected Italy, North Africa, or Gaul.[83] Few towns had problems of a scale that made priorities for the distribution of church resources an explosive issue. In Alexandria, the bishop had to choose between shirts for the poor and the itch to build;[84] the bishops of the West, by contrast, found that they had to invent new ways of spending money.

Building and the increase of ceremonial in connection with new foci of worship was the only way out. And where better than at the graves of the martyrs? The practical and social problems of building within the walls of the town would be avoided.[85] Only a cemetery area could have taken shrines the size of those which Alexander had placed outside Tebessa and Paulinus outside Nola.[86] Furthermore, building and ceremonial at such shrines would sum up more appositely than anywhere else the paradox of episcopal wealth. For this was "non-wealth:" it was not private.[87] So it would be deployed at a "non-grave," standing in the middle of a cluster of "very fine and private places." Furthermore, such wealth and ceremonial would be deployed in the invisible presence of a figure who had taken on all the features of a late-Roman *patronus*. The saint was the good *patronus:* he was the *patronus* whose intercessions were successful, whose wealth was at the disposal of all, whose *potentia* was exercised without violence and to whom loyalty could be shown without constraint. The bishop could stand for him. Lavish building, splendid ceremonial, and even feasting at such a shrine washed clean the hard facts of accumulated wealth and patronage, as they were now practiced in real life, even by bishops, a short distance away within the walls of the city of the living.[88] The cult of the saints was a focus where wealth could be spent without envy and *patrocinium* exercised without obligation.[89] It was a solution both more clear-cut and antiseptic than almost any outlet for the display of wealth and power that had been previously found in the civic life of the classical world. It is not surprising that, in the late fourth century, the saints suddenly began to "stand out" in such high eminence. As Bishop Alexander stated in his inscription at Tebessa,

> Here where you see walls crowned with gleaming roofs,
> here where the high ceilings glitter and the holy altars stand:
> this place is not the work of any noblemen, but stands
> forever to the glory of the bishop, Alexander.[90]

Furthermore, the Christian communities on which the bishops came to lavish so much wealth connected with the cult of saints had their own reasons to need precisely such a cult. For now that the Christian congregation could begin to identify itself with the majority of the inhabitants of each great city in the Roman world, the Christian church was placed under pressure to offer its own definition of the urban community and to provide rituals which would make this definition manifest. The Christian definition of the urban community was notably different from that of the classical city. It included two unaccustomed and potentially disruptive categories, the women and the poor. The cult of the saints offered a way of bringing precisely these two categories together, under the patronage of the bishop, in such a way as to offer a new basis for the solidarity of the late-antique town.

Let us look first at the role and the positioning of the shrine itself in relation to the existing urban community. As we have seen, the cemetery areas in which the graves of the saints lay were pointedly peripheral to the city of the living.[91] In worshiping the saints, Jerome said, "The city has changed address," *movetur urbs sedibus suis.*[92] There was much to be gained from such a shift. Christians who trooped out, on ever more frequent and clearly defined occasions as the fourth century progressed,[93] experienced in a mercifully untaxing form the thrill of passing an invisible frontier: they left a world of highly explicit structures for a "liminal" state. As Victor Turner has pointed out, the abandonment of known structures for a situation where such structures are absent, and the consequent release of spontaneous fellow feeling, are part of the enduring appeal of the experience of pilgrimage in settled societies.[94] The accustomed social world looks very different from even a short walk outside the town. William Christian has described the effect of processions to nearby shrines of the saints in northern Spain:

> As images of social wholeness, the processions have an added significance. The villagers for once in the year see the village as a social unit, abstracted from the buildings and location that make it a geographical unit.[95]

Precisely such a scene moved Prudentius, when he writes of the crowds that streamed out into the countryside to the shrine of Saint Hippolytus. Here was the *true* Rome: Rome shorn for a blessed day of its blatant social and topographical distinctions:

> The love of their religion masses Latins and strangers together in one body. . . . The majestic city disgorges her Romans in a stream; with equal ardor patricians and the plebeian host are jumbled together, shoulder to shoulder, for the faith banishes distinctions of birth.[96]

Being placed along the roads that led from the city into its countryside, they could even provide a joining point not only for the townsmen among themselves, but between the townsmen and the alien, despised villagers on whose foodstuffs the city depended.[97] In the case of the shrine of Saint Felix at Cimitile, the pilgrimage center could redress the balance between town and country in Campania. It came to act as the meeting point of a loose confederacy of hill villages whose importance had grown throughout the fourth century at the expense of Nola, the traditional urban center of the region.[98]

It was on such occasions, also, that the greatest cleavage of all in late-antique urban society was bridged: for a delightful and perilous moment, the compartments segregating the sexes in public broke down. If not actually mixed with the men in the crowds, women were certainly available to the public gaze in a manner rare in a late-antique urban context.[99] Of one holy man it could be said, by his biographer, that he had remained chaste all his life: and this, although he had frequently attended the festivals of the martyrs as a young man![100] The frequent denunciations of shocked clergymen, and the history of successful love affairs initiated at such high moments—from the young Augustine in the great basilicas of Carthage, right up to the early middle ages, when young Muslim "bloods" would go out to see the pretty Christian girls in the great Palm Sunday processions of northern Iraq and an eleventh-century emir of Tunis learned, as Augustine had done, in the same hot nights of seven hundred years before, "to love, for love of you, the Christian feasts, and savor the sweet melodies of chanted psalms"—show that we are dealing with a heady elixir.[101] *Indiscreta societas*, "unregulated sociability:"[102] though linked by Christian moralists with pilgrimages and festivals of the saints, and invariably condemned, these moments of unstructured meeting carried with them a warm breath of hope for a lost solidarity and for the lowering of social boundaries that haunted the urban Christian communities of the Mediterranean world.[103]

Yet these exciting moments did not happen every day. The festivals of the saints always had to compete with robust traditions of secular high holiday that could offer, in more traditional form, similar moments of controlled release from explicit structures. It would be foolish to underestimate the continued vigor and heavy charge of diffused religiosity of the non-Christian ceremonial life of the late-antique town.[104] Yet the shrines of the saints reaped the advantages that came from their unique placing and their unique clientele.

For women in the ancient world, the cemetery areas had always been a zone of "low gravity," where their movements and choice of company were less subject to male scrutiny and the control of the family.[105] The new shrines, when not crowded on days of festival, were oases of peace and beauty, with flowing water, rustling trees, filled with the cooing of white doves.[106] In the shrine of Saint Stephen at Uzalis, we can see how the vast tranquillity of a shrine could engulf and heal a woman caught in the rigidities of her urban setting.

Megetia was a noblewoman from Carthage. She had dislocated her jaw from violent vomiting in the fourth month of her pregnancy, in a manner that was both debilitating and grotesque: it was a cause of constant shame to a noblewoman committed to a round of solemn visiting and respectful kissing.[107] By the seventh month her child had died in the womb.[108] Megetia's solution was to break with a setting made heavy with shame and dishonor. Her menfolk gave her and her mother permission to travel to nearby Uzalis.[109] There she was able to lie in sackcloth and ashes before the shrine, totally unashamed despite her high status.[110] Throughout that time, her only companions and advisors were women.[111] Even when Saint Stephen appeared to her in a dream, he did not behave, as Megetia unconsciously expected him to behave, lifting her jaw to him to be examined, as by her male doctor.[112] Instead, he merely reminded her of a sin she had not confessed. The shame of a disfigured noblewoman, who had failed in pregnancy, was mercifully transmuted into a private guilt, with which she wrestled successfully.[113] The stages of her recovery are marked by visits to the shrines—of Saint Stephen at Uzalis and Saint Cyprian at Carthage. In a society where the bonds of the kin tended to draw closer around the individual, offering protection and control in a less certain world,[114] the saints, as Ambrose pointed out, were the only in-laws that a woman was free to choose.[115] Their shrines offered to half the inhabitants of every late-Roman town respite and protection which they lacked the freedom to find elsewhere.[116]

The women were joined by the poor. The mood of solidarity and ideal giftgiving associated with their ceremonies made the shrines of the saints the obvious place for the poor to congregate.[117] But the poor could have found their support at the doors of Christian town houses.[118] It was the peripheral position of the cemetery areas that gave charity performed in them an added appositeness. They provided a vantage point from which the Christian church could intervene in a debate that reached its climax at the turn of the fourth and fifth century: Who was a full member of the urban community?

In a most felicitous manner, Evelyne Patlagean has shown that one of the principal changes from a classical to a postclassical society was the replacement of a particularized political model of society, in which the unit was the city, its composition defined in terms of citizens and noncitizens, by a more all-embracing economic model, in which all society was seen, in town and country alike, as divided between the rich and the poor, the rich having a duty to support the poor, which was expressed in strictly religious terms as almsgiving.[119] Nowhere was this change acted out more pointedly than in Rome.

In Rome, the old urban structures had retained their full symbolic vigor: within the walls of Rome, the Roman *plebs* continued to receive allowances of food at traditional distribution points,[120] and they received largesse in the course of traditional urban celebrations, linked to traditional locations.[121] They received such gifts because they were there, not because they were poor: they were the *plebs Romana*. Yet, at just this time, the population of Rome was kept at a high level, almost certainly through immigration from the small towns and farms of an afflicted countryside, and was supported by food from that countryside.[122] As a result, the members of the *plebs Romana*, though the only full members of the Roman community, would rub shoulders with the beggar, the vagrant, and the immigrant on terms equal in everything but status. At the first touch of famine, however, every outsider, whether the broken farmers of the hills or the *honestus advena* Ammianus Marcellinus, would be driven from the city.[123] The secular leaders of Rome had left room in their world only for their traditional clients, the *plebs Romana*.[124]

In a society where membership of the community was expressed most convincingly in terms of the patron-client relationship, and where the giving of gifts was the traditional symbol of this relationship,[125] the almsgiving associated with the cult of the saints was far more than a laudable form of poor relief. It amounted to nothing less than a claim by the new leaders of the Christian church to redraw the immemorial boundaries of the urban community. Hence, by the middle of the fourth century, the shrine of Saint Peter on the Vatican Hill had achieved a symbolic significance, as an antithesis to the Circus Maximus and the Colosseum, quite out of proportion to the comparatively modest sums spent there among the poor. In 365, the urban prefect was Lampadius,

> a man who took it very ill if even his manner of spitting was not praised, on the ground that he did so with greater skill than anyone else. . . . When this man, in his praetorship, gave magnificent games and made very rich distributions of largesse, being unable to endure the blustering of the commons, who often urged that many things should be given to those who were unworthy of them, in order to show his generosity and contempt of the mob, he summoned some beggars from the Vatican and presented them with valuable gifts.[126]

It was the mocking tribute of old Rome to the new sense of community developing on its fringes, around the Christian shrines.

The Christian church not only redefined the bounds of the community by accepting a whole new class of recipients, it also designated a new class of givers. For women had been the other blank on the map of the classical city. It was assumed that giftgiving was an act of politics, not an act of mercy; and politics was for men only. By contrast, the Christian church, from an early time, had encouraged women to take on a public role, in their own right, in relation to the poor:[127] they gave alms in person, they visited the sick, they founded shrines and poorhouses in their own name and were expected to be fully visible as participants in the ceremonial of the shrines.[128]

By the end of the fourth century, the traditional view of the place of women in upper-class Roman society had come under strain. The core of senatorial residents in Rome tended to gravitate around the accumulated wealth and indefinable prestige of a small group of senatorial heiresses. The *Historia Au-*

*gusta* tells of how senatorial ladies had founded "a little Senate house of women," to ensure that they did not lose their senatorial nobility when forced by circumstances to marry upwardly mobile politicians.[129] Yet for all their jealously preserved residue of private status, the senatorial women of Rome had been given no public role. A law of 370 expected women to pay for games promised by their late husbands on behalf of their sons; but the same law continued that it was "quite out of place and shameful" if, on such occasions, they were to make a public appearance in the full insignia of a praetor.[130] To appear in the circus box, encased in heavy silks, to receive the acclamations of the assembled *plebs Romana* was a solemn moment reserved for men only;[131] yet senatorial ladies had plainly needed to be reminded sharply of their place.

It is, therefore, significant that after the Gothic siege and sack of Rome, which tested to breaking point the traditional image of the urban community,[132] the womenfolk of the leading Christian families achieved a new prominence through participation in Christian charity and church building associated with the cult of the saints. They were encouraged to do this under their own names by their *patroni* and advisers, the bishop and clergy.[133] Demetrias was the granddaughter of the great Petronius Probus, the doyen of the *gens Anicia*.[134] In 412, she publicly dedicated herself to virginity, taking the veil from the bishop of Carthage.[135] This happened at a time when, as refugees and members of a family which was thought to have disrupted the traditional solidarities of Rome,[136] the Anician ladies might have been forced to rescue the fortunes of the family by a politic *mésalliance*. As Jerome pointed out, in his letter of congratulation, Demetrias, as one man's bride, would have been known in one province only; now she would enjoy the acclaim of the Christian *orbis terrarum*.[137] Resettled in Rome, Demetrias emerged as the builder of a shrine of Saint Stephen. The inscription leaves us in no doubt: it praises *Demetrias Amnia virgo*.[138] As devoted client of Saint Stephen, Demetrias had found a way, in those hard years, to remain very much an Anician lady, with her nobility intact. The cult of saints had guaranteed her a public role in the Christianized city.

Developments such as these, which are vividly documented

for Rome but are by no means confined to that city, lead us to sense the weight of the pressures of the urban community as a whole which forced the cult of saints into ever greater prominence. Far from betraying an amiable recidivism in relation to the pagan past, expenditure of wealth and ceremonial at the graves of the saints is marked by a sense of urgency. For in this cult the townsmen of the western Mediterranean had found a new idiom with which to express and control the disturbingly new situation in which they found themselves at the turn of the fourth and fifth centuries.

I trust that the reader will pardon me for having presented a somewhat schematic and deliberately *grisaille* analysis of a complex development, rich in intimate religious feeling. But if we are to shake the "two-tiered" model from our minds, we must be prepared to offer an alternative. If this alternative has any merit, it is in directing our attention to different areas of the late-Roman scene. Beliefs, for instance, must be set precisely against their social context, for the simple reason that, without some form of orchestration, beliefs such as those that surround the graves of the saints can lie faceless for generations. What we have seen is not the growth of new beliefs within the Christian communities, but the restructuring of old beliefs in such a way as to allow them to carry a far heavier "charge" of public meaning. We must also redefine "popular." Let me suggest that we take seriously its late-Roman meaning: the ability of the few to mobilize the support of the many. We are in a world where the great are seldom presented in art without an admiring crowd.[139] One of the most interesting features of late antiquity indeed, is the capacity of its elites to strike roots that worked themselves downwards into deeper layers of the populace than had apparently been true in the classical Roman Empire. So much of what we call the "democratization of culture" in late antiquity is democratization from on top.[140]

Last of all, we can appreciate, perhaps, how an alternative model can open up to us the minds and the hearts of a remarkable generation. As far apart as Cappadocia and Rouen, men and women were prepared to place at the disposal of the articulation of the cult of saints all the resources of the upper-class culture of the late-Roman world. For, far from describing a grudging or politic concession to the mindless force of habits formed among the "common herd," we have met a group of *impresarios*, taking initiatives, making choices, and, in so doing, coining a public language that would last through western Europe deep into the middle ages. We are now free to leave the crowds for a moment and to attempt, in the next two chapters, to enter the minds of the men who, in differing ways, threw up around the graves a new structure of relations between heaven and earth.

# Chapter Three

## The Invisible Companion

The philosophers and the orators have fallen into oblivion; the masses do not even know the names of the emperors and their generals; but everyone knows the names of the martyrs, better than those of their most intimate friends.[1]

It is in these terms that Theodoret bishop of Cyrrhus sought to convey the extent of the triumph of Christianity: by the mid-fifth century, the cult of the saints had ringed the populations of the Mediterranean with intimate invisible friends. "The invisible friend"—ἀόρατος φίλος;[2] the "intimate friend"—γνήσιος φίλος:[3] these are terms on which Theodoret and his contemporaries dwelt lovingly in relation to the saints. What we shall follow in this chapter is the manner in which new invisible companions came to crowd in around the men and women of late antiquity and the early middle ages. In so doing, we shall touch upon the subtle transformation of immemorial beliefs that was involved when Mediterranean men and women, from the late fourth century onwards, turned with increasing explicitness for friendship, inspiration and protection in this life and beyond the grave, to invisible beings who were fellow humans and whom they could invest with the precise and palpable features of beloved and powerful figures in their own society.

A tradition of scholarship for which any personal relationship whatsoever with an invisible

50

intermediary figure, whether a god, a *daimon*, a guardian angel or a saint, tends to be relegated to the suspect category of "popular beliefs," has not been sufficiently sensitive to the implications of such a change. As all such relationships might seem to betray a uniform "reflux of the human mind" into polytheism, the differences between them have not received the attention they deserve. Yet to seek the face of a fellow human being where an earlier generation had wished to see the shimmering presence of a bodiless power is no small change; and it is a change made all the more clear by the manner in which the Christian writers who expressed their intimate relationships with the new invisible companions still drew on ancient ideas whose momentum lingered on perceptibly in a new setting. This enables us to follow with some precision the slow changing of an age.

We begin with an ancient map of the relations between the human and the divine. The men of the second and third centuries had an acute sense of the multiplicity of the self and of the chain of intermediaries that reached, yet further still, from the self to God. Plutarch had been firm on this issue. Contrary to popular belief, he wrote, the soul is not a simple, homogeneous substance: it is a composite, consisting of many layers. Above the layers of which the individual is immediately conscious, there lies a further layer, the "true" soul, that is as immeasurably superior to the soul as we know it, as the soul itself is superior to the body.[4] Thus, the self is a hierarchy, and its peak lies directly beneath the divine. At that peak, late-antique men placed an invisible protector. Whether this protector was presented as the personal *daimon*, the *genius*, or the guardian angel, its function was the same: it was an invisible being entrusted with the care of the individual, in a manner so intimate that it was not only the constant companion of the individual; it was almost an upward extension of the individual.[5] For the individual had been entrusted to it at birth, and continued under its protection after death. The abiding identity of the self was in its keeping. There was nothing strange, therefore, in late-antique etiquette, in addressing a person simply as "Your Angel."[6] As Ammianus Marcellinus wrote,

The theologians maintain that there are associated with all
men at their birth . . . certain divinities of that sort, as direc-
tors of their conduct; but they have been seen by very few,
whom their manifold merits have raised to eminence.[7]

The great men of the third century had been those whose
visions made plain that they enjoyed an exceptional degree of
closeness to their invisible guardians. In 240, the young Mani
began his career as a preacher with experiences of contact with
his protector so intimate as to culminate in the fusing of his
subjective identity with that of his higher self, his heavenly
twin:

Coming to me, the spirit (the heavenly twin) chose me,
judged me fit for him, separated me by drawing me away
from the sect in which I was reared. . . . I made him mine, as
my very own.[8]

In 310, Constantine prepared carefully for his conquests with
a vision of *his* Apollo: "You saw him and recognized yourself in
him . . . young and gay, a bringer of salvation and of exceeding
beauty."[9]

Nor was such intimate care reserved only for the great. For
Origen, benevolent presences pressed in around the average
Christian: the guardian angels could be treated as his "kinsfolk
and friends . . . who make their presence felt intimately to those
who pray to them."[10] What this could mean is shown in the
autobiographical work of a pupil and admirer of Origen, the
*Speech of Thanksgiving and Praise of Origen*, presented by Gregory Thaumaturgus in 234. Gregory had much to explain in his
life. He was a *déraciné*. He and his relatives had moved on the
edge of the imperial administration from the back country of
Pontus on the Black Sea to Palestine, passing through the
schools of Roman Law at Beirut. He was an anxious and ambiti-
ous young man of apparently Christian background, whose
career resembles closely that of the young Augustine. When he
came across the study circle of Origen at Caesarea he felt that he
had steered, at last, into a safe harbor. In making clear to himself and to others the nature of his conversion Gregory fell back
naturally on the concept of the guardian angel:

Indeed, neither I nor any of my kinsmen could see what was best for me. . . . For a long time, that angelic presence has nourished me, has formed me, and led me by the hand. Above all, he joined me to that great man—to a man who had no previous relationship with me; to a man who was no kinsman and no neighbor; to a man who had not come from my province, and was unacquainted with my home.[11]

Thus, whether in times of crisis, or in the day-to-day search for protection and inspiration, the religious sensibilities of late-antique men had long been molded by an intense dialogue with invisible companions. At the end of the fourth century, the *Hymns* of Synesius of Cyrene express in exquisitely traditional language the warmth of which such a relationship was capable:

And give me a companion, O King, a partner, a sacred messenger of sacred power, a messenger of prayer illumined by the divine light, a friend, a dispenser of noble gifts, a guard of my soul, a guard of my life, a guard over prayers, a guard over deeds.[12]

While Synesius, the philosopher, wrote these and similar lines, Pontius Meropius Paulinus, a nobleman whose family estates and those of his wife were scattered from Bordeaux to Barcelona, brought a decade of increasing withdrawal to an end by settling as a priest at Nola, where he owned family property, where he had served in 381 as governor, and where an ancestor had been acclaimed in the city as *patronus ex origine*. By 394, he had sloughed off much of his family property, and had shocked senatorial opinion by adopting a life of ascetic continence, thereby bringing a great family name to an end. His past behavior demanded explanation, both to himself and to others: an anxious withdrawal "up country" following the assassination of his brother and the threat of confiscation, in the wake of the suppression of the usurpation of the emperor Maximus, around 389; the death of a newborn son; ordination as a priest forced upon him by the congregation at Barcelona, followed brusquely by a definitive withdrawal at Nola in 394.[13] His breach with Gallo-Roman aristocratic society was registered in a public exchange of poems between himself and his teacher, Ausonius,

then over sixty, the doyen of the cultivated classes of southern
Gaul and, for a happy moment, the *éminence grise* of a court
open to the influence of the traditional landowning families, of
which Paulinus had been so successful a member.[14] Throughout his life, Paulinus remained something of an exhibit:
*Paulinus noster* Augustine would call him when he wrote on
detachment from wealth in the *City of God*.[15]

Apart from Augustine himself, few Christian writers in the
Latin West were exposed to such constant pressure to com-
municate their destinies to a curious Christian audience. None
communicated this destiny more frequently and with greater
poetic skill in terms of a relationship with an invisible companion, than did Paulinus in the poems on Saint Felix, which
he came to write after he had settled in Nola, lavishing attention
on Felix's shrine first as priest and then as bishop of Nola:

> Nunc ad te, venerande parens, aeterne patrone
> susceptor meus, et Christo carissime Felix,
> gratificas verso referam sermone loquellas.
>
> [Now let me turn my poet's tongue in thanks to
> you, Felix, revered father, everlasting patron,
> Felix my nurse, Felix, dear friend of Christ.][16]

Paulinus's relationship with an invisible figure has been
justly compared with the notoriously overarticulate liaison enjoyed by the second-century rhetor, Aelius Aristides, with his
healing god, Asclepius.[17] However, the egocentrism and
hypochondria that makes Aristides' *Sacred Tales* such a disturbing and fascinating document are notably absent. The "vast
gentleness"[18] of Paulinus has, if anything, done him a dis-
service. We take his relationship with Saint Felix for granted, as
Aelius Aristides ensured that we would never take his dealings
with Asclepius for granted. As a result, Paulinus's activities at
Nola tend to be passed over: they have come to be regarded as
idyllic, a little fussy, and, above all, not very surprising;[19] they
are treated as no more than we might expect from an eccentric
aristocrat who had found new ways to spend the boundless
wealth and leisure of the senatorial class[20] at a time when we
assume that, in any case, the cult of saints was rising like a
ground mist throughout the western Mediterranean.[21] We as-

sume that Paulinus, no theologian but a well-groomed classical poet, had found in Felix and his shrine a comfortable place of retirement, a new subject for versifying and an avatar of the old gods of the city.[22]

Yet we must never forget that Paulinus was the contemporary and the close friend of Sulpicius Severus, author of the classic *Life of Martin*.[23] Both men have much in common: around the turn of the century, they were struggling to express new forms of relationship between the ordinary man and his holy protectors. Whether these spiritual *patroni* had recently been living and visible, as was Saint Martin, or were long dead—or, rather, living and *in*visible—as was Saint Felix, both Sulpicius and Paulinus placed human beings firmly in the forefront of Christian Latin literature. The fact that both succeeded in such a way as to set western Christian attitudes to the saints on a steady course from that time onwards should not lead us to underestimate the novelty of their enterprise and the skill with which they redistributed many of the ancient themes of Mediterranean religious thought in such a way as to give new prominence to their heroes.[24] If, in Nietzsche's words, "die Originalen sind zumeist auch die Namengeber gewesen,"[25] then Paulinus, precisely because of the seemingly unthinking certainty with which he found apposite names for the haunting presence in his life of Saint Felix, deserves a place alongside the mighty Augustine, as a founder of Latin Christian piety.

Yet, with Paulinus, we can see an ancient landscape changing all the more evidently through catching sight of so many of the old landmarks viewed from a different angle. Thus, when Paulinus writes about his relationship with Saint Felix, he pointedly and lovingly transfers to a dead human being all the sense of intimate involvement with an invisible companion that men in previous generations had looked for in a relationship with the *non*human figures of gods, *daimōnes,* or angels. Precisely because Paulinus makes so clear how much of his relationship with Felix follows an ancient outline, we can measure how intimate a figure the patron saint could become for the men of late antiquity. At the same time, the fact that the relationship can be expressed as one between two human beings means that the rich blood of late-Roman bonds of friendship and dependence now flows into the tissue of the invisible world. Felix has a human face. Relations with him are modeled on expectations molded by human experience. What is more important, perhaps, is that this human experience carried with it so much of the precise flavor of the day-to-day life of the men of the late fourth and early fifth centuries. Felix was not a timeless idealized figure: he was very much a *patronus* and an *amicus* as Paulinus and his readers recognized such beings, only too well, in the tight-knit world of the Roman aristocracy and its dependents.

Let us begin, however, with the ancient background, with the manner in which Felix steps into his role as invisible companion. For Paulinus deliberately pins his identity on his relationship with Felix, and, in so doing, he carries over to the human saint much of the language used previously of the *daimōn*, the *genius*, and the guardian angel. The weight of the centuries of belief that linked the layers of the self to the divine through a close-knit chain of nonhuman intermediaries presses Felix deep into the life and personality of Paulinus. He is far more than a distant intercessor before the throne of God; he is a guardian of Paulinus's identity and, almost, at times, a personification of that identity. Paulinus's poems make plain that, for late-antique and early medieval men, the patron saint still has the ancient quality almost of an unconscious layer of the self.

Thus we seldom lose sight of a chain of intimately joined beings. The *daimōnes* themselves enjoyed gods as their protecting spirits.[26] It came to be accepted with increasing enthusiasm that the exceptional man, also, could enjoy the same privileges as a *daimōn*, by having a god or God as his direct personal protector.[27] The average man had his *daimōn* or genius allotted to him by God.[28] Astrological belief gave a further precision to the moment at which the guardian and the individual were joined at birth: for the horoscope revealed the alloy of the *genius* that lodged with the person at that moment.[29]

We find the same structure of closely interdependent figures in the poems of Paulinus. Felix, having enjoyed the intimate guardianship of Christ throughout his life,[30] has come yet closer to him after the grave.[31] The richness of this close bond in

Heaven spills over from Felix to Paulinus, his charge on earth:
"Now let me speak of you . . . I, whom Christ has handed over
to you, his dear friend, to be your own from my first years on
earth."[32] Paulinus is a poet of intimacy: for him "contempt for
the world" was always associated with the opportunity to sink
every deeper "into the companionship of Christ."[33] In an
extraordinary joining of images, he can write of a dead man
scaling the stars to lay his head on Jesus' breast.[34] But the language he uses of Felix is not merely the language of human
friendship or human patronage: it has kept an ancient ring.
Paulinus feels the closeness of Felix with all the inevitability of a
link in the tranquil structure of the universe. For Felix is more to
Paulinus than a protector who has made his care known to him
by single acts of intercession; these acts themselves reveal a
stable, hidden bond.[35] In a way, Paulinus was born with Felix;
and by baptism and ascetic withdrawal, he has been "reborn"
with Felix. Felix's festival, the day when Felix, by dying, was
"born" from earth to Heaven, has become Paulinus's true
birthday:

> I have always honored this day in such a way that I would
> treat it as my own birthday rather than that day on which I
> was born. . . . Ill-starred the day when I came forth, from
> evil stock to evil deeds; blessed the day when my protector
> was born for me to Heaven.[36]

This is a carefully chosen paradox, charged with ancient associations. For only a linking of the identity with an ideal invisible
companion thought of as a bond as close as the joining of the
*genius* to the person at birth, could console Paulinus and his
austere friends for the sadness of finding themselves born into
the flesh.

It is not surprising, perhaps, that the cult of the patron saint
spread most quickly in ascetic circles: for an identity placed at a
nadir of uncertainty by the ascetic's deep sense of sin cried out
for some intimate thread of stability. Paulinus's portrait of Felix
is very much the warm and colorful antithesis of Paulinus's
refusal to paint his own, as too sadly modeled on the flaking
image of Adam to merit copying.[37]

If we turn to Gregory of Nyssa's life of his sister Macrina, we can see what this could mean in a cultivated Christian family. Macrina, Gregory writes, was only her public name; she had a true, secret name, revealed in a vision. For when her mother was giving birth to her, she dreamed three times that she was holding her child while a majestic figure, the virgin martyr Thecla, gave her the name of Thecla. She was really giving birth to a second Thecla.[38] The dream was crucial for Macrina's mother, a young woman, who had married unwillingly, merely to gain the protection of a husband when her parents had died, and for whom this was the first experience of childbirth: the labor became easy, and Macrina was born with her identity secured. The sadness of physical birth had been redeemed. Macrina would soon be joined by a succession of formidable brothers. But with her identity reinforced and a trifle over-shadowed by her mysterious link to the exemplary virgin Thecla, Macrina always remained different. As a child, she had lived "as if she was still in her mother's womb;"[39] as head of a convent, her life trembled on the invisible frontier between the human and the angelic.[40]

The later spread of Christian names reflects the need to link the identity of the individual to a saint. A Christian name stood for a new identity associated with a new birth. For the "rebirth" promised at Christian baptism derived its full meaning from an ancient model of the formation of the personality. Baptism can-celed the influence of the stars that had first formed the person-ality, by giving the initiate a new protecting spirit, in such a way as to free him from a personality in which the quality of the original *genius* itself had been woven into a tangled web by the conflicting influence of the planets.[41] In Syria, for instance, we can follow the name Sergius, spreading through the towns and villages along routes that radiate from the baptisteries that flanked the shrines of the saint.[42]

Yet these protecting figures are now human beings. We can see what this means if we turn for a moment to the art of the fourth century. In the late-third- or early-fourth-century burial chamber of the Vincentii, we can see the lady Vibia led by the hand into the feast of the gods by her *angelus bonus*.[43] In 396, the lady Veneranda is shown in her burial chamber behind a mar-tyr's shrine, flanked by another elegant late-Roman woman, the martyr saint Petronilla.[44] Petronilla was the daughter of Saint Peter. She was a somewhat improbable saint: in Rome, she did not even survive late antiquity. But in the late fourth century she was perfectly apposite as the protectress and "double" of a lady who was anxious to appear a "good daughter" to Saint Peter and the Roman church.

The immediate outcome of the shift can be seen in the poetry of Paulinus. For the role of Saint Felix as the guarantor of Paulinus's identity, and in some way, as the heir of the *genius*, though important, is an ancient palimpsest compared with the new role of Felix the *amicus* and the *patronus*. On that subject, the cult of saints tapped a wellspring of articulateness in Paulinus the aristocrat, who had moved since birth in a world held together by the *religio amicitiae*.[45] To stroll in a garden hand in hand with a companion had always been Paulinus's idea of happiness.[46] Three days before he died, when all hope of his recovery had been abandoned, the visit of two neighboring bishops revived him so completely that he sat up in bed, "forgetting his physical weakness, and showed himself to them as lively and refined as an angel."[47]

Yet there is always more to Paulinus's poetry than the ceremoniousness of late-Roman senatorial etiquette. Rather, it reveals the other side of that etiquette: a class which defined itself by its culture was accustomed to expressing the deep warmth that always welled up in ancient Mediterranean men around the figure of the beloved teacher and spiritual guide. Hence the poems which Paulinus wrote to Ausonius justifying his break with the world were about issues that deeply preoccupied a *Geistesadel*: they explore rival forms of inspiration;[48] and they convey the full *pathos* of conflicting loyalties to two beloved teachers:[49]

> ... prius ipsa recedat
> corpore vita meo quam vester pectore vultus.[50]
>
> [Thee shall I hold, in every fibre woven ...
> Shall I behold thee, in my mind embrace thee,
> Instant and present, thou, in every place.][51]

This is the mold into which Paulinus, in the following decade, poured his new relationship with Saint Felix. He never lost the capacity to gather heroes around him. Just before he died, he asked in a clear voice if his "brothers" Januarius (San Gennaro, martyred bishop of Naples) and Martin (Martin of Tours, then dead for thirty years) were present. Reassured, he raised his hands with the Psalm "Levavi oculos meos ad montes."[52]

To speak of a man like Paulinus as if he had merely replaced the worship of the old gods by his attachment to Saint Felix is to use too inert a model for the change. Men of the late-Roman aristocracy such as Paulinus found that they could obliterate their pagan past because they could add something new: the warmth of late-Roman senatorial *amicitia* and the intensity of late-Roman loyalty to *patroni* and to beloved teachers suffused their newly forged style of relationship with the other world.

Characteristically, Augustine was one of the first to realize the implications of this change. Augustine approached the role of the saints from a very different angle from that of Paulinus. He himself notably lacked that register of senatorial feeling for personalized ties of friendship and patronage which had enabled Paulinus to give such full-blooded expression to the course of his new life as the *alumnus* and *famulus* of Saint Felix. The *Confessions* are in a category of their own precisely because Augustine's tongue is still heavy with the ancient language of the Psalms, that is, the language of a man speaking directly to God.[53] We glimpse a full range of Christian devotion in them; but in Augustine's portrayal of his own evolution, the landmarks of Paulinus's world are notably absent: he has no patron saints, and we catch only a few chill hints of the demons in the *Confessions*.

Yet it is the very abstractness of Augustine's approach that enabled him, in the years around 416, to draw out clearly the change that such intense links with dead human beings could imply. For in the years when he was welcoming and establishing the cult of Saint Stephen in North Africa, Augustine had begun to write the amazing book 10 of the *City of God*. This was a book devoted to redefining the nature of the true intermediaries between God and men. Unlike the rebel angels, these beings would link men to God by being equally his servants, and so committed to forwarding his will among men as their fellow servants.[54] The cult of the martyrs, therefore, presented a paradox that enabled Augustine to invert the traditional hierarchy of the universe. Men who had shown themselves, as martyrs, to be true servants of God, could bind their fellow men even closer to God than could the angels.[55] For belief in the ministrations of angels, even of those most obedient to God's will, had tended to place a cliff face of beings of a different order from themselves between the human race and God.[56] This ancient sense of difference was the corollary, in the chain of mediation between God and man, of the fault that ran through the universe, separating the stars from the earth. Only the martyrs, heavy with the humility of human death, could bridge that fault. As Augustine put it in a sermon which he preached on Saint Stephen while writing these chapters of the *City of God*: when, in the Apocalypse, John the Divine saw the angel, he worshiped it; but the angel said: "Arise: adore the Lord: I am your fellow servant."

Per conservum beneficia sumamus.

[Let us take the benefits of God through him, our fellow servant.][57]

Augustine's solution summed up a drift in Christian sensibility: the need for intimacy with a protector with whom one could identify as a fellow human being, relations with whom could be conceived of in terms open to the nuances of known human relations between patron and client, is the hallmark of late-fourth-century Christian piety.[58] It insensibly tended to oust reverence for beings, who, as gods or angels, had owed their position to their role as intermediaries between men and beings other than men in the soaring hierarchy of the late-antique universe.[59]

There was even something cozy about the cult of the martyrs. Preaching in a small town, Maximus of Turin could point out that the local martyrs had once come to Turin to spread the gospel: in that way, they were fellow citizens of Turin,[60] and their graves stood among the graves of the parents and grandparents of his congregation.[61] At a time when, in Maximus's estimation, no one of importance seemed to notice the town, when the great landowners hunted all spring far from the city[62] and coldly abandoned the region to its fate at the first rumor of barbarian invasion,[63] the intimate link between the Christian community and its humble dead was no small matter.

Such a link was both intimate and eminently intelligible. For to emphasize the shared humanity of a saint meant that the saint's role could be understood all the more clearly in terms of those human relationships which late-Roman society had been most skilled at articulating.[64] Nothing is more characteristic of the late fourth century than the speed with which the patron saint gained a precise profile in Christian art. Previously, belief in the role of the holy dead as intercessors had been strong: but it had been expressed in a remote language, closely tied to a terminology of atonement taken from the Old Testament.[65] It happened; but it could not be shown to happen.[66] The art of late antiquity, however, had been at its best precisely in expressing the relationships between outstanding figures and their dependents. It was the willingness to express the role of the saint in terms of the kind of social relations which fourth-century art had learned to convey so well that ungagged the doctrine of the intercession of the saints and allowed it to speak out clearly on the walls of the catacombs.[67] In the late-fourth-century painting in the Coemeterium Maius, we find an artist who knew how to express, in an idiom refined by a century of imperial art, what it was like for a couple to kneel for protection on either side of the still, upright figure of the martyr—*famuli* approaching their *patronus*.[68]

Indeed, one of the unconsidered strengths of Christianity in the late fourth century was the sensitivity with which it could replicate, in its model of relations with the other world, the social experience of the contemporary Roman Empire. What we often study in isolated detail as so many examples of literary, legal, and iconographic borrowings from the secular world, if taken altogether add up in themselves to a clue to the success of the Christian church: for Christianity could express itself in terms that rapidly shook themselves free from the archaic language of previous generations; and, in so doing Christian piety gained the incalculable advantage of being firmly rooted in day-to-day experience.[69] In poetry, in art and in liturgy, Christian writers and patrons of the late fourth century were able to work the leaven of specifically late-Roman human relationships into the heavy dough of a religious language taken, through the Old Testament, from the cultic practice of the ancient Near East. In the middle of the third century, Cyprian of Carthage plainly foreshadows Ambrose; but his tongue is still checked by the rigidities of an ancient language; that rich combination of power and intimacy that is the hallmark of the late-Roman *grand seigneur* is lacking.

By stressing this process of replication in the Christian church, I do not wish to trivialize it. Christian writers did not mindlessly create a mirror in Heaven that reflected, in rosy tints, the hard facts of patronage and *prepotenza* that they had come to take for granted on the late-Roman earth. The role of replication in late antiquity was subtly different: it enabled the Christian communities, by projecting a structure of clearly defined relationships onto the unseen world, to ask questions about the quality of relationships in their own society. The cult of the saints in late antiquity, therefore, did more than dress the ancient dead in contemporary upper-class costume. It was a form of piety exquisitely adapted to enable late-antique men to articulate and render manageable urgent, muffled debates on the nature of power in their own world, and to examine in the searching light of ideal relationships with ideal figures, the relation between power, mercy, and justice as practiced around them.

We shall have much occasion, in our last two chapters, to follow this theme in the Christian communities of the fifth and sixth centuries. What we have still to understand is what it meant for men like Sulpicius and Paulinus to see the joining point between themselves and their invisible companions in terms of the intensities of a late-Roman patron-client relationship. For this is the heart of the change. The invisible companion may be as close to them and as abiding as a guardian angel had once been; but the relationship itself no longer has the calm inevitability of ascending stages of the universe. It is tinged, now, with the sense of risk as with the warmth of a late-Roman relationship of friendship and patronage.

For the *impresarios* of the cult of saints were studiously anxious men. Sulpicius and Paulinus shared the strong link, during the years between 394 and 398, of having very recently and at no small cost of suffering and scandal, abandoned their previous social identities. In their writings we have no sense of leisured literary play around themes that either could take for granted. Gibbon might write that

> The life of Saint Martin and the Dialogues conerning his miracles contain facts adapted to the grossest barbarism in a style not unworthy of the Augustan age.[70]

But there is nothing of the age of Augustus about Sulpicius himself: like Paulinus, he had done nothing less than hang his identity on his hero.

I would suggest that only language shot through with the *grandeur et misère* of friendship and patronage could do justice to so potentially hazardous an enterprise. This can be seen on many levels. In the first place, in a world marked by increasingly explicit patronage, it was a fact of late-Roman life that for everybody, from the humblest villagers of Syria and Egypt upwards, freedom of maneuvre could only be gained by playing off conflicting patronage networks.[71] Paulinus did this with great success. He consistently presented himself as the *famulus* of Felix, *his* patron. By belonging to Felix alone, Paulinus belonged to nobody else.[72] Behind his poetry and the known facts of his career in Nola, we sense the quiet determination of the aristocrat who had mastered that most profitable late-Roman art of remaining an outsider. As a result, Paulinus and the shrine of his *patronus*, a little outside Nola, became the joining point of a whole provincial society.[73] Paulinus's emergence at Nola from being the self-styled humble doorkeeper to Saint Felix in 394 to acting as imperial arbiter in the disputed papal election of 419 was an adventure whose success could not be taken for granted.[74] It was a venture in self-assertion for which any late-antique man would have had to draw heavily on his invisible companion.

Yet Paulinus and his contemporaries had a deeper need for patronage. We should not forget the speed with which, in all areas of the Mediterranean world, the ascetic movement had articulated and, in so doing, amplified, Christian anxieties about sin and the last judgment. Augustine was far from being the only man whose clear sky came, increasingly, to be clouded over.[75] Nor was this merely a victory of pessimism. Sin and the last judgment came to bulk so large in the late fourth century not because more sin was happening or because the last judgment was thought to have drawn appreciably nearer. Instead we have to reckon with a growing determination on the part of the Christian leaders to present the world and the play of human action within it in terms of a single, all embracing principle of explanation, as so many direct consequences of sin and its remission.[76] The dark cloud of ascetic piety, therefore, had a clearly visible silver lining, the perpetual hope of amnesty.

It is this hope of amnesty that pushed the saint to the forefront as *patronus*. For patronage and friendship derived their appeal from a proven ability to render malleable seemingly inexorable processes, and to bridge with the warm breath of personal acquaintance the great distances of the late-Roman social world:[77] in a world so sternly organized around sin and justice, *patrocinium* and *amicitia* provided a much-needed language of amnesty.

This is the secret of the appeal of Sulpicius's Martin. As Aline Rousselle has written of Sulpicius and his circle, in the tense years that marked the beginnings of their ascetic vocations: "Ce petit groupe considère Martin comme un intercesseur plutôt que comme un modèle."[78] The miracle by which Martin comes to be recognized for the first time in his community as not only holy but as *potens et vere apostolicus*, owes its drama less to the fact that he could bring a catechumen back to life: its wonder lay in the intimate manner in which the friendship and patronage of Martin was thought to be able to reach across the faceless horror of the underworld.[79] It is the same with Sulpicius himself.[80] In giving a clear face to Martin through his *Life of Martin*, Sulpicius ensured that that smiling face would reassure him in the dark world to come. *Praemisi patronum:* "I have sent my patron on ahead" is his reaction to the news of Martin's death.[81]

It is the same with the less-sheltered Ambrose. Preaching at the funeral of his brother Satyrus, he knew that the gospel miracle of the raising from the dead of Lazarus (which scene may have been carved on the side of the sarcophagus in which he would so soon place his brother) would not happen. But the late-Roman miracle of *commendatio*, by which Satyrus became a *commendabilis,* a man with a record of favor from the great, might yet happen at the last judgment.[82] And it was a miracle that would be all the more certain to happen because it could be imagined to happen in a vivid and humane idiom provided by the conventions of late-Roman art. In the late-fourth-century catacomb of Hermes, the soul of the dead man stands, his hands raised in fervent prayer, at the foot of the "dread judgment seat of Christ," while the apostles stand to either side of him, one pointing toward him with a reassuring motion of the right hand.[83]

Behind the need to find the recognizable face of a human being, whose behavior could be rendered intelligible in terms of the tacit disciplines of late-Roman patronage relationships, we can sense a pressure of anxiety. In ascetic circles a crevasse begins to open in the late-classical image of the human person. For late-classical belief had emphasized, above all, the peaceable continutiy between the self and the divine; and it did so by presenting the self as the last link in an unbroken chain of intermediary beings. The identity of a person, therefore, could be thought of as sharing in the calm order of the universe.[84] Even when, in the face of physical death, this identity seemed least certain, the stability of the link with the guardian spirit was thought to survive the splintering of the body. Tertullian could expect that the Christian would awaken in another world, looking into the clear face of his angel.[85]

By the end of the fourth century a profound change had taken place. It is important that we should characterize it accurately, in order to begin to explain it. Certain explanations can be ruled out. Knowing what we do of the moral texture of the third-century Christian communities, we do not need to think that, when it came to sinning, worldliness, and feigned adhesion, the conversion of Constantine heightened to any appreciable extent activities in which the contemporaries of Origen and Cyprian had already shown themselves capable of a high all-round level of performance. As with the idea of "mass conversions," so with the idea of the "corruption of the church" after its establishment by Constantine, we are dealing with labor-saving formulas that take us much less far than we might think in understanding the precise moral tone of the late fourth century.[86]

Furthermore, it has been suggested that the cult of saints was the natural result of men who, either as new converts or as members of an increasingly worldly church, had hoped, by multiplying intercessors on their behalf, to find an easier road to Heaven than the straight and narrow path that had been offered by the early Christian communities. It has been said of the new devotion to patron saints, that it is "the expression of a piety which had long ago given up the effort to take on to itself the demands of holiness."[87]

Yet it may be possible to regard the change in tone as having come about for other, more intimate reasons, with more far-reaching consequences. For the *impresarios* of the new cult are precisely those who had taken on themselves the crushing weight of holiness demanded by the ascetic way of life. As we saw in the last chapter, they were not the kind of men who allowed themselves to be dispirited by the average members of their congregation; nor were they in any mood to make concessions to "superstitious" beliefs.[88]

What has really changed throughout the Christian world is the late-classical sense of the stability of the identity. Augustine's sad musing on this theme is only one example of the dark thoughts of ascetic "servants of God" scattered throughout the Mediterranean.[89] We have seen what an urgent issue it was for Sulpicius and for Paulinus: both men looked to new invisible companions as role models and intimate protectors in order to find a thread of continuity in their lives. At death, the crevasse came to open wide. No one could be secure at that awful moment. Macrina, sitting upright in bed facing the setting sun, prayed the long, somber prayer of the dying, which put into ancient words a sense of perilous uncertainty: "Place beside me an angel of light, to lead me by the hand . . . and may the Envious One not stand against me on my way."[90] After a portrait of Monica in book 9 of the *Confessions,* where the somewhat idealized and threatening figure of his mother as it was communicated in earlier books takes on the shades of human flesh, through now being built up in loving brush strokes by small tales of childhood peccadillos,[91] Augustine breaks out into the same somber language of risk: "Her soul let no one wrench from Thy protection; let not, by force or stealth, the lion or the dragon bar her way."[92] As his disciple said to Apa Daniel:

> "O my father, do you fear, also, you who have become perfect in such measure?"
>
> "O my son, if Abraham, with Isaac and Jacob were in my presence now and said, 'you are just,' I would still have no confidence."[93]

Only the saints could have such confidence on one's behalf; only they could reach across the crevasse of uncertainty with a known human gesture of acceptance:

> On the twelfth of the kalends of June, Petrus entered the jaws of the underworld. But may the martyr Baudelius, on the day he also suffered death, commend to the Lord his own dear charge.[94]

We are dealing with men who have turned their backs on the towering order of the universe to seek reassurance in the tight web of known human relationships: and they have done this in part because, against this immemorial backdrop, they have, for good or ill, turned to discover themselves.

# Chapter Four

## The Very Special Dead

One of the most moving fragments of late antiquity is now attached to the wall of the Mediterranean room in the Louvre. It is the epitaph of a little Sicilian, Julia Florentina, "a most dear, innocent child," who died at the age of eighteen months, having received Christian baptism, experienced a momentary remission, "and lived on four hours longer, just as she had once been before."

> While her parents bewailed her death at every moment, the voice of [God's] majesty was heard at night, forbidding them to lament for the dead child. Her body was buried in its tomb in front of the doors of the shrine of the martyrs.[1]

We have here a glimpse of a Mediterranean family thinking about the unthinkable fact of death. Their inscription is a reminder of the force of the tensions latent in early Christian attitudes to death and the afterlife.

For, compared with the Christian piety of later ages, the early church tended to leapfrog the grave: the long processes of mourning and slow adjustment to the great sadness of mortality tended to be repressed by a heady belief in the afterlife. The *vox maiestatis* in the night intervened to cut short the mourning of the little girl's parents. The ceremonial of the funeral procession was presented as a foretaste of the clarity of the resurrection:

> Patet ecce fidelibus ampli via lucida iam
> paradisi.[2]
> [See now for the faithful a shining way lies open
> to the spacious garden of paradise.]

The gleaming white shrouds, the incense, the strict control of demonstrations of grief[3] were a triumphal reminder of Christ's triumph over "black death."[4] Tombs in the late-Roman Christian cemetery at Pécs even show a trellis fence that identified the grave with the "spacious garden of paradise."[5]

Yet the sadness of the tomb survived. Of all late-antique thinkers, one might have expected Gregory of Nyssa and his circle to have been the one whose thought had equipped him best to gaze through that sadness to another world.[6] Far from it. When he had to place the body of his sister Macrina beside her parents in the family tomb, an ancient horror of the dead gripped him. Fear came over him "remembering the divine command, 'Do not uncover the shame of thy father or thy mother.'" He did not wish to look upon "the common shame to which all human beings come." The bodies of his parents had to be covered with a new shroud before he leant over the tomb to place his sister above them.[7] Outside the town, the harsh Anatolian landscape was dotted with derelict tombs, their contents partially exposed. Gregory assumed that, for all members of his congregation, this could not be other than an ugly and deeply disturbing sight.[8] The "shining way to Paradise" of Christian art and liturgy had in no way rendered translucent the facts of death for the average Mediterranean man.

Hence the emotional force that thrust the graves of the martyrs into prominence. Here, at least, were the graves of the very special dead. They had died in a special way; they lay in the grave in a special way; this fact was shown by the manner in which all that was most delightful and most alive in late-antique life could be thought of as concentrated in their tombs and even (perhaps, as we shall see, particularly) in detached fragments of their dead bodies. Hence the final consolation of the parents of Julia. She at least would lie beside those very special dead for whom mourning was unthinkable. The late-antique cult of the martyrs represents, therefore, a consistent imaginative determination to block out the lurking presence, in the cemeteries of the Mediterranean world, of "black death."

We should not underestimate the psychological momentum behind this effort. In itself belief in the afterlife does little to explain it. What we shall have to follow in this chapter is the working of an imaginative dialectic which led late-antique men to render their beliefs in the afterlife palpable and directly operative among the living by concentrating these on the privileged figure of the dead saint. Let us begin with the sadness of late-Roman cemeteries. They were very large and full of very ordinary people. In the Polyandrion, the "place of the great majority" outside Autun, the silence of the night was broken only by a few mysterious echoes of chanted psalms, which betrayed the presence, among so many thousands, of "a few tombs of faithful souls worthy of God."[9] We should never forget this sharp streak in late-antique Christian piety, especially as it was expressed by those ascetic leaders whose anxieties we described in the last chapter. The all too solid shame of the grave had been transmuted by very few.

For the martyrs and the other holy dead were the predestinate: Gregory of Tours writes of them as "the snowwhite number of the elect."[10] Late-antique men in the Latin West did not suffer from post-Reformation anxieties about the identity of the elect. The elect could be identified, if only posthumously, with absolute certainty. Thus, the late-fourth-century cult of the saints as practiced in North Africa and elsewhere provided Augustine with the solid ground course on which he raised his dizzying doctrine of predestination. For Augutine's problem in his last years had been to fit the nonelect, that is, the damned, into the dark weave of God's wisdom.[11] The elect, by contrast, were the one clear thread. They presented no problem to Augustine or his contemporaries. Even in those last treatises that "bruise human reason"[12] when they speak of the justice of God in hardening the hearts of the many, the elect have reassuringly familiar features. Their qualities are securely rooted in the expectations of late-antique Christian piety.[13] They are those who have received from God the gift of perseverance: they had enjoyed

> a liberty . . . protected and made firm by the gift of perseverance that this world should be overcome, this world in all its deep loves, in all its terrors, in all its countless ways of going wrong.[14]

And who had persevered unto death more magnificently and more publicly than had the martyrs?

It is the same with the deeper levels of Augustine's thought. The cult of the martyrs is the secure reference point of some of his seemingly most vertiginous speculations. The unmoved certainty with which the divine protection had overshadowed the person of Christ had been extended to the elect: "Let thy hand be upon the man of thy right hand, upon the son of man whom thou madest strong for thyself."[15] In a profound manner, the elect were members of his mystical body: "Christus . . . totus, cum membris suis."[16] To Augustine and his contemporaries, the martyrs were the *membra Christi* par excellence.[17] The hand of God that had rested with unshakable constancy above Christ rested also above his elect: a fifth-century relic case shows just this hand of God holding a crown above the martyr, a fragment of whose body it contained.[18] The martyr himself, and later the holy man, is often shown in the pose of the Crucified.[19] This identified him not only with the sufferings of Christ, but also with the unmoved constancy of his election and the certainty of his triumph.

In the sermons on the martyrs which Augustine preached at the very end of his life, we are left in no doubt as to what the *donum perseverantiae,* the gift of perseverence unto death, meant to him. They are extraordinary as evocations of the strength of the love of life, and of the intimate grip of the human flesh from which the soul is torn so unwillingly:

> They really loved this life; yet they weighed it up. They thought of how much they should love the things eternal if

they were capable of such deep love for things that pass away.[20]

The cult of the martyrs reenacted at regular intervals throughout the year the memory of those men and women to whom the gift of perseverence had been given and had been seen to be given. If Pelagius's teachings on free will and the possibility of perfection had it in them to turn the Christian congregations into a community of saints,[21] then Augustine's doctrine of predestination had the incalculable advantage that it could explain to these congregations how they had once produced heroes.

Thus, if the elect were the stars in God's Heaven, God had scattered a Milky Way of such stars over the Christian world in the form of the graves of the saints:[22] Saint Felix's shrine outside Nola was where that "star" had come to rest on earth.[23] Yet not everybody could live as comfortably in the contemplation of these few pinpoints of light as could the *impresarios* of the cult of the martyrs. For in breaching the ancient barrier between Heaven and Earth, the cult of the saints was in danger of setting up an equally firm barrier on earth: the difference between their graves and the thousands of ordinary graves that surrounded them could seem as irremovable as the ancient fault between earth and the untouchable glow of the Milky Way. Their unflecked light merely served to sharpen the darkness around them and so insensibly increased the abiding opacity of ordinary death.

The works of Gregory of Tours, for instance, show a man for whom a sense of the universal ravages of sin left only the graves of the saints intact. This is how Gregory and his contemporaries chose to remember Attila's invasion of Gaul:

> For they say that before those enemies of the faith came, a man of faith saw in a vision the blessed deacon Stephen conferring with the holy apostles Peter and Paul, and speaking as follows: "I beg you, my lords, to prevent by your intercessions the burning of the city of Metz. . . ." And they replied to him: "Go in peace, beloved brother, your oratory alone the fire shall not burn. But as for the city, we shall not prevail, because the sentence of the will of the Lord has already gone out over it."[24]

In the many burnt-out cities of early medieval Gaul, contemporaries tended to note that only the shrines of the saints
had remained standing.[25]

It was not a reassuring prospect. If an age gets the heresies
that it deserves, as statements in more consequential and radi-
cal terms of the unexpressed assumptions and tensions of contemporary belief, then Gregory got the heresy he deserved—a
priest who doubted the resurrection of the dead. Christ had
risen, he said; but why extend this privilege to fallen men? The
martyrs' shrines, which held the attention of his bishop, were
too few and far between compared with the dull weight of·death
in the overwhelming majority. Surely, the "sentence of the will
of the Lord" that had flattened Metz, had flattened all the
human race since the fall of Adam:

> For dust thou art and to dust thou shalt return.

> For the wind passeth over him and he is gone, and the place
> thereof shall know him no more.[26]

It is against this chilly background that we should place the
outburst of poetry, art, and healing by which the men of late
antiquity strove to block out such dark thoughts around the
graves of the martyrs.

In his impressive study of the gravestones of Puritan New
England, Allan Ludwig quotes the private devotional poems of
Edward Taylor:

> For thou [Christ] has farely Washt Death's grim
> grim face
> And made his Chilly finger-ends drop grace.

To this he adds the following comment:

> Apparently our understanding is no longer dialectical
> enough to encompass both life and death in one symbol. No
> grouping of New England symbols has aroused more con-
> troversy than those symbols of transformation which pur-
> port to change grim death into sweet grace before our
> eyes.[27]

I quote this partly so as to measure the distance between
early-modern Christian attitudes to death and those applied in

late antiquity to the cult of the martyrs. The martyrs had triumphed over death; the iconography of the saints in late antiquity made no attempt to encompass "grim death" and "sweet grace" in one symbol. As André Grabar has written, "The imagery of a martyr's relics is never in any case an imagery of the *memento mori;* rather it strives by all means in its power to proclaim the suppression of the fact of death."[28] Plainly, at such a place "Death's grim grim face" had already been "farely Washt."

Yet I would suggest that the dialectic continued at a deeper imaginative level. It is difficult to explain the geyserlike force with which belief in miracles of healing at the tombs or in connection with the relics of the martyrs burst out throughout the Mediterranean world if we do not bear in mind the pressure which such a dialectic had built up. Consideration of such pressures, and not only the impeccably orthodox statements on the afterlife and the resurrection of the dead with which Gregory answered his doubting priest, bring us closer to the warm capacity of the Christian congregations to identify themselves with such potentially unattainable stars as the martyrs, and to do so, above all, in close proximity to their physical remains.

Our dialectic begins, as Gregory of Tours would have wished it to begin, with consideration of the doctrine of the resurrection of the dead, and of the nature of the repose of the souls of the saints before this resurrection.[29] As Gibbon put it,

> Whatever might be the condition of vulgar souls in the long interval between the dissolution and the resurrection of their bodies, it was evident that superior spirits of the saints and martyrs did not consume that portion of their existence in silent and inglorious sleep.[30]

> Let the martyrs make plain to us [said Maximus of Turin] how much refreshment God lavishes upon the dead.[31]

So many of the miracles associated with the tombs of the saints are miracles that made visible the invisible refreshment of the saints; they are the early-Christian imagery of Paradise in action. Bleak in his observations of human nature as practiced around him in sixth-century Gaul, Gregory is at one with the Christian poets of the late fourth century in scanning the world for places where men could catch a glimpse of Paradise. His hagiographical work is full of subdued music and of mysterious perfumes that brought into the basilicas of Gaul a touch of Paradise.[32] For Paradise was a mountain covered with trees in full bloom, its air "fragrant and filled with music."[33]

Take the trees that flourish at the graves of the saints. A modern student of "popular religion" might see in them unchanging avatars of those holy trees which Saint Martin had chopped down vigorously.[34] Yet this is too inert and consequently too imprecise a continuity to do justice to the exact associations which these trees had for a man such as Gregory. He fastens on one aspect of them: they flourish every year. Following the poetic image of Prudentius, Gregory emphasizes that the very way that they decked themselves out with petals like dove's down brought the heavy bloom of paradise into the courtyards of the shrines.[35] Flourishing vegetation rendered palpable the vigor of a blessed soul: at the tomb of Severus, dried-out lilies spring to life every year, as an image of how the man within "flourishes like a palm tree in paradise."[36]

Yet in the midst of all this poetry, we are never far from "Death's grim grim face." When Gregory visited the tomb of a martyr, "everyone of our party filled our nostrils with the scent of lilies and roses."[37] Yet when a priest of Clermont was locked up by his bishop in a tomb of Parian marble, Gregory writes: "Years afterwards he used to describe the fetid stench which clung about the dead man's bones."[38]

The tombs of the very special dead were exempt from the facts of death. This was not only because the souls of the occupants are in Paradise: the deep peace of their sleep before the resurrection shows in their bones. It is the repose of the body of Saint Felix that moves Paulinus so deeply. Dust pouring from the sarcophagus had made him fear that an animal had disturbed Felix's bones; but on lifting the lid, he saw them for the first time, lying in an awesome stillness.[39]

In other writers, the resurrection could come yet closer still. In his funeral poem, Prudentius describes the color flowing back into the remade body. It is a reminder of how dearly late-antique men loved a good complexion:

These cheeks which now are wan and white with wasting shall have beauteous skin tinged with the bloom of blood more charming than any flower.[40]

Such taste, like Vergil's, was a little *art nouveau*. Take Gregory of Tours's ancestor, Gregory of Langres:

His face was so filled with glory that it looked like a rose. It was deep rose red, and the rest of his body was glowing white like a lily. You would have said that he was even now ready for the coming glory of the resurrection.[41]

It is this pushing forward into the present of God's power to remake the human body at the resurrection which comes to impress itself on Augustine when he wrote and preached in his old age about the graves of the saints. His accounts of the miracles at the shrine of Saint Stephen, in the last book of the *City of God*, were far from being a capitulation to the "silly stories" current among the "common herd."[42] For Augustine they are surreal rather than "silly." They betray the effort by which Augustine, a man formed in the most austerely immaterialist current of Neo-Platonic thought available to an educated man of his age, had come to think the unthinkable concept of a future integration of flesh and spirit. The recorded miracles of healing at the shrines show God's power and his abiding concern for the flesh. And this power, Augustine now believes, is shown most appropriately at the places where those dead now lie, who had been prepared to lose their close-knit bodies in the faith of the unimaginable mercy of the resurrection.[43] Miracles that had once struck Augustine, the contemplative, as of little significance, as so many lights dimmed by the sun of God's harmonious order, now take on a warmth and a glow of their own, as Augustine pays more heed to the instinctive fears and yearnings of the once-neglected body:[44]

I know you want to keep on living. You do not want to die. And you want to pass from this life to another in such a way that you will not rise again as a dead man, but fully alive and transformed. This is what you desire. This is the deepest human feeling; mysteriously, the soul itself wishes and instinctively desires it.[45]

Augustine's evolution was singular as only he could make it, and it has now been studied as carefully as it deserves.[46] It is a reminder that an intellectual breakthrough of the first order lies behind what is too often presented as a belated concession to the mindless weight of "popular belief."

Yet Augustine's formulation of his later views, and his decision to add the records of local cases of healing to his final cannonade against all the unquestioned assumptions of the pagan philosophical world view, are only special cases in the working out of the imaginative dialectic surrounding the very special dead. The result of this dialectic had been not merely to block out the negative associations of physical death with all the resources of an imagery of paradise, but to raise the physical remains of the saints above the normal associations of place and time. At their graves, the eternity of paradise and the first touch of the resurrection come into the present. In the words of Victricius of Rouen: here are bodies, where every fragment is "linked by a bond to the whole stretch of eternity."[47]

It is with such a remark, perhaps, that we can touch on some of the reasons for the rapid and flagrant departure from pagan and Jewish practice involved in the Christian transfer of relics. The relic is a detached fragment of a whole body: as Victricius said, "You see tiny relics, a little drop of blood."[48] But it is precisely the detachment of the relic from its physical associations that summed up most convincingly the imaginative dialectic we have described. For how better to suppress the fact of death, than to remove part of the dead from its original context in the all too cluttered grave? How better to symbolize the abolition of time in such dead, than to add to that an indeterminacy of space? Furthermore, how better to express the paradox of the linking of Heaven and Earth than by an effect of "inverted magnitudes," by which the object around which boundless associations clustered should be tiny and compact? Detached fragments of the saints in gold and silver caskets, or in their miniature marble shrines, had some of the measureless quality of an *objet trouvé*.[49] The exquisite little golden tube in which Paulinus enclosed a sliver of the Holy Cross heightened, by the staggering contrast in sizes, the overpowering associations of that cross, where once "the Lord of Majesty had hung attached, as all the universe trembled before him."[50] The disparity of sizes further emphasized the magnificence of God's mercy, falling in such clear, tiny drops "like the gentle dew from Heaven."[51]

Yet, in detaching the relic from direct association with physical death, the imaginative dialectic was, if anything, heightened. For what was being brought were tiny fragments around which the imaginative associations of a very special kind of death could cluster undisturbed. And this very special kind of death had been almost invariably unpleasant. "What you see before you," Victricius had insisted "is blood and dust."[52]

At the root of every miracle of healing at a martyr's shrine of late antiquity there lay a miracle of pain:

> Let not a day pass, brethren [Victricius urged the congregation at his new shrine] when we do not dwell on these tales. "This martyr did not blanch under the torturer; this martyr hurried up the slow work of the executioner; this one eagerly swallowed the flames; this one was cut about, yet stood up still."[53]

For the sufferings of the martyrs were miracles in themselves. The accounts of their deaths, in the *Passiones* and the *Gesta martyrum,* was one point only in a long chain of manifestations of the power of God throughout their lives, continued up to the present at their shrines. As the *Decretum Gelasianum* put it,

> We must include also [for public reading] the deeds of the saints in which their triumph blazed forth through the many forms of torture that they underwent and their marvelous confession of the faith. For what Catholic can doubt that they suffered more than is possible for human beings to bear, and did not endure this by their own strength, but by the grace and help of God?[54]

The heroism of the martyrs had always been treated as a form of possession, strictly dissociated from normal human courage. When Felicitas had been in labor in prison,

> one of the assistants of the prison guards said to her: "You suffer so much now—what will you do when you are tossed by the beasts?" "What I am suffering now," she replied, "I suffer by myself. But then Another will be inside me who will suffer for me, for I shall be suffering for him."[55]

Hence the callousness with which Christian leaders dismissed displays of physical or moral courage by a rival: for the exemplary courage of the martyrs and apostles had been lifted by God out of the domain of mere human physical endurance and mere human moral strength.[56]

Thus, the original death of the martyr, and even the long, drawn-out dying of the confessor and the ascetic, was vibrant with the miraculous suppression of suffering. Memories of it set up an imaginative vortex in the minds of those who thronged to the shrine. This was all the more powerful because much of the overt expression of these suferings had been blocked. The explicit image of the martyr was of a person who enjoyed the repose of Paradise and whose body was even now touched by the final rest of the resurrection. Yet behind the now-tranquil face of the martyr there lay potent memories of a process by which a body shattered by drawn-out pain had once been enabled by God's power to retain its integrity.[57]

In the ancient world, the cure of illness was frequently associated with potent fantasies of violent dismemberment and reintegration. Aelius Aristides wrote:

> I believe that he dreamed that the God [Asclepius], together with Telesphorus, said to him in regard to me, that it was necessary to remove my bones and put in nerves, for the existing ones had failed . . but the god [also] said, in consolation and instruction, not directly to knock out the bones and cut out the existing nerves, but that there needed to be, as it were, a certain change of those existing, and thus there was need of a great and strange correction.[58]

It is from this angle perhaps that we can usefully approach the genre of the *passio*, the story of the sufferings of the saints. They touched a layer of associations in the minds of the Christian audience which facilitated the "great and strange correction" of healing.

As historical documents, the *passiones* make dispiriting reading:

> Il ne fallut donc pas plusieurs siècles, comme on aimerait à s'imaginer, pour franchir l'abîme qui sépare les émouvants récits crées dans le feu de la persécution de la littérature insipide et prétentieuse qui les a fait trop souvent oublier.[59]

Dismissed in this manner as yet another document of the dismal victory of the tastes of the "common herd," the surviving *passiones* of late antiquity have seldom been studied in their own right.[60] "Insipid and pretentious" they might be to a sober scholar of the history of the early church: but it is precisely that quality of repetitiveness and melodrama that gave their reading at the great festivals of the saints a momentum that echoed the rhythms of cure among the hearers.

In the first place, the *passio* abolished time. The deeds of the martyr or of the confessor had brought the mighty deeds of God in the Old Testament and the gospels into his or her own time. The reading of the saint's deeds breached yet again the paper-thin wall between the past and the present.[61] As a study of the iconography adopted by Paulinus in his shrines at Nola and Fundi has made plain, time was concertinaed at a shrine: "In ihren "geschichtliche" Darstellung, Zustandsbild und Zukunftsvision ineinander übergehen."[62]

Hence the insistence of writers at shrines, such as Paulinus, that unlike the classical poets, who dealt with imaginary figures in the distant past, they were describing present true facts.[63] There was more to this than validating by a standard literary device propaganda that put a strain on the reader's credulity.[64] For the hagiographer was recording the moments when the seemingly extinct past and the unimaginably distant future had pressed into the present. Hence a loving circumstantiality and a belief, unique in ancient authors, that you can prove anything by statistics. Paulinus's poems on miracles at the shrine of Saint Felix have some of the unashamed vigor of those late-Roman carvings associated with the *arte plebeia* of the early fourth century, where the classical mythological decor has been ousted by realistic little vignettes of the hunt, of trading, or in the Arch of Constantine, of warfare and the frank exercise of power.[65] Where can we turn other than to the hagiographic works of Gregory of Tours to learn the truly important facts about Merovingian Gaul: the dimensions of Lac Leman and the superior quality of its trout;[66] the temptations of civet de lapin in the Lenten season;[67] the first mention of the *omelette à la provençale?*[68] The very "concrete and fastidious" nature of this genre upsets the critic and delights the social historian in search of fragments of "local color": it betrays the urgency with which men like Paulinus and Gregory sought to trace the joining of past and future in their own time. For, as Gregory frequently repeats, if healing and mercy did not happen in his own days, who would believe that they had ever happened or ever would happen again?[69]

So the *passio* brought the past into the present. Coinciding as it did with the high point of the saint's festival, the reading of the *passio* gave a vivid, momentary face to the invisible *praesentia* of the saint. When the *passio* was read, the saint was "really" there: a sweet scent filled the basilica,[70] the blind, the crippled, and the possessed began to shout that they now felt his power in healing,[71] and those who had offended him in the past had good reason to tremble.[72] We shall see how the ceremonial of the saint's festival, particularly in sixth-century Gaul, high-lighted the excitement of his *praesentia*, and raised to a high pitch the hope that his *potentia* would be immediately available: for the saint's power was all the more efficacious because, like all great men of late antiquity, the saint knew how to maximize its impact by prolonged inaccessibility. "Insipid and preten-tious" though such *passiones* might seem for us, like their equally maligned secular predecessors, the panegyrics, their perfor-mance was a recognized moment in a ritual of power.[73] Without a *passio* the *praesentia* of the saint lacked weight. Take the exam-ple of Saint Patroclus of Troyes:

> The men of that place had paid little reverence to this mar-tyr, because the story of his sufferings was not available. It is the custom of the man in the street to give more attentive veneration to those saints of God whose combats are read aloud.[74]

Yet merely to speak in terms of excitement is not enough. It seems to me that the public reading of the *passio* was, in itself, a *psychodrame* that mobilized in the hearer those strong fantasies of disintegration and reintegration which lurked in the back of the mind of ancient men. Thus, of the Coptic passions of the martyrs, those that recount in the most grisly detail the break-ing up and miraculous reintegration of the martyr's body are precisely those associated with well-known healing shrines.[75]

Let us turn to some Latin Christian authors. There is already a strong element of the *psychodrame* in the *Crowns of Martyrdom* of Prudentius. His poems linger on the dissolution of the bodies of the martyrs and on the final preservation of their integrity. The fragilities of the body are laid bare with macabre precision.[76] Prudentius wished his readers to feel the dissolution of the Fall working every moment in their every fiber: "Membra morbis exedenda, texta venis languidis."[77] The sufferings of the martyrs complete the unraveling of "this limp skein of flesh on which disease preys endlessly."

> Set to, then, torturer, burn and cut,
> Dissect the parts of this compacted clay,
> It is an easy thing to break such fragile stuff.[78]

Having been made to feel the full horror of the dissolving body, the reader is reassured by the triumph of integrity over its disintegration. For, while the body is "painted with wash on wash of blood," its core, the soul, remains all of one piece.[79]

For Prudentius, integrity resided primarily in the survival of the untouched soul. The later author of the *passio* of Saint Eulalia goes further: the body itself has become symbolic of the triumph of the martyr over disintegration. Its scars covered with gleaming white snow, Eulalia's body hung on the scaffold for three days, "whole and untouched."

> O worthy martyr, who has granted so superb a display [*tam gratissimum expectaculum*] to your fellow townsmen, conquering past weakness, strengthening our present, teaching future ages.[80]

The *gratissimum expectaculum* of Eulalia's prolonged suffering had given merciful form to processes by which shattering pain could be resolved and the body regain a stability and an untouched purity.

In Gregory's account of his own relations with those shrines where the sufferings of the saints were publicly reenacted in the *passio* and remembered by their devotees, we can trace an imaginative dialectic at work at its deepest level. So many of the cures that he himself experienced took place at spots connected with a precisely congruent moment in the suffering of the martyr. The very intimacy of the emotional bond between the believer and his invisible companions, on which we dwelt in the last chapter, made this identification appear quite natural. Gregory, *peculiaris alumnus* of Saint Julian of Brioude[81] was cured of a splitting headache caused by sunstroke by dousing his head in the fountain of Saint Julian, that is, in the spring where the martyr's own head had been washed clean after the shattering pain of decapitation.[82] Often we go beyond identification to a form of emotional inversion. "Death's grim grim face" is washed so clean by the martyr that a torture that had once caused exquisite suffering is now the most apposite vehicle for relief. The stone sockets into which the feet of Saint Benignus had been set with molten lead, was now a place where soft water rested, drops of which cured Gregory from the scalding pain of an eye infection.[83]

The emotional inversion of suffering was a theme which never failed to bring out the most enthusiastic in Latin Christian poets. Traveling through the cities of Gaul, Venantius Fortunatus's verses on the shrines of the martyr-saints glory in such inversions:

> Et corpus lacerum corpora multa fovet.
> He whose good health was ended by an evil death
> Now both gives life to many and retains his own.[84]

Gregory and Venantius are the last Latin authors with which this study is concerned. Both men sum up the sensibility of a whole epoch. It is conventional to make a stark contrast between them, as if they stood for the passing of one age into another, to juxtapose the protomedieval rigors of Gregory the bishop of Tours with the classical *dulcedo* of Venantius the wandering Italian. Helen Waddell once wrote:

> And in the grim if humorous world of Gregory of Tours, brutal and debauched, his [Venantius's] *aperçus* of lovely things, a green parrot on a tapestry, violets and primroses on the altar at Easter, moonlight on a church floor, are a proof that the sense of beauty lingered.[85]

What we have seen is, if anything, the opposite to a "lingering" of the passing beauty of the classical world. We have been treated, instead, to a carefully maintained crescendo of beauty in poetry, in ceremonial, and in shimmering art around a new and obsessive theme. Gregory and Fortunatus share in the extraordinary emotional feat connected with the rise of the cult of saints in late antiquity. Both men turned the *summum malum* of physical death preceded by suffering into a theme into which all that was most beautiful and refined in their age could be compressed. Without this feat, the "perennial Hellenism" associated with the beauty of the faces in the rows of saints in Paradise who looked down on Venantius as he grew up in Ravenna, whose classical grace still haunts the visitor to that town, might have had less cause to linger in the West.

# Chapter Five

## Praesentia

In a characteristic moment of penetrating disapproval, Hegel wrote of the piety of the middle
ages:

> The Holy as a mere thing has the character of
> externality; thus it is capable of being taken
> possession of by another to my exclusion; it
> may come into an alien hand, since the pro-
> cess of appropriating it is not one that takes
> place in Spirit, but is conditioned by its qual-
> ity as an external object. The highest of
> human blessings is in the hands of others.[1]

Hegel was speaking of the role of the clergy as
the guardians of the Eucharist in the middle
ages. But in the cult of relics also, late-antique
and early-medieval piety lived down with gusto
to his strictures. This cult gloried in particularity.
*Hic locus est:* "Here is the place," or simply *hic*, is
a refrain that runs through the inscriptions on
the early martyrs' shrines of North Africa.[2] The
holy was available in one place, and in each such
place it was accessible to one group in a manner
in which it could not be accessible to anyone
situated elsewhere.

By localizing the holy in this manner, late-
antique Christianity could feed on the facts of

distance and on the joys of proximity. This distance might be physical distance. For this, pilgrimage was the remedy. As Alphonse Dupront has put it, so succinctly, pilgrimage was "une thérapie par l'espace."[3] The pilgrim committed himself or herself to the "therapy of distance" by recognizing that what he or she wished for was not to be had in the immediate environment.[4] Distance could symbolize needs unsatisfied, so that, as Dupront continues, "le pèlerinage demeure essentiellement départ": pilgrimage remains essentially the act of leaving.[5] But distance is there to be overcome; the experience of pilgrimage activates a yearning for intimate closeness. For the pilgrims who arrived after the obvious "therapy of distance" involved in long travel found themselves subjected to the same therapy by the nature of the shrine itself. The effect of "inverted magnitudes" sharpened the sense of distance and yearning by playing out the long delays of pilgrimage in miniature. For the art of the shrine in late antiquity is an art of closed surfaces. Behind these surfaces, the holy lay, either totally hidden or glimpsed through narrow apertures. The opacity of the surfaces heightened an awareness of the ultimate unattainability in this life of the person they had traveled over such wide spaces to touch.[6]

In Tebessa, the approach to the shrine, as it wound past high walls, swung under arches, crossed courtyards, and finally descended into a small half-submerged chamber, was a microcosm of the long journey of pilgrimage itself.[7] At the shrine of Saint Lawrence at Rome, the first sign of patronage by a Christian emperor involved a heightening of the effect of distance; Constantine installed flights of stairs leading up and down from the grave, and "shut off" the grave itself with a grille of solid silver weighing a thousand pounds, thus keeping the tomb of Lawrence still at a short distance from the pilgrims.[8] At the shrine of Saint Peter, a whole ritual of access was played out:

> Whoever wishes to pray there [writes Gregory of Tours] must unlock the gates which encircle the spot, pass to where he is above the grave and, opening a little window, push his head through and there make the supplication that he needs.[9]

Golden keys to open these gates were treasured and potentially miraculous relics of the Roman pilgrimage,[10] as were the little cloths, the *brandea,* which the pilgrims lowered on to the tomb below, drawing them up heavy with the blessing of Saint Peter.[11] When the young prince Justinian wrote from Constantinople for a fragment of the priceless body of Saint Peter itself, he was flatly refused, and was sent instead one such cloth, inserted from a special window.[12] A yearning for proximity kept so carefully in suspense occasionally exploded. The Carthaginian noblewoman Megetia, as we have seen, had committed herself to the "therapy of distance" by traveling away from her family to the shrine of Saint Stephen in nearby Uzalis.[13] But she could not rest at that:

> While she prayed at the place of the holy relic shrine, she beat against it, not only with the longings of her heart, but with her whole body so that the little grille in front of the relic opened at the impact; and she, taking the Kingdom of Heaven by storm, pushed her head inside and laid it on the holy relics resting there, drenching them with her tears.[14]

The carefully maintained tension between distance and proximity ensured one thing: *praesentia,* the physical presence of the holy, whether in the midst of a particular community or in the possession of particular individuals, was the greatest blessing that a late-antique Christian could enjoy. For, as we have seen in previous chapters, the *praesentia* on which such heady enthusiasm focused was the presence of an invisible person. The devotees who flocked out of Rome to the shrine of Saint Lawrence, to ask for his favor or to place their dead near his grave, were not merely going to a place; they were going to a place to meet a person—*ad dominum Laurentium.*[15] We have also seen how the fullness of the invisible person could be present at a mere fragment of his physical remains and even at objects, such as the *brandea* of Saint Peter, that had merely made contact with these remains.[16] As a result, the Christian world came to be covered with tiny fragments of original relics and with "contact relics" held, as in the case of Saint Peter, to be as full of his *praesentia* as any physical remains.[17] Translations—the movement of relics to people—and not pilgrimages—the movement of people to relics—hold the center of the stage in late-antique and early-medieval piety. A hectic trade in, accompanied by frequent thefts of, relics is among the most dramatic, not to say picaresque, aspects of western Christendom in the middle ages.[18] Only comparatively recently have medievalists succeeded in rendering this startling behavior intelligible.[19]

Let us consider for a moment the immediate profile and consequences of the beliefs that first encouraged the translation of relics in the late fourth century. If relics could travel, then the distance between the believer and the place where the holy could be found ceased to be a fixed, physical distance. It took on the shifting quality of late-Roman social relationships: distances between groups and persons were overcome by gestures of grace and favor,[20] and the dangerously long miles of the imperial communications system were overcome by a strenuously maintained ideology of unanimity and concord.[21] Those who possessed the holy, in the form of portable relics, could show *gratia* by sharing these good things with others, and by bringing them from the places where they had once been exclusively available to communities scattered throughout the Roman world. Behind every relic that was newly installed in its shrine throughout the Mediterranean, there had to lie some precise gesture of good will and solidarity. The inscription on an African shrine records merely the fact of distance overcome: "A piece of the wood of the Cross, from the Land of Promise, where Christ was born."[22] But Paulinus, writing inscriptions for his friend Sulpicius Severus, leaves us in no doubt of the reassuring touch of human friendship behind the "moment of high and terrible emotion"[23] of the arrival of such a fragment at Nola:

> Hoc Melani sanctae delatum munere Nolam
> Summum Hierosolymae venit ab urbe bonum.
> [Brought as a gift to Nola by the holy Melania,
> this, the highest of all goods, has come from the
> city of Jerusalem][24]

As a result, the transfer of relics, especially from the Holy Land to the Christian communities of the Western Mediterranean, can serve the historian as a faithful "trace element" that enables him to take an X-ray photograph of the intricate systems of patronage, alliance and gift-giving that linked the lay and the clerical elites of East and West in the late Roman Empire. In recent years, the theme of notable pilgrimages and translations of relics has passed from the sober domain of hagiographical antiquarianism into a series of elegant studies of patronage and politics among the Christian governing classes of the late fourth and early fifth centuries—I refer particularly to the work of David Hunt in England and of Ken Holum of the University of Maryland.[25]

I would like to point out some of the implications of this development. The yearning of pilgrimage and a "therapy of distance," associated with the neutral fact that a particular landscape lay at an unchangeable distance from other centers, came to be detached from a purely geographical setting: the holy could be brought ever closer through gestures of concord and gift giving which the men of late antiquity and the early middle ages treasured as the cement of their social world. A network of "interpersonal acts," that carried the full overtones of late-Roman relationships of generosity, dependence, and solidarity, came, in one generation, to link the Atlantic coast to the Holy Land; and, in so doing, these "interpersonal acts" both facilitated and further heightened the drive to transmute distance from the holy into the deep joy of proximity.

Without an intense and wide-ranging network of late-Roman relationships of *amicitia* and *unanimitas* among the late-fourth-century *impresarios* of the cult of saints, relics would not have traveled as far, as fast, or with as much undisputed authority as they did. If this had not happened, if the translation of relics had not gained a major place in Christian piety, the spiritual landscape of the Christian Mediterranean might have been very different. It might have resembled that of the later Islamic world: the holy might have been permanently localized in a few privileged areas, such as the Holy Land, and in "cities of the saints," such as Rome. There might have been a Christian Mecca or a Christian Kerbela, but not the decisive spread of the cult of major saints, such as Peter and Paul, far beyond the ancient frontiers of the Roman world, as happened in Europe of the dark ages. Elsewhere, the holy might have been tied to the particularity of local graves that enjoyed little or no prestige outside their own region.[26] By the early fifth century, the strictly "geographical" map of the availability of the holy, which had tied the *praesentia* of the saints to the accidents of place and local history, had come to be irreversibly modified by a web of new cult sites, established by the translation of relics, which reflected the dependence of communities scattered all over Italy, Gaul, Spain, and Africa on the enterprise and generosity of a remarkable generation of distant friends.

Recent studies of the social and political contexts of translations of relics have revealed with such delightful, and even damaging, circumstantiality the relations and the motives of the principal human participants, that we should not forget the prime giver of good things, who was thought by late-antique men to stand behind the busy story of the discovery, the transfer, the accumulation—even, at times, the bare-faced robbery—of the holy. God gave the relic; in the first instance, by allowing it to be discovered, and then by allowing it to be transferred. As Augustine said in a sermon on Saint Stephen: "His body lay hidden for so long a time. It came forth when God wished it. It has brought light to all lands, it has performed such miracles."[27] Nowhere did the silver lining of God's amnesty shine more clearly from behind the black cloud of the late-antique sense of sin that in accounts of the discovery and translation of relics. For these accounts are shot through with a sense of the miracle of God's mercy in allowing so precious a thing as the *praesentia* of the holy dead to become available to the Christian congregations in their own place and in their own times.

Behind the awkward Latin of the account by the priest Lucianus of the discovery of the body of Saint Stephen in a field outside the village of Caphargamala, in 415, we can sense the hopes and fears of the Aramaic speakers of the region.[28] Lucianus is warned to announce the good news to the bishop of Jerusalem:

> For it is especially fitting that we should be revealed in the time of your priesthood. . . . For the world is in danger, from the many sins into which it falls every day.[29]

When the coffin of Saint Stephen finally made its appearance, the touch of the divine mercy was overwhelming:

At that instant the earth trembled and a smell of sweet perfume came from the place such as no man had ever known
of, so much that we thought that we were standing in the
sweet garden of Paradise. And at that very hour, from the
smell of that perfume, seventy-three persons were healed.[30]

This mercy was further ratified by a downpour of rain which
ended the cruel winter drought:

And the earth drank its fill, and all here glorified the Lord,
because of Stephen his holy one, and because our Lord Jesus
Christ had deigned to open to this imperiled world the
heavenly treasure of his mercy and lovingkindness.[31]

The discovery of a relic, therefore, was far more than an act of
pious archaeology, and its transfer far more than a strange new
form of Christian connoisseurship: both actions made plain, at
a particular time and place, the immensity of God's mercy. They
announced moments of amnesty. They brought a sense of deliverance and pardon into the present.

They could condense moods of public confidence. Thus,
there is nothing strange in the decision of the church historian
Sozomen to end his history with the story of the discovery and
translation to Constantinople of the relics of the prophet
Zechariah. Such an event made more plain even than did the
cessation of barbarian invasion and civil wars the mood of
public confidence on which the writer deemed it politic to end
an account of the prosperity enjoyed by the Eastern Empire
under Theodosius II. God had made manifest his approval of
the reign of Theodosius by making accessible to the inhabitants
of his empire the *praesentia* of the long-buried dead.[32]

A sense of the mercy of God lies at the root of the discovery,
translation, and installation of relics. In such a mood, the relic
itself may not have been as important as the invisible gesture of
God's forgiveness that had made it available in the first place;
and so its power in the community was very much the con-
densation of the determination of that community to believe
that it had been judged by God to have deserved the *praesentia*
of the saint. It is in this light that we can best see the steady
drain of relics into the new capital, Constantinople.[33] The precise events of the discovery of the relic and the ceremonies

surrounding its arrival and installation counted for more than the mere fact of its presence in the city. Many relics lapsed into obscurity after their arrival. What mattered was the arrival itself. This was an unambiguous token of God's enduring capacity to forgive the inhabitants of the rapidly growing, tension-ridden city.[34] As recognitions by God of the "manifest destiny" of the new capital and its right to survive, translations of relics were carefully remembered in art and liturgy on the same footing as those blessed moments when God had brought to a halt the awesome rumble of earth tremors.[35]

The discovery and the installation of a relic, therefore, was surrounded by a sense of amnesty and a heightening of morale. Precisely because of this, late-Roman men felt free to seek, in the ceremonies surrounding the cult of saints, a positive replication of social relations that preoccupied them so deeply. For the ravages of sin in late-antique social and personal relationships were suspended on those high moments when the invisible persons took up their place in the community: the *praesentia* of the saint could be associated with unambiguously good happenings in a world only too cluttered with bad happenings. As a result, the ceremonial and literature that surrounded the arrival, the installation, and the annual celebration of the cult of a patron saint in the western Mediterranean, from the late fourth to the sixth centuries, built up a carefully articulated model of ideal relationships. This model helped the inhabitants of the towns to make sense of the seedy and ambivalent facts of life in the western provinces during the last century of the Western Empire and the first century of barbarian rule. If, as Ortega y Gasset once wrote, "The virtues which count most for us are those we do not possess," then the cult of saints, from the fourth century onwards, made plain the virtues which late-Roman men lacked and wished for most: concord and the unsullied exercise of power. Let us examine the manner in which the cult of saints articulated these two themes in the public life of the Christian communities. First, the theme of concord.

In the first place, the translation of relics symbolized the newly achieved solidarity of an empire-wide class. The late fourth century saw the formation of a new Christian elite of bishops and noble pilgrims. Much as the Sophists of the second century A.D. had found that the patronage of the Roman emperors and alliance with Roman governing families had raised them suddenly from positions of a purely local importance to a role in the empire as a whole that was "conspicuous and stunning,"[36] so the bishops and the upper-class pilgrims of the fourth century found themselves increasingly committed to the wide and dangerous world of the new Christian empire. As Macrina used to remind her brother,

> Your father enjoyed a considerable reputation in his time for his culture; but his fame reached no further than the law courts of his own region. Later, he became known as a teacher of rhetoric throughout all Pontus. But all he wished for was fame within the bounds of his own home country. You, however, are a name to conjure with in far cities, peoples and provinces.[37]

The new members of this Christian elite were in an exceptionally strong position to encourage the discovery and translation of relics. Their wide journeys and their unanswerable social prestige made it easy for them to appropriate and to give the stamp of authority to fragments of the holy. Yet there were also deeper reasons: the cult of saints, as I have described it in chapter 3,[38] rendered eminently intelligible the social position of these restless figures. Like those who were committed to permanent ascetic withdrawal, such as Paulinus at Nola, highly placed strangers in foreign parts needed the constant presence of invisible companions on their journeys, both for protection and as supernatural extensions of their own immense prestige. Members of a class held together, ideally, by tenacious bonds of friendship, they throve on the frequent interchange of visible tokens of their *unanimitas*.[39] Relics offered a way of expressing both protection and solidarity. Their discovery and transfer rendered tangible, as the mere sense of the overshadowing of a guardian angel could not have done, the distinctly proprietary relationship which lonely and enterprising men and women had always been expected to establish with their invisible guardians.[40] Thus, the passing of relics from one community to another, or their discovery, heightened the special status of the

members of the Christian elite by making them privileged
agents, personally involved in administering the lovingkindness of God. As Ambrose said of his own role in the discovery
of the bodies of Gervasius and Protasius,

> Although this is a gift from God, yet I cannot deny the grace
> and favor which the Lord Jesus has bestowed on the time
> of my priesthood; for because I have not gained the status
> of a martyr, I have at least acquired these martyrs for you.[41]

Later, in the age of Sidonius Apollinaris and his colleagues[42]
and of Gregory of Tours, we see the bishops of Gaul, in frequent discoveries and translations of relics, discreetly backing
into the limelight of the newly found *praesentia* of the saints. It
was their *merita*, their personal high standing with God, that
had gained the mercy of new protectors for their community.[43]

Gaudentius of Brescia is one example of the new type of
traveler. A wealthy man of ascetic leanings and strong antip-
athy to the Arian views then dominant in northern Italy,
Gaudentius had decided to travel to the Holy Land. In Cappadocia he had received from the nuns of Caesarea relics of the
forty martyrs of Sebaste, which they had received from none
other than Saint Basil.[44] The community had "deigned to be-
stow" these on him as "faithful companions" of his journey:[45]
the gift in distant Cappadocia had been a gesture of acceptance
and solidarity.[46] Gaudentius echoed the gesture on his return.
He called the church in which he placed these and other relics in
Brescia "The Gathering of the Saints," *concilium sanctorum*.[47]
Preaching in around 387 at a time when only a few of his colleagues had been able to travel to Brescia for fear of an im-
pending barbarian invasion,[48] his "Church of the Gathering of
the Saints" stood out, for Gaudentius, as a monument of hap-
pier days of ideal solidarity in a less dislocated world.

It was the same, a decade later, with Victricius of Rouen. We
meet him first in a small circle of ascetics: Paulinus, Saint Martin, and he had once coincided at Vienne.[49] But Victricius's
world soon became dangerously wide. As bishop of Rouen, he
had come to live on the frayed edges of the Roman Empire,
among the barbarians and pirates of the Seine estuary.[50] Along
the English channel, the administrative unity on which the

solidarity of Victricius's class had rested was rapidly vanishing.[51] Throghout northern Gaul, the Mediterranean had come to seem a long way away.[52] Yet, in these years, Victricius maintained his correspondence with Paulinus, now settled in Nola, visited Rome around 403,[53] wrote to Pope Innocent for examples of the custom of the Roman church to apply in his diocese,[54] and had even visited Britain around 394 to reestablish the concord of the churches.[55] Solidarities emphasized in the relatively safe environment in which Gaudentius had obtained and installed his relics in Brescia now needed yet more explicit tokens of ideal concord and of supernatural protection. Victricius had traveled to Britain with relics that came to him from northern Italy:[56] "habeo vestrarum praesentiam majestatum."[57] In a world less certain than the well-patroled pilgrimage routes of Asia Minor and the Near East, Victricius could "enjoy the company of these majestic presences." Secure in his own close relationship to his invisible companions, Victricius now placed the protection they had offered him at the disposal of the whole Christian congregation.[58] It was a reassuring gesture of distance shrinking to a community in danger of becoming an isolated sub-Roman region. For by the effect of "inverted magnitudes" which, as we have seen, so impressed his friend Paulinus, Victricius was able to bring to Rouen tiny fragments that condensed the solidarity of the whole Christian world: "So great a multitude of citizens of Heaven . . . so mysterious a unity of heavenly power."[59] In his sermon *De laude sanctorum* Victricius deliberately presented the installation of his relics as an event heavy with paradox: the splinters of bone and drops of blood were mysteriously joined to an immense invisible unity that embraced the cult sites of the entire Mediterranean. It was a moment for the distant congregation in Rouen to linger on the ideal of "a perfect and total concord."[60]

The late-Roman preoccupation with concord can be seen on every level of public life. The sermons of Gaudentius and Victricius allow us to sense its weight on an empire-wide scale. For the massed fragments of relics gathered together in one place both condensed the ideal unity of the Christian church, as it had first been fused together by the Holy Ghost at Pentecost, and could be spoken of in a language also heavy with late-Roman secular ideals of concord and solidarity between distant friends and distant regions.[61] Yet the relics also emphasized the concord of the local community. The unity of the little fragments, some of them quite indistinguishable from each other,[62] summed up the ideal concord of the community in which they had come to rest. It is interesting to note how frequently late-Roman Christian communities emphasized the fact that they had more than one saint in their midst. While later centuries seem to have been more content to have one, single patron saint as protector, many late-Roman communities chose, instead, to opt for doublets: Peter and Paul in Rome, Felix and Fortunatus in Aquileia.[63] What we know about the associations of the cult of Peter and Paul in Rome makes us suspect that such an emphasis was deliberate: the feast of a pair of saints was a feast of concord in a potentially deeply divided city.[64] The festival of a pair of saints reenacted a highly pertinent "foundation myth" for the Christian community. It stressed the specifically late-Roman miracle by which two brothers—even two clergymen!—had managed to end their lives in perfect harmony. As Chromatius of Aquileia said, in his sermon on Saints Felix and Fortunatus: they "have adorned our own unity with a glorious martyrdom."[65] Such festivals gave an explicit, clerical interpretation to the spontaneous and largely unthinking outbursts of fellow-feeling associated with the shrines of the saints.[66]

If we look at the ceremonial of the saints in later centuries, we find the same pattern. The world of Gregory of Tours is full of serried ranks of saints. For the tombs of the individual saints are rarely allowed to stand alone in their neighborhood. Not every city had a single patron saint.[67] Rather, the bishops wove around each shrine a web of invisible colleagues that did justice to the enduring sense of the solidarity of the senatorial episcopate of Gaul. Centuries-old memories of senatorial and imperial concord stirred on the festivals of the saints. At the shrine of Saint Julian of Brioude, an area slightly set back from the towns, and precisely for that reason a joining point for the whole Auvergne, the possessed shout out: "Why do you bring in strangers to this place? You have gathered a whole council of the saints."[68] *Adgregasti concilium:* it is an image of united power, such as Gaudentius had appealed to over a century previously in his church foundation at Brescia. In a Gaul where the old yearnings for *concordia* among the great had lost none of their relevance,[69] the martyrs maintained some sense of awesome solidarity as they worked together "in the triumphal train of Christ."[70]

It is in the light of this double preoccupation with concord and the exercise of power that we should approach the ceremonial that welcomed the saint into the community in the first place and then reenacted each year at his festival the arrival of the saint's *praesentia* among his people. The *De laude sanctorum* of Victricius of Rouen, and later evidence, make plain that such ceremonies were consciously modeled on the ceremonial of the emperor's *adventus,* or "arrival in state" at a city.[71] In order to understand their full meaning, therefore, we must look for a moment at the associations and the function of that basic ceremony. For it is easy to be misled by late-Roman ceremonial. It has so often been presented exclusively as a device by which the majesty of the emperor was made plain to his subjects, and his person rendered inaccessible and awesome. Yet a more differentiated treatment of imperial ceremonial has made plain that such ceremonies were not played out merely to astonish and overawe the emperor's subjects: they were subtly orchestrated both so as to enlist and to register the participation of the urban communities who attended the imperial *adventus.* Thus, far from being ceremonies limited to the court alone and devoted exclusively to the exaltation of the emperor's person, the ceremonies of the imperial *adventus* had always meant as much to the community which welcomed the emperor as they did to the emperor himself and his entourage. They registered a moment of ideal concord. For all groups in the community could unite in acclaiming the emperor's presence among them.[72] Each separate category within the city—young and old, men and women, tradesmen and nobility, foreigners and locals—had its rightful place in the ceremony of welcome.[73] The *praesentia* of the Emperor, therefore, was held to embrace the whole, undivided community.[74]

It is this aspect of the ceremony of *adventus* as a moment of ideal concord between the separate components of a small town that emerges most clearly from the sermon of Victricius and in the practice of the fifth- and sixth-century church in Gaul. Victricius used the solemn occasion of the arrival of his relics to place new social categories on the map of the Christian community of Rouen. For Victricius was not only a bishop. He was an admirer of Saint Martin and a patron of the new, frequently suspect, ascetic movement.[75] By treating the arrival of his relics as analogous to that of an emperor, he was not only emphasizing their invisible majesty; he was ensuring that their arrival would be an occasion for the Christians of Rouen to find room, in their view of their own community, for a further category. A solemn cortège of chanting monks and virgins now paraded alongside the traditional ranks of the clergy.[76]

Thus, the ceremonial of the saints came to be used in Gaul both to differentiate and to widen the Christian community. The saint's festivals were occasions when room had to be found for all categories of Catholic Christians, new and old alike. A few generations after Victricius preached in Rouen, the novel choirs of monks were joined by equally disturbing outsiders—the Frankish counts of the city, surrounded by their alien bodyguards.[77] Without the studiously all-inclusive ceremonial life that had been developed for the festivals of the saints, it would have been difficult to find a place for these outsiders in the life of the little towns of southern Gaul of the sixth century, whose capacity for deep rancor Gregory of Tours had described so well and so frequently. The Catholicism of the Franks meant, above all, their right to participate in great ceremonies of urban *consensus*.[78] It was by patronizing the basilicas of the saints and by appearing at their festivals, for instance, that Willithruta of Paris, a striking Frankish blonde from a warrior family of exemplary tribal ferocity, could gain acceptance in her community as "Roman in her devotion, if barbarian by birth."[79]

The ceremonials of *adventus*, therefore, as these were continued in the cult of the saints, could widen the bounds of the Christian urban community by giving a place to each one of the various groups within it. They might do more than that. For the festival of a saint was conceived of as a moment of ideal consensus on a deeper level. It made plain God's acceptance of the community as a whole: his mercy embraced all its disparate members, and could reintegrate all who had stood outside in the previous year. Hence the insistence that all Catholic Christians should be able to participate fully in the saint's festival. The terror of illness, of blindness, of possession, or of prison resided in the fear that, at that high moment of solidarity, the sinner would be seen to have been placed by his affliction outside the community:

> "Oh woe is me," a blind woman had cried to Saint Martin, "for blinded by my sins, I do not deserve to look upon this festival with the rest of the people."[80]

Hence the miracles which Gregory of Tours treasured at the festival of Saint Martin were miracles of reintegration into the community. The barriers that had held the individual back from the *consensus omnium* were removed. "With all the people looking on," the crippled walk up to receive the Eucharist.[81] The prisoners in the lockhouse roar in chorus to be allowed to take part in the procession, and the sudden breaking of their chains makes plain the amnesty of the saint.[82] The demons loose the bonds by which they had held the paralyzed and the possessed at a distance from their fellow men.[83] At that moment the amnesty of the saint's presence was proclaimed in the manner most astonishing to late-Roman men: the Christian community had, for a blessed moment, become one again.[84]

The translation of relics had made plain in clear and abiding ritual gestures the structures of patronage and the solidarities that bound together the Christian elites of the Western Roman Empire in its last century. The ceremonial of their installation and the annual celebration of their festival further emphasized the urgent need for concord on the local level. But the *praesentia* of the saint also spoke to the Christian congregation about yet another urgent concern; the nature of the exercise of power in their midst: and it did so in a manner shot through with the imaginative dialectic that we traced in the last chapter.

We must not forget that, while the relic might be discovered, transferred, installed, and the annual memory of the saint be celebrated in an atmosphere of high ceremony associated with unambiguously good happenings, the relic itself still carried with it the dark shadows of its origin: the invisible person, whose *praesentia* in the midst of the Christian community was now a token of the unalloyed mercy of God, had not only once died an evil death; but this evil death had been inflicted by an evil act of power.[85] The martyrs had been executed by the persecutors, or, in the case of Saint Martin, his life as a confessor had been punctuated by dramatic conflicts with unjust and proud authorities.[86] Their deaths, therefore, involved more than a triumph over physical pain; they were vibrant also with the memory of a dialogue with and a triumph over unjust power. If the *passio* of the saint played the same ceremonial role in registering the invisible *adventus* of the saint as had the panegyric on the occasion of the imperial "arrival in state," then we are dealing with a very strange panegyric indeed: for with the reading of the *passio*, the shadow of an act of unjust power, dramatically described, edges across the bright ceremony of the arrival of the saint in imperial majesty. Just as the fact of an evil death is suppressed by the imagery of the saint in Paradise, and its memory made all the more potent for being thus excluded, so, in the *De laude sanctorum* of Victricius, the memory of the ceremonial of the arrival of an emperor, with which the saint is now identified, is flanked by the memory of a scene of judgment and execution that is now all the more conspicuous for its absence:

We see no executioner now on this spot, no bared sword. We approach the altars of the divine authorities; no blood thirsty enemy is present . . . no torturer hovers in the background.[87]

We should not underestimate the gusto with which the Christian communities of the western Mediterranean turned the celebration of the memory of the martyrs into a reassuring scenario by which unambiguously good power, associated with the amnesty of God and the *praesentia* of the martyr, overcame the ever-lurking presence of evil power.[88] The feasts of the martyrs, and the reading of their *passiones* on that occasion, did more than allow individuals to live through a drama of the resolution of pain and illness; the local community as a whole could live through, at the martyr's feast, a tense moment when potent images of "clean" and "unclean" power came together.

The long drawn-out interrogations, the exchange of black jokes, and the gruesome descriptions of torture that are so obtrusive a feature of Prudentius's poems on the martyrs offer more than the spectacle of triumph over pain: they paint, in heavy tones taken from the known horrors of late-Roman judicial practice, the dark side of the ideal "clean" power now associated with the *praesentia* of the saints.[89]

The healing of the evils of power plainly preoccupied the crowds that gathered in the shrines almost as much as did the healing of the evils of the body. The priest who preached to the crowds of pilgrims assembled from Carthage and its neighborhood at the shrine of Saint Stephen at Uzalis warmed readily to such themes: for these registered the impact of the power of the saint in a full public setting.[90] Florentius was a man known to the community. As municipal accountant for Carthage, he had been accused of embezzlement. Dragged before the proconsul, "the angry authority rose up with a terrible voice." It was a bad moment: "At once, a deep chill went through the hearts of all present."[91] Florentius was hung up for interrogation on the rack. With that high good humor common among agents of the law in its more painful processes, the torturer nudged him in the ribs at that juncture and said: "Now is the time to pray to Saint Stephen." Lifting his eyes to the proconsul, he noticed the bench on which the assistants and friends of the proconsul were sitting, both as his legal advisers and as the *patroni* of the community grouped round the imperial representative. Instead of the unpleasant face of one of these, "ugly and scoured with wrinkled age," he saw a young man with a shining complexion: Stephen had become the *patronus* and *suffragator* of Florentius beside the proconsul, and was gesturing to him with the right hand not to worry. The proconsul cooled off, so that Florentius saw in him "no longer a judge but a father."[92]

It was a story which plainly lost nothing in the telling. What is revealing is the manner in which, through the intervention of

Saint Stephen, the exercise of power in a situation where local opinion had been prepared to favor the culprit, had been "washed clean" to everyone's satisfaction: Florentius was very literally "let off the hook"; the patronage system of the late-Roman courts was made to work by the substitution of Saint Stephen for the ill-favored old man; and the proconsul could step back into his ideal role as father of the city.[93]

Carthage at that time was still a carefully governed city. The unpleasant experience of Florentius was only a small part of a series of brutal purges: Saint Stephen, it appears, had done little to protect Augustine's friend Marcellinus from summary execution in those years.[94] Stephen's intervention merely washed clean, in an ambiguous case, the undisrupted workings of imperial strong government. Other, more rudderless regions soon found themselves without a central government to "wash clean." Here the saint intervened in a situation created by competing patronage systems. In communities where *de facto* social power was frequently exercised by groups that were increasingly unacceptable to the Catholic congregations, either as non-Catholics or as barbarians, the saint could cover with his "clean" power the frequently abrasive process by which the power of the Catholic bishop, backed by his congregation, attempted to come up to level up with, or to hold in check, forms of "unclean" power created by the structure of secular government.[95]

Such was the situation precipitated by the arrival of the relics of Saint Stephen at Mahon in Minorca in 417.[96] That part of the island had long been dominated by well-established Jewish families.[97] For the Christians this had created an ambivalent situation. In their opinion, under a Christian empire, "clean" power should have been exercised by the bishop, or at least by Catholic noblemen. In fact, the secular structures of the Empire had unambiguously designated a Jewish doctor of the law and father of the synagogue, Theodorus, as the unchallenged leader of the community: he had been exempted from municipal burdens, had acted as *defensor* of the city, and was now its *patronus*.[98] Theodore and his relatives stood at the head of a community where Jews and Christians had learned to coexist, sharing, for instance, in the same haunting beauty of their chanted Psalms.[99] Yet, at the time of the Vandal invasion of Spain, the secular structures of the empire which had given unchallenged power and privilege to Theodorus and his relatives seemed far away from the Balearic Isles. The arrival of the relics of Saint Stephen, coinciding as it did with a temporary absence of Theodorus in Mallorca, provided the opportunity to bring to an end his ambiguous position on the island. Stephen was the true, the "clean" *patronus,* who could replace the tainted and ambivalent power of a Jewish *patronus.*[100]

Much of what followed was violent and highly unpleasant; the reader must bear with me if, in describing a thoroughly dirty business, where violence and fear of yet greater violence played a decisive role, I limit myself to the perspective of bishop Severus, our only source, and speak of the *patrocinium* of Saint Stephen as "clean" power.[101] We sense, as in a few ancient texts, the horrid onset of communal religious violence, as Jews and Christians suddenly and ominously ceased to greet each other in the streets.[102] The synagogue was destroyed,[103] and the Jewish families driven for a time on to the bleak hillsides.[104] Yet it was something marginally more decent than a mere *pogrom.* Bishop Severus is careful to present these events, at least in retrospect, as part of the emergence of Stephen as the true *patronus* of the city, capable, as Theodorus had been, of embracing both Jews and Christians, in what was now the "clean," unambivalent exercise of power. This emphasis imposed subtle restraints, if not on what happened, at least on the manner the Christian community chose to remember an otherwise brutal takeover. For, because Stephen was the ideal *patronus,* his arrival on the island was not seen as an occasion to "purge" the island of Jews.[105] Rather it was seen as a bid to establish the consensus of a divided community on a new, "clean" basis. Within a few weeks, Theodorus and his relatives had made their peace with the bishop. Though becoming Christians, they maintained their full social status within their own community, though now subject to the higher *patrocinium* of Saint Stephen, and seated beside the Christian bishop as Christian *patroni.*[106] Thus, far from being eradicated, the "unclean" power of the established Jewish families has been "washed clean" by being integrated into the Christian community under Saint Stephen. And Saint Stephen was a *patronus* skilled in the arts of *consensus*. He played his part by offering good Jewish miracles. Jewish women see him as a globe of fire;[107] he scatters sweet manna on the hillside;[108] at his touch, sweet water springs from a cave.[109] As in Uzalis, so at Minorca, Stephen, by resolving the tensions between intertwined and potentially conflicting strucutres of power, had emerged as the *patronus communis*, "the patron of all."[110]

It is in this way that little communities for whom the structures of the Roman Empire either meant little, or had ceased to exist, grappled with the facts of local power in a changing world. The *praesentia* of the saints had been made available to them in gestures that condensed the poignant yearning for concord and solidarity among the elites of the Western provinces in its last century; yet, once available, the imaginative dialectic that surrounded the person of the saint insured that the shrine would be more than a reminder of the ideal unity of a former age: the shrine became a fixed point where the solemn, necessary play of "clean power"—of *potentia* exercised as it should be—could be played out in acts of healing, exorcism and rough justice.

# Chapter Six

## Potentia

To visit a late-antique Christian shrine could be a noisy and frightening experinece. Jerome wrote of the first impact of the tombs of the prophets in the Holy Land on the Roman pilgrim Paula:

> She shuddered at the sight of so many marvelous happenings. For there she was met by the noise of demons roaring in various torments, and, before the tombs of the saints, she saw men howling like wolves, barking like dogs, roaring like lions, hissing like snakes, bellowing like bulls; some twisted their heads to touch the earth by arching their bodies backwards; women hung upside-down in mid-air, yet their skirts did not fall down over their heads.[1]

Catholic Europe, as presented to a newcomer of the late sixth century, was mapped out in terms of the places in which such things happened. For possession and exorcism in the great basilicas of Catholic Gaul was held to be the one irrefutable sign of the *praesentia* within them of the saints. Thus Nicetius of Trier wrote to Chlodoswintha, the wife of the Lombard king Alboin, newly arrived in Italy from the Danube and toying with the Arian heresy of his Ostrogothic predecessors:

106

Let him send his men to the Lord Martin, on the day of his festival, on the eleventh of November.... And what can I say of the Lord Germanus, the Lord Hilarius, or the Lord Lupus, where so many marvelous happenings take place that I can hardly find words to express them: when the possessed, that is, those who have demons in them, float in the air, and the demons in them are put to the torture to confess that these saints are indeed the "lords" of which I speak. Does this happen in the churches of the Arians? By no means; for God and the lords the saints are not sensed to be present there. For the demons cannot deny the place where the saints reside.[2]

To a late-Roman man the drama of exorcism was the one demonstration of the power of God that carried unanswerable authority. In the healing of the possessed, the *praesentia* of the saint was held to be registered with unfailing accuracy, and their ideal power, their *potentia*, shown most fully and in the most reassuring manner. For the solemn and dramatic course of possession and exorcism formed an exact fit with expectations of the exercise of "clean" power which, as we have seen, clustered around the tombs of the saints. Late-antique and early-medieval men were not merely impressed by the melodramatic associations of exorcism: they felt that in such a drama they witnessed more clearly and with greater precision the manner in which God, through his lords the saints, could stretch forth into their midst the right hand of his healing power. The *medicabilis divinae potentiae dextera*,[3] from whose touch all miracles sprang, was shown at its most "mysterious and terrifying" in the shouts of the demons speaking through the possessed at the shrines of the saints.[4]

Let us begin, therefore, by following carefully the rhythm of a cure by exorcism at a shrine, and, having seized this rhythm, examine the implication for late-Roman and early-medieval society as a whole of the decision of the Christian church to accept such a cure as the paradigm of the exercise of the *potentia* of the saints.

It is hardly surprising that, when faced with such noisy and disturbing a phenomenon, modern scholars have, like the delicately nurtured Paula, blanched at the scenes enacted round the shrines of late antiquity. Sober historians of the Christian

church have declared that such phenomena, like the noisy celebrations at the saints' festivals, "are more problems of crowd
psychology than of Christian piety."[5] In so doing, they have
declared the study of exorcism, possibly the most highly rated
activity of the early Christian church, a historiographical
"no-go" area. Yet even "crowd psychology" has its surprises:
the work of Natalie Z. Davis, for instance, on the horrors of
religious violence in sixteenth-century France and on the up-
roarious carnivals of the post-Reformation cities, has demon-
strated how historians who are prepared to study such
phenomena with alertness and a strong stomach, can find that
they can catch behind what first strikes them as a cacophony of
random violence or exuberance, the strains of an alien music.[6] It
is the same with exorcism. Abundant anthropological material
has made the phenomenon of spirit possession eminently intelligible in observed, living societies.[7] Combined with
exhaustive treatments of the theme of exorcism and the demonic in the ancient world,[8] these studies have made plain that
we are not dealing with some rare aberration of "popular" religion, but with the regular verbs in a stable grammar of the
impingement of the supernatural in society that stretches from
the New Testament deep into the middle ages.

Let us examine some aspects of the rhythm of possession and
exorcism as these contributed to build up a model of the working of the power and presence of the saints in late-antique
society. Most important of all for a late-antique man were the
heavy judicial overtones of the process of exorcism at a shrine.
Exorcism had always taken the form of a dialogue in which the
invisible authority behind the human agent of exorcism could
be seen to be pitted against the power of the demons who spoke
through the possessed human sufferer.[9] What was spelled out
with unfailing clarity at a late-Roman shrine was that this dialogue was a judicial inquiry. The horrors of a late-Roman
courtroom, which included the application of tortures in the
process of interrogation, the *quaestio*, were reenacted with
gusto, in invisible form, in the dialogue between the saint and
the demons in the possessed.

Nothing gave a more palpable face to the unseen *praesentia* of
the saint than did the heavy cries of the possessed. As Gregory

of Tours said of the outburst of shouting by the possessed at the tomb of Saint Julian at Brioude,

> In this way they bring home the presence of the saints of God to human minds, that there should be no doubt that the saints are present at their tombs.[10]

But this shouting was so convincing to late-Roman bystanders because these were believed not to be random cries: they were the audible and visible side of an inaudible and invisible judicial inquiry. The *praesentia* of the saint is rendered manifest because it is the *praesentia* of an active late-Roman judge, using late-Roman methods of interrogation.

The imaginative dialectic, to which I have referred in my last two chapters, was fully worked through in such a scene. The original act of "unclean" power, by which the martyr had been tortured and condemned is transmuted into its reverse. Now the martyr is the judge; and the gods of paganism, the demons who had stood behind his persecutors, are the culprits under interrogation.[11] As Victricius of Rouen made plain, "clean" power could not be shown in a more convincing manner. At an altar from which the shadow of the memory of physical tortures and execution has been studiously banished, an invisible *quaestio* could now be reenacted:

> A torturer bends over the unclean spirit, but is not seen. There are no chains here now, yet the being who suffers is bound. God's anger has other hooks to tear the flesh and other racks to stretch invisible limbs.[12]

We should remember that in the late-Roman *quaestio*, torture was not an end in itself: it was applied only to gain the truth. The dramatic dialogue between judge and culprit carried with it a sincerity that pain alone could guarantee.[13] The demons in the possessed, therefore, were not being punished by torture: they were confessing the truth under torture.[14] Their recognition of the *potentia* of the saint was all the more authoritative for having been extracted in that way. When alive, the authority of Saint Martin had elicited, in the agonized cries of the possessed who flocked to him, a roll call of the names of the ancient gods: this amounted to a definitive recognition by the demons, who bore the names of the gods, of the superior *potentia* of Martin and his God.[15]

It was, indeed, the liberating precision of exorcism that commended itself so strongly to late antique men. It was a deeply reassuring drama for men anxious about themselves and their society. For the truth behind confusing and complex situations could be seen to emerge through the invisible questioning of the saint. The horror of the demonic was its very facelessness. The demons "did their business in the darkness," in the sense that they stood for the intangible emotional undertones of ambiguous situations and for the uncertain motives of refractory individuals.[16] The vast prestige of Saint Martin came from the fact that, as an exorcist, he could concretize and, so, mercifully delimit and render manageable tense moments, by being able to perceive and isolate the demon lurking within them. Just as he enjoyed the nourishing converse of angels, so "the devil also was clearly visible to his eyes— conspicabilem et subjectum oculis."[17] His conflict with the refractory Brictio was rendered explicable by Martin's ability to see, in Brictio, the sullen demons of competition;[18] the terror caused by a rumor of the advance of the barbarians on Trier was "defused" by the manner in which Martin exorcized, from one of the possessed, the demon who had spread an infectious mood of panic.[19]

We should not underestimate, therefore, the strong "confessional" overtones of the scenario of exorcism. At a time when the public penitential system of the Latin church was suffering from the strains imposed by its ancient mechanisms, the old ideal of public penance and forgiveness could be spasmodically reenacted in the dramatic dialogue of exorcism.[20] By the seventh century, the roll call of defeated gods that Martin once elicited, had settled down to a more humdrum, but equally precise, list of the sins that had exposed each sufferer to possession:

> Each one of them confessed to their individual fault: one because he had drunk a glass of water without making the sign of the cross; another had exposed himself by gluttony, another by perjury, another by theft, another by murder.[21]

Throughout we are dealing with a phenomenon which, beneath its flamboyant forms of acting out, still moved to the steady rhythms of Roman justice and preserved the values of the early-Christian penitential discipline.

Possession and exorcism was not only a *psychodrame* which the Christian community found peculiarly consonant with its preoccupation with power and justice: it was a drama in which the individual might have a good reason to be implicated, as a "possessed" sufferer. It is far from certain that all who came to the shrine came because they had been possessed; some, at least, came in order to be possessed:[22] and in so doing they could place the rights and wrongs of their case before the *praesentia* of the saint rather than expose themselves to the hard justice of their fellows. The evidence from sixth-century Gaul suggests that not all the possessed came to the shrines already in a state of extreme disturbance. The borderline between voluntary and involuntary possession was as fluid in late antiquity as it has been observed to be in other societies. As a result, the possessed became a regular part of the life of the shrine. They were a recognized group. They would be blessed daily. They were given food. They were set to scrub the floor of the basilica.[23] At the shrine of Saint Martin, they would join the other category, the beggars, in taking up sticks and stones to defend the honor of their saint.[24] Occasionally, they took the chestnuts out of the fire by speaking the truth in public: some could be hired to abuse a bishop;[25] another, having praised a bishop and abused a king, discreetly vanished.[26] Evidently, the invisible *quaestio* of the saint could be an occasion for much plain speaking in the midst of the Christian community. The basic reason for such articulateness was that the exercise of the *potentia* of the saint differed from the exercise of "unclean" power: not only was the *quaestio* mercifully intangible; its aim was the reintegration into the community of the individual human being through the assertion against the demonic of the abiding resilience of his human nature.

The weight of violence was directed away from the human sufferer onto the demonic. For the possessed was always thought of as totally dissociated. It was the demon within the human being, and not the human being himself, which acted as it did, writhing and leaping as it cried out in pain and anger at the interrogation of the saint: "Clamantes propria aliena per ora daemones [It is their own pains the demons shout through others' mouths].[27] Hence the drama of exorcism was not merely a drama of authority: it was a drama of reintegration. The human being who had been swept far away from the human community was solemnly reinstated among the warm mass of his fellows. The process might begin, as Paula had witnessed it, with the horror of the collapse of the categories that defined a human being.[28] The possessed might howl like an animal[29] or flail in mid-air in the nonhuman region of the demonic.[30] It ended, after the demon had been investigated, judged and excluded, with the recuperation of the full human personality: "Iam totus vel solus homo in sua jura reversus [Now the man alone returns entirely to his rightful place]"[31] Hence the imaginative importance of the great prayers of exorcism that maintained and articulated, in liturgical form, the expectations of the group at the shrine. These stressed the solemn ordering of the universe at the Creation, the position of the sufferer as a temple of God, and the awesome reentry of God into his temple.[32] They were majestic assertions of true order and rightful possession in a harsh and disorderly world. Such prayers were mirrored in the overpowering visual impression of the great basilicas themselves: with their harmonious rows of columns, with their brilliant mosaics and gilded ceilings in which the sunlight seemed trapped forever, with the subtle play of light and shadow around their great candelabra,[33] the shrines caught an echo of the solemn joy of the first morning of man's creation:

> For he who fixed the bounds of light and dark
> Is he who drives black chaos from the martyrs'
> tombs.[34]

The regaining of the harmony of God's original creation implied the regaining for the individual of a place among his fellows. The hard boundaries of the group had to open to make way for the human being who had, in so palpable a manner, been delivered by the *potentia* of the saint from the demon that had kept him apart. At the shrine of Gervasius and Protasius, Augustine wrote, thieves who confessed their deeds in a state of possession could make reparation for their robberies.[35] Compared with the vengeance demanded by the outside world, the justice of the saint was all that justice should be—it was manifest, swift and remarkably mild.[36]

The *potentia* of the saint was made plain by a further consequence. Frequently in the work of Gregory of Tours, we find
that those who had been healed at the shrine gain from this
healing a change of social status. Serfs are emancipated from
their former owners, and become part of the *familia* of the saint,
either at the shrine itself, or on the estates of Saint Martin.[37] Not
that this necessarily amounted to a marked improvement.
When, in the eighth century, we find the monks of a great
monastery in Upper Egypt recruiting to their estates children
who had been healed at the shrine of the monastery's saint, we
are dealing with yet another harsh method by which great
landowners mobilized their labor force. A young man who was
present when his family discussed with the abbot the terms of
work to which the healing at the shrine had made him liable,
plainly heard nothing to his liking: he slipped away, took a boat
downstream to Cairo and was never seen in the village again.[38]
The healed became the property of the invisible "lord" to the
exclusion of all other lords.

What every stage of the process of exorcism, and, more generally, of healing, spelled out for a late-antique man was that
healing and deliverance from the consequences of sin had to
pass through a precise set of interpersonal relations. Seldom
had "the power of the healing right hand of God" been
stretched forth to mankind so palpably and so exclusively
through human links that maintained the fully panoply of the
late-Roman judicial system and the full implications of late-
Roman forms of dependence. Even a bull was remembered as
having approached the shrine of Saint Julian, "not tossing with
his horns, but filled with a sense of fear, as if appearing before
the tribunal of a judge."[39]

We need only look outside the Christian communities to realize how distinctive this overwhelming emphasis on an interpersonal relationship as the basis of all acts of healing could be.
Let us turn to the work of an almost exact contemporary and
fellow countryman of Saint Martin of Tours, to the *De
medicamentis* of the physician Marcellus of Bordeaux.[40] To compare the miracles of healing, and especially of exorcism performed by Martin, with the recipes for cures contained in the
work of Marcellus, is to enter another world. We must be careful, however, to define clearly in what way the two worlds

differed. For they plainly overlapped in many ways. The ministrations of Martin often took place at the country houses, or with the full permission, of the same senatorial landowners for whom Marcellus wrote.[41] It would be wrong to think of exorcism as appealing merely to a "lower-class" segment of the populations of Gaul. If anything, it is Marcellus, who includes in his book "the simple and efficacious remedies of common country folk"[42] and gives the Celtic names of many medicinal plants including the shamrock,[43] who brings us far closer to popular Gallic practice than do the drastic and ceremonious rituals of exorcism which Martin performed in palaces and towns.

Nor should we blur the differences between the two men and the two worlds which their attitudes to cure reveal. If we do this, it is because the "two-tiered model" has seldom been more tenacious than in the study of medicine in late antiquity. If we judge the two men by the standards of modern rational medicine, Marcellus, the purveyor of exotic recipes and folk medicine, and Martin, the exorcist, fall equally far below an acceptable level of intellectual respectability. The differences between the two, and the implications of these differences, are obscured in a fog of modern disapproval. It is habitual to read through the *De medicamentis* with raised eyebrows, noting the rich layers of folklore and superstition that lie beneath the thin veneer of Hippocratic empiricism.[44]

It we are to understand the implications of the Christian model of healing, and the significance of its rise to prominence as the paradigm of healing in the dominant shrines of Christian Gaul, we must step aside from modern attitudes. Late-antique medicine and healing cannot be judged from the single viewpoint of whether or not its practices measure up to our own image of rational science. We must accept the medical pluralism of an ancient society. As Vincent Crapanzano has remarked of modern Morocco: "In Morocco there is no single, socially chartered therapeutic system with final authority."[45] In late antiquity, as in modern Morocco, the individual found himself faced with a choice of therapeutic systems;[46] and, in making his or her choice, the patient would appeal to criteria that reflected a precise social milieu. For the patient would depend on a "support group" of relatives and acquaintances for information about healing and, more generally, would draw on shared attitudes that would designate one therapeutic system rather than another as congruent with the expectations of the group on that occasion. When no therapeutic system has final authority, as is the case in parts of modern Morocco and was certainly the case for the society of late-Roman Gaul, the process of choice is frequently gone through, and, as a consequence, the social and cultural criteria behind the choices are frequently mobilized:

In the morning, I decided to go to the *fqih*. My husband said, "No it is necessary to go to the hospital." I answered, "No, it is not an illness for the hospital, it is an illness for the *fqih*. . . . I too knew that it was an illness for the *fqih* and the saint. When an infant falls sick and has fever and breathes with difficulty, it is an illness which is for the *fqih*. But when a child eats and vomits, when he is sick in the intestines, then it is an illness for the hospital. Also, if he chokes when he vomits, it is an illness for the hospital. I learned to tell them apart from the neighbors."[47]

Late-Roman men passed their therapeutic systems through a similar process of implicit accountancy.

What is noteworthy in the contrast between the therapeutic system that was "socially chartered" at Christian shrines and the system to which Marcellus appealed, was the studious absence in the therapeutic system of Marcellus of a high-pitched idiom of relationships of dependence. Those who drew their cures from the traditions to which Marcellus appealed, and who adopted the methods which he recommended, plainly lived in a world where the exercise of *potentia,* and the dependence of the individual on a clearly designated *dominus* and *patronus,* were not elements from their social world that needed to be acted out in the process of healing. The choice between Martin and Marcellus was a choice of which types of human relations were considered desirable to mobilize and to replicate in the process of cure. Intense dependence on the *potentia* of another is tacitly excluded, in the work of Marcellus, by a large measure of "autarky" on the part of the patient. As Aline Rousselle has written, in her seminal treatment, the reader of Marcellus has to work out his own salvation, with the means placed at his disposal in the book:

Il devient sujet actif de sa guérison. Le malade sait que de sa concentration volontaire dépend l'efficacité des formules et amulettes. Il bénéficie donc, au niveau de la pratique, d'une thérapie globale. L'homme est engagé, corps et esprit, dans sa propre guérison.[48]

There are some obvious reasons for this distinct approach. The *De medicamentis* is written in the first place to teach men to do without doctors and, especially, without surgery.[49] The greatest benefit that Marcellus promises in his preface is that his book will enable the reader to cure himself, *sine medici intercessione.*[50] As such, the *De medicamentis* fits into a long tradition of handbooks of do-it-yourself medicine, which were always particularly favored by great landowners who traveled frequently and who would have found themselves separated from urban medical services on their estates.[51] The medical manuals of the early colonies of America are the direct descendents of the *genre:* "Let all your victuals be light and temperate; and your drink, Beer brewed with Sorrel Leaves, Pine Tops, Root of Ash and a little Old Iron."[52] Such manuals convey an image of the body that assumes that the patient can avoid dependence on a drastic and expensive therapeutic system: simple ingredients, self-control, and a due sense of the blessings of the environment can confer on him a large measure of autarky in the preservation of his health.

Heaven be praised, there is little occasion to say anything of the stone in the Bladder, there being few instances of it in this Colony. Among the Gentry, the Madeira Wine, which has but little Tartar in it, and the Molasses Beer, being soft and cleansing, are happy Defences against the scourge of Luxury and Laziness.[53]

Behind even the most banal remedy, we can sense the unspoken decision of a small society on what specific resources, social and moral as well as strictly medical, it can mobilize against disease, and with what it can dispense. For Marcellus makes his reader self-sufficient by making him dependent on something other than his doctor. The links of dependence, therefore, are subtly shifted from a precisely designated person to a diffused tradition to which the sufferer can have easy access on his own terms.

Here we meet Marcellus, the descendant of the "religious aristocracy" of Gaul.[54] From the dawn of time, he writes, the gods have made known to men the virtues of plants and the correct combinations of spells and remedies.[55] A profound sense of the unstinting generosity of the natural world and of the constant gentle prompting of the gods in making its beneficent properties easily available to men runs through the *De medicamentis*.[56] It accounts for the exclusively pagan tone of a book whose author was possibly a Christian writing for a largely Christianized upper class. For Marcellus's paganism is part and parcel of his therapeutic system: if healing was available to all men, independent of the monopoly established by medical expertise, this was because, for any learned late-antique doctor such as Marcellus, the availability of healing implied a view of the medical tradition whose roots went back to those days when mortals communed with the gods.[57] It is the same with Marcellus's incorporation of local material. The *De medicamentis* has allowed scholars to scan the Gallic world in the last century of paganism, collecting from it fragments of the Gallic language and echoes of long-forgotten Celtic spells.[58] This is not because Marcellus, a doctor in Bordeaux, who may have attended Athaulf and talked to the formidable Jerome when on pilgrimage in the Holy Land, is the last of the Druids;[59] it is because the generosity of the gods had showered on men both the learned traditions of an educated elite whose works and remedies spanned the ancient Mediterranean[60] and the immemorial wisdom of their native lands.[61]

The religious affiliations of Marcellus and the precise religious roots of many of his remedies remain vague. What emerges clearly, however, is the firm manner in which both the *genre* of the book itself and the assumptions which led Marcellus to write such a book offer a model of direct and unmediated dependence of the individual on his environment. The book sums up the wisdom latent in that environment: "like music in an Italian street," it is available to all; and Marcellus thinks it an act of mercy to tell them so.[62] This environment is presented, in most spells and remedies, as part of a wider world of magical sympathies that can be approached with unaffected ease by the patient. No *psychodrame* of dependence and authority need ever be played out.[63] A prayer on seeing the first swallow, accompanied by bathing the eyes in spring water, is enough to ward off eye-diseases throughout the year.[64] One thinks, by way of contrast, of the awesome association of pain transmuted into majesty which Gregory of Tours saw behind the equally banal eye salve provided by Saint Benignus.[65] As Aline Rousselle says, speaking of the healing sanctuaries of Celtic Gaul: 'Le contact du patient et du divin se fait en partie directement.'[66] Impressive though the pagan sanctuaries of fourth-century Gaul might still have been, a visit to them, and contact with the gods through the healing medium of water or of sleep, was deemed enough.[67] These ancient methods appear to have been untouched by the harsh and up-to-date late-Roman language of *potentia* exercised by persons that contemporaries associated with Christian shrines. They had the voiceless power of nature itself behind them.

The *potentia* of the saint in his shrine assumed a "vertical" model of dependence. The saint's power held the individual in a tight bond of personal obligation that might begin, days of hard journey away, in a need to visit the saint's *praesentia* in the one place where it could be found; it could make the patient pass through the drama of a late-Roman court scene, and it might even end in a palpable and irreversible act of social dependence, by which the recipient of healing became the serf of the church in which his invisible *dominus* resided. By contrast, Marcellus sums up a world for which a "horizontal" model is still dominant: the patient is tied directly by a web of Lilliputian threads to the diffuse and seemingly bottomless traditions of his own environment. Such a model tacitly but firmly excluded the intervention from outside of a *potentia* that might dislodge the individual from the environment in which he could still feel safely embedded. Seen in this light, what we call the spread of Christianity in Gaul, as it radiated from those great shrines where the *praesentia* of the saints was dramatically revealed by acts of power, amounts to a conflict of two models of healing, each heavy with assumptions on the position of man in his society and in his environment. It is to this conflict that we must now turn.

For this is the conflict which holds the attention of Gregory of Tours. It is summed up for him in two words: *reverentia* and its antithesis, *rusticitas*. *Reverentia* implied a willingness to focus belief on precise invisible persons, on Christ and his friends the saints—the *amici dominici*[68]—in such a way as to commit the believer to definite rhythms in his life (such as the observation of the holy days of the saints), to direct his attention to specific sites and objects (the shrines and relics of the saints), to react to illness and to danger by dependence on these invisible persons, and to remain constantly aware, in the play of human action around him, that good and bad fortune was directly related to good or bad relations with these invisible persons. *Reverentia*, therefore, assumed a high degree of social and cultural grooming. It was not a luxuriant undergrowth of credulity or neopaganism. It involved learning an etiquette toward the supernatural, whose every gesture was carefully delineated. Hence the importance for Gregory of its antithesis, *rusticitas*, which is best translated as "boorishness," "slipshodness"—the failure, or the positive refusal, to give life structure in terms of ceremonious relationships with specific invisible persons.[69]

Gregory's use of the word *rusticitas* throws light on the position of Christianity in parts of Gaul, and, by implication, in western Europe as a whole, at the end of the late-antique period. It is a situation which requires some delicacy of interpretation. For a sharp dichotomy between "town" and "country," "Christian" and "pagan" does not do justice to its nuances. *Rusticitas*, as Gregory observed its ravages, overlapped considerably with the habits of the rural population; but it was by no means limited exclusively to these. *Rusticitas* could be committed by most people on most days—and especially on Sundays, as when the inhabitants of Arles irrespective of class and culture brought upon themselves the solemn warnings of their bishop, Caesarius, by behaving like *rustici* in making love to their wives on the Lord's Day.[70] Still less can it be identified with "rural paganism." For what we have seen is that, although therapeutic systems such as those assumed by Marcellus depended on knowledge inherited from the pagan past, they formed an intractable enclave of *rusticitas* less because they were closely connected with any precise forms of pagan worship, as because they tacitly denied any rhythm of cure that

involved explicit dependence on the *potentia* of an invisible
human being: the kin, the neighbors, especially the cunning
men and women of the locality, were thought to be able to
provide all that the sufferer needed.[71] When members of Gregory's own entourage, traveling to Brioude to avoid the plague,
resorted to the use of amulets applied by local diviners to cure
one of their fellows, what angers him is not that they were
behaving like pagans, but that they had lost their sense of *reverentia* for the saints. It provokes in him a characteristic outburst:

> Quaerat patrocinium martyrum . . . postolet adiutoria con-
> fessorum, qui merito amici sunt dominici nuncupati.
>
> [Let the patronage of the martyrs be what the sufferer
> seeks. . . . Let him pray for the help offered by the confessors,
> who are truly called friends of the Lord.][72]

Thus, in any place where a Christian shrine lay close to hand,
the diffuse resources of the neighborhood, as these had been
applied in the form of amulets and divination, were met by a
precisely delineated image of ideal human relations sketched
out by bishops such as Gregory with a certainty of touch that
betrayed the long grooming of late-Roman aristocratic society.

It is in a conflict of models of healing, therefore, that we can
sense the impact of the rise of Christianity. Throughout the
Mediterranean world, whether it is in a little wooden chapel on
an estate in the Limousin,[73] as described by Gregory, or in the
vigorous "mopping up" by Bishop Theodoret of Cyrrhus of the
sectarian villages of the hinterland of northern Syria, perched
on their mountain ridges, above the disciplined life of the
plains in a countryside where, as an eighteenth century traveler
observed, "we see despotism extending itself over all the flat
country and its progress stopt towards the mountains, at the
first rock, at the first defile, that is easy of defence,"[74] the advance of Christianity beyond the towns was the advance of the
*praesentia* of the saints.[75] Throughout this book, we have seen
how such a *praesentia*, in the form of a relic and its shrine, was
heavy with a whole cluster of specific associations, involving
human interaction with an invisible, ideal human being,
wielding ideal *potentia*.

Only too frequently in late antiquity, the *praesentia* of the saint in the countryside ratified disruptive processes that had been at work for centuries. For we are dealing with a silent change, larger by far than the rise of the Christian church. In Gaul and Spain, the spread of Latin at the expense of local Celtic dialects, and the consequent emergence of the Romance languages, betrays the final death of cultures that had existed since prehistory. The Christian church inherited the results of this change.[76] By the sixth century, the only major settled civilization that maintained a paganism reaching back without dislocation to the preclassical world, west of India and east of Ireland, was the Zoroastrian culture of Sasanian Iran: elsewhere, in Egypt, in Mesopotamia, in Anatolia, and in western Europe, the ancient preclassical world had come to a definitive end.[77] It was a silent subsidence more drastic than the decline and fall of the Roman Empire, and more irreversible than the passing of the urban gods of Greco-Roman paganism. In the countryside and the towns of Gaul and Spain the *praesentia* of the saints reaped the fruits of a belated and largely unwitting triumph of Romanization. For the spread of Christian *reverentia* made final the processes by which the indigenous cultures of the western Mediterranean had been imperceptibly eroded by a slow but sure pressure from on top exercised through the grid of administration and patronage relationships that had reached ever outwards over the centuries from the towns and from the country villas of the great.[78] A century after the end of the Western Empire, Gregory and his contemporaries could now be certain that, if all roads no longer ran to Rome, in the Touraine, at least, they would all run to Tours, *ad dominum Martinum:* a speck of dust from his shrine was worth more than all the imemorial cunning of the village healers.[79]

For, as we have seen throughout this book, the *reverentia* that Gregory expected derived its force from an unremitting if discreet process of "socialization," taking place in a world whose expectations of the supernatural had been pieced together, lovingly and with a certain urgency, from the workings of power and protection observed among the Late Roman aristocracy in a largely urban environment. The language of the cult of saints breathed this quite distinctive atmosphere; and the rhythms and preoccupations that supported it were acted out most convincingly either at urban shrines, under the patronage of aristocratic bishops, or, as at the shrine of Saint Julian of Brioude, in a rural area dominated by an aristocracy with widespread, urban connections.[80] When this *reverentia* reached out into areas where such "socialization" was less available, it was met by the tacit resistance of life styles that were less amenable to urban and aristocratic grooming. Throughout the late-antique and early-medieval period, the process of Christianization was brought to a standstill by the silent determination of human groups who would not alter the immemorial patterns of their working life to pay reverence to the saints,[81] or to bend their habits to please yet another class of *domini*.[82] Zones of "raw rusticity" hemmed in Gregory's ceremonious world.[83]

Occasionally, however, the new *praesentia* of the saint might be used to condense and resolve the ambiguities of scattered agrarian communities whose members felt enmeshed in conflicting networks of obligation.[84] Gregory's hagiographic work is punctuated by incidents that allow us to glimpse the malaise of a countryside faced by baffling or oppressive forms of power. For the *praesentia* of the saint often sparked off heady enthusiasm, associated with the arrival of new, "clean" power in areas where, until then, the villagers had had no choice but of forms of "unclean" dependence. When the relics of Saint Julian passed through the fields of Champagne at a time when these were crowded with hired laborers drawn from the neighboring villages, their passage was marked by scenes as dramatic and as ominous as any later pursuit of the millennium:

> Look at the most blessed Julian drawing near to us! Behold his power! Behold his glory! Run, lads, leave your ploughs and oxen; let the whole crowd of us follow him![85]

The transient *praesentia* of the saint had brought to these tired men the touch of an ideal dependence that could set them free, if only for a moment, from the harsh demands of Gallo-Roman landowning in a labor-intensive cereal-growing area.[86] Many of the afflicted individuals who were emancipated from their lords[87] or who abandoned their families on finding healing at the shrines of the saints came from peripheral areas.[88] Faced by the ambiguities of the patronage system in which they were caught, those with no other defense, often the women, opted dramatically for dependence on an ideal *dominus* at his distant shrine, rather than for dependence on the all too palpable wielders of power in their locality.[89]

Gregory registered this trickle of uprooted men and women with approval: for it is the demons that speak in them, recognizing, in unexceptionable form, the ever-widening range of the *potentia* of the saints.[90] What angers him deeply, however, is any attempt on the part of the population to sidestep the demands of *reverentia* by creating for themselves indigenous pockets of *praesentia* which escaped the control of the bishop. Yet his *libri historiarum* and other later sources are full of incidents that reveal the explosive situation which the dominance of the urban saints of Gaul had created. Whenever communities were faced by threats with which the conventional therapeutic systems could not cope, as in the frequent recrudescences of the plague after 543, their immediate response to the situation was a reassertion of the "horizontal" model of healing, if now in a new, Christian form.[91] Soothsayers appeared, empowered by visions of the saints, to circulate new forms of remedies and to enunciate new rituals of propitiation.[92] Prophets established penitential rituals, based on their ability as diviners to detect thieves, to recover stolen goods, and to read thoughts.[93] These movements betrayed a poignant need to bring the *praesentia* of the saints, often of the most authoritative and unimaginably distant of these, such as Peter and Paul, straight into the local community. And they claimed to do this without the crushing demands of *reverentia* mobilized around the urban shrine and its bishop.[94] Even Gregory met his match in such men:

> [After a bad year, in 587] there appeared at Tours a man named Desiderius, who proclaimed himself one above the common, asserting his power to work many miracles. He boasted, among other things, that messengers passed between himself and the apostles Peter and Paul. As I was absent, the country people flocked to him in multitudes,

bringing with them the blind and the infirm, whom he
sought to deceive rather by the false teaching of hellish arts,
than to heal by the power of holiness.[95]

What worried Gregory was that this was not an isolated case.[96]
These incidents stretched from the early sixth century deep into
the middle ages.[97] We can sense in them the reaction of men
and women who had been pushed tragically to one side by the
rise of the Christian church, and by the extension of its structures into the countryside. Religion in its fullness, and full participation in the beneficence of the saints, happened elsewhere,
in the towns.[98]

For this was the paradox of late-antique Christianity as it
came to be crystalized in the cult of saints. A universal and
exclusive religion, Christianity claimed to have spread to every
region of the known world.[99] In fact, having spread, it lay
around the shrines of the saints like pools of water on a drying
surface. For only in certain places, and in certain precisely delimited social milieux, could the language of the *praesentia* and
the *potentia* of the saints echo with satisfying congruence the
deepest wishes of the Christian communities. Outside the areas
where *reverentia* could be limned in with a full palette of late-
Roman associations, there lay wide zones where Christianity
could only be painted in so many washes of gray, over a countryside where many of the tints of indigenous paganism had,
long previously, grown pale.[100] It is a sad prospect: Christian
*reverentia* created a situation which the elites of the Greco-
Roman world had never envisaged in so sharp a form;[101] the
population was now divided between those who could if they
wished be full participants in the grooming of a universal religion, and large areas and classes condemned, by physical distance and the lack of "socialization," to a substandard version
of the same religion.[102] The death of paganism in western society, and the rise of the cult of saints, with its explicitly aristocratic and urban forms, ensured that, from late antiquity onwards, the upper-class culture of Europe would always measure
itself against the wilderness of a *rusticitas* which it had itself
played no small part in creating.[103]

We also look out on a natural world made passive by being
shorn of the power of the gods. It seems to me that the most

marked feature of the rise of the Christian church in western Europe was the imposition of human administrative structures and of an ideal *potentia* linked to invisible human beings and to their visible human representatives, the bishops of the towns, at the expense of traditions that had seemed to belong to the structure of the landscape itself.[104] Saint Martin attacked those points at which the natural and the divine were held to meet:[105] he cut down the sacred trees,[106] and he broke up the processions that followed the immemorial lines between the arable and the nonarable.[107] His successors fulminated against trees and fountains, and against forms of divination that gained access to the future through the close observation of the vagaries of animal and vegetable life.[108] They imposed rhythms of work and leisure that ignored the slow turning of the sun, the moon, and the planets through the heavens, and that reflected, instead, a purely human time, linked to the deaths of outstanding individuals.[109] What is at stake behind the tired repetitions of antipagan polemic and the admonitions of the councils in sixth-century Gaul and Spain is nothing less than a conflict of views on the relation between man and nature.

Alphonse Dupront has made this point clear when he speaks of the nature of the Christian pilgrimage site:

> Le lieu dans la plénitude du sens est réalité cosmique, quelque accident physique qu'en chaque cas il consacre. Et toute l'histoire du pèlerinage chrétien vise à baptiser le païen— c'est à dire à anthropomorphiser le cosmique. . . . L'écran humain ou "l'hominisation" sont actes cohérents à toute considération chrétienne du lieu de pèlerinage.[110]

This was certainly the opinion of the fifth-century bishop of Javols, as his activities were remembered by Gregory. When he spread Christianity into the Auvergne, he found the country folk celebrating a three-day festival with offerings on the edge of a marsh formed in the volcanic crater within a mountain top. "Nulla est religio in stagno," he said:

> There can be no religion in a swamp. But rather acknowledge God and give veneration to his friends. Adore Saint Hilarius, the bishop of God, whose relics are installed here. He can act as your intercessor for the mercy of God.[111]

What happens later may seem no great change. The pilgrimage to the mountain top continued.[112] But the *religio* has well and truly gone out of the swamp. Instead, we have a human artifact—a stone building; the *praesentia* of a human being—the relics of Saint Hilarius; and Saint Hilarius's power is supposed to operate through the quintessentially human relationships of friendship and intercession. The site itself is incorporated into an administrative structure dependent on the authority of human beings resident in a town far removed from the significant folds of the once holy landscape: it has become a church in the diocese of the bishops of Javols. Seen in this way, the rise of Christianity in Western Europe is a chapter in the "hominization" of the natural world.[113]

This is a triumph which the modern scholar need not witness with quite the same degree of enthusiasm as did Gregory of Tours. Faced with the majesty of the mountain tops and with the long, slow wisdom of pre-Christian Europe, Gregory's *reverentia* seems brittle and not a little abrasive: it reflects the comparatively rapid growth of an inward-looking institution, gripped to the point of obsession with the need to understand relations with the unseen in a language of human interaction hammered out within the narrow confines of late-Roman urban and aristocratic society.[114] Wherever we look, in the early centuries of the cult of saints, we see the victory of a language drawn from observed human relations over the less articulate and less articulable certainties of an earlier age.

Yet we must also do justice to the resolution of the four remarkable generations that stretched from Paulinus's decision to settle in Nola, through the end of Roman rule in western Europe, to the childhood memories of Gregory of Tours. The old world had its limitations: as Sir James Frazer said in his *Golden Bough:* "God may pardon sin, but Nature cannot."[115] God and his human friends had come to pardon sin. Among the men we have met in these chapters, to opt so obsessively for a patterning of expectations of the supernatural that reflected current relationships of dependence always meant more than to opt for a language topheavy with associations of the exercise of power and patronage. In late-Roman conditions, *potentia* had a more gentle reverse side. Patronage and dependence, even the exigencies of aristocratic *amicitia*, might seem hard, binding relations to us; but it was through these that late-Roman men hoped to gain that freedom of action from which the miracle of justice, mercy, and a sense of solidarity with their fellow humans might spring. We, who live in a world where justice, mercy, and the acceptance of the majority of our fellows is quite as rare and as fragile a suspension of the observed laws of society as was that blessed moment of amnesty associated with the *praesentia* of the saints in a late-Roman community, should learn to look with greater sympathy and, hence, with greater scholarly care, at the dogged concern of late-antique Christians to ensure that, in their world, there should be places where men could stand in the searching and merciful presence of a fellow human being.

# Notes

N.B. Of the original authors that I have cited, almost all the secular writers, and many of the ecclesiastical, are available in the bilingual editions of the Loeb Classical Library (London: Heinemann; New York: Putnam; and Cambridge: Harvard University Press). The subdivisions of each text to which I refer are those employed in this and other standard editions. I frequently cite the volume and column numbers of the *Patrologia Latina* (*PL*) and *Patrologia Graeca* (*PG*) of J. G. Migne, *Patrologiae cursus completus* (Paris, 1844 onwards) for ease of reference to the passages mentioned. I have used the following editions of works by the following authors, citing some of these throughout in abbreviated form:

Augustine, *De cura gerenda pro mortuis*

   *Corpus Scriptorum Ecclesiasticorum Latinorum* 41 (Vienna: Tempsky, 1890).

Augustine, *City of God. De Civitate Dei*

   *Corpus Christianorum* 47 and 48 (Turnhout: Brepols, 1955).

Gregory of Tours

   Greg. Tur. *LH:* Gregorii episcopi Turonensis, *Libri historiarum*, ed. B. Krusch and W. Levison, *Monumenta Germaniae Historica: Scriptores Rerum Merovingicarum* 1, 1 (Hanover: Hahn, 1951).

The following five works are to be found in Gregorii episcopi Turonensis, *Miracula et opera minora,* ed. B. Krusch, *Monumenta Germaniae Historica: Scriptores Rerum Merovingicarum* 1, 2 (Hanover: Hahn, 1885).

Greg. Tur. *GM: Liber in gloria martyrum*

Greg. Tur. *VJ: Liber de passione et virtutibus sancti Iuliani martyris*

Greg. Tur. *VM: Libri I–IV de virtutibus sancti Martini episcopi*

Greg. Tur. *VP: Liber vitae patrum*

Greg. Tur. *GC: Liber in gloria confessorum*

Paulinus *Carmina*

*Corpus Scriptorum Ecclesiasticorum Latinorum* 30, 2 (Vienna: Tempsky, 1894).

Venantius Fortunatus *Carmina*

Ed. F. Leo and B. Krusch, *Monumenta Germaniae Historica: Auctores Antiquissimi* 4 (Hanover: Hahn, 1881).

*ILCV*

E. Diehl, *Inscriptiones latinae christianae veteres,* vols. 1 and 2 (Zurich: Weidmann, 1925 and 1961).

The reader may find the following translations of texts used in the argument of this book helpful:

Augustine *De cura gerenda pro mortuis*

*The Care to be Taken for the Dead,* in *Saint Augustine: Treatises on Marriage and Other Subjects,* trans. J. Lacy, The Fathers of the Church 27 (New York: Fathers of the Church, 1955).

Gregory of Tours *Libri historiarum*

*The History of the Franks,* trans. O. M. Dalton (Oxford: Clarendon Press, 1927) and Lewis Thorpe (Harmondsworth: Penguin, 1974).

Gregory of Tours *Miracula*

M. L. Brodin, *Livres des miracles,* in Société de l'histoire de la France 88 and 103 (Paris: J. Renouard, 1857 and 1860).

We can expect translations of the *Miracles of Saint Julian* and the *Miracles of Saint Martin* from John Corbett of Scarborough College, University of Toronto, in the Pontifical Institute for Medieval Studies Series.

Jerome *Contra Vigilantium*

*St. Jerome: Letters and Select Works*, trans. W. H. Fremantle, in *A Select Library of Nicene and Post-Nicene Fathers*, ed. P. Schaff and H. Wace (New York: Christian Literature, 1893).

Paulinus *Carmina*

P. G. Walsh, *The Poems of St. Paulinus of Nola*, Ancient Christian Writers 40 (New York: Newman Press, 1975).

Paulinus *Epistulae*

P. G. Walsh, *Letters of St. Paulinus of Nola*, Ancient Christian Writers 35 and 36 (New York: Newman Press, 1966 and 1967).

Prudentius *Cathemerinon* and *Peristephanon*

*Prudentius*, ed. and trans. H. H. Thomson, Loeb Classical Library (London: Heinemann, 1961; Cambridge: Harvard University Press, 1969).

*Prudentius: "Hymns for Every Day" and "The Martyrs' Crowns,"* trans. M. C. Eagan, The Fathers of the Church 43 (Washington: Catholic University of America Press, 1962).

Sulpicius Severus *Vita Martini* and *Dialogi*

Trans. B. M. Peebles, *Niceta of Remesiana, Sulpicius Severus, Vincent of Lerins and Prosper of Aquitaine*, Fathers of the Church 7 (New York: Fathers of the Church, 1949).

*The Works of Sulpitius Severus*, trans. A. Roberts, in *A Select Library of Nicene and Post-Nicene Fathers*, 2d. series, 11 (Ann Arbor, Michigan: Cushing, 1964).

Victricius of Rouen *De laude sanctorum*

R. Herval, *Origines chrétiennes, de la iie Lyonnaise gallo-romaine à la Normandie ducale (ive–xie siècles): Avec le texte complet et traduction du "De laude sanctorum" de saint Victrice (396)* (Paris: Picard, 1966).

Preface

1. F. W. Maitland, *Domesday Book and Beyond* (Cambridge: At the University Press, 1897): 596.

Chapter One

1. Peter Brown, *The Making of Late Antiquity* (Cambridge: Harvard University Press, 1978): 16–18.
2. Augustine *Sermon* 18.1.
3. F. Cumont, *Astrology and Religion among the Greeks and Romans* (London: Constable, 1912; reprint ed., New York: Dover Books, 1960): 92–110.
4. *ILCV* 391. 3–6: "Mens videt astra, quies tumuli complectitur artus." See Lidia Storoni Mazzolani, *Sul mare della vita* (Milan: Rizzoli, 1969) for a sensitve commentary on such inscriptions. See also E. Nordström, *Ravennastudien* (Uppsala: Almqvist and Wiksell, 1953): 31 on the meaning of the star-studded dome of the mausoleum of Galla Placidia.
5. Plutarch *Romulus* 28. 6.
6. Prudentius *Cathemerinon* 10. 29. See Richmond Lattimore, *Themes in Greek and Latin Epitaphs* (Urbana: University of Illinois Press, 1962): 311–13 on the stability of such views.
7. G. Sanders, *Licht en Duisternis in de christelijke Grafschriften*, 2 vols. (Brussels: Vlaamse Akademie voor Letteren, 1956), 1:502–13 and "Les chrétiens face à l'épigraphie funéraire latine," in *Assimilation et résistance à la culture gréco-romaine dans le monde ancien*, Travaux du VIᵉ Congrès International d'Etudes Classiques, ed. D. M. Pippidi (Bucharest: Editura Academiei; Paris: Les Belles Lettres, 1976): 283–99.
8. *ILCV* 1070. 5.
9. *Midrash Ps.* 16. 2: H. L. Strack and P. Billerbeck *Kommentar zum Neuen Testament aus Talmud und Midrasch* (Munich: C. M. Beck, 1926), 1: 892.
10. This development has been studied with particular reference to Gaul: J. Hubert, "Evolution de la topographie et de l'aspect des villes de la Gaule du IVᵉ au Xᵉ siècle," *Settimane di Studio del Centro Italiano di Studi sull'Alto Medio Evo* 16 (Spoleto: Centro di Studi sull'Alto Medio Evo, 1959): 529–58; P. A. Février,"Permanance et héritages de l'antiquité dans les villes de l'Occident," *Settimane di Studio* 21 (1974): 41–138; M. Vieillard-Troïekouroff, *Les monuments de la Gaule d'après les oeuvres de Grégoire de Tours* (Paris: Champion, 1976).
11. Greg. Tur. *VM* 2. 50. 194.
12. E. Le Blant, *Les inscriptions chrétiennes de la Gaule* (Paris: Imprimerie Impériale, 1856), 1: 240.
13. Venantius Fortunatus *Carm.* 3. 7. 41 and 46:

Fulgorem astrorum meditantur tecta metallo
. . . . . . . . . . . . . . . . . . . . . . . . . . . . . . . . . . . . . . . .
Et terram stellas credit habere suas.

14. Artemidorus *Oneirocriticon* 1. 51.

15. Carl Andresen, *Einführung in die christliche Archäologie* (Göttingen: Vandenhouck and Ruprecht, 1971): 27–28, surveys a vast literature.

16. B. Kötting, *Der frühchristliche Reliquienkult und die bestattung im Kirchengebäude* (Cologne: Westdeutsche Verlag, 1965). J. Guyon, "La vente des tombes à travers l'épigraphie de la Rome chrétienne," *Mélanges d'archéologie et d'histoire: Antiquité* 86 (1974): 594: "La levée de l'interdit religieux sur la sépulture *intra muros,* vieux d'un millénaire . . . est le signe d'une véritable mutation historique." G. Dagron, "Le christianisme dans la ville byzantine," *Dumbarton Oaks Papers* 31 (1977): 11–19.

17. T. Klauser, "Christliche Märtyrerkult, heidnischer Heroenkult und spätjüdische Heiligenverehrung," *Gesammelte Arbeiten,* ed. E. Dassmann (Münster in Westfalen: Aschendorff, 1974): 221–29.

18. I would stress this. I do not wish to imply that classical Greece and Rome were marked by an automatic sense of pollution by the dead, or that Christianity suddenly removed that sense. Other peoples' dead were the problem: one's own dead, or those of one's city if sufficiently validated by custom, were not an object of repugnance or a source of supernatural danger.

19. F. Pfister, *Der Reliquienkult im Altertum,* 2 vols. (Giessen: Töpelmann, 1909–12).

20. It has remained a hotly debated topic: E. Dyggve, *Dødekult, Kejserkult og basilika* (Copenhagen: P. Branner, 1943); A. Grabar, *Martyrium* (Paris: Collège de France, 1946); T. Klauser, "Von Heroon zur Märtyrerbasilika, " *Gesammelte Arbeiten,* pp. 275–91; J. B. Ward-Perkins, "Memoria, Martyr's Tomb and Martyr's Church," *Journal of Theological Studies* 17 (1966): 20–38, with Grabar's reply in *Cahiers archéologiques* 18 (1968): 239–44.

21. But see the nuances of A. D. Nock, "The Cult of Heroes," *Harvard Theological Review* 37 (1944): 141–74 in *Essays in Religion and the Ancient World,* ed. Zeph Stewart (Oxford: Clarendon Press, 1972), 2: 575–602.

22. L. Gernet, *Le génie grec dans la religion* (Paris: Albin Michel, 1932): 264: "Il est frappant que les héros ne soient pas

conçus comme intercesseurs. Avec la divinité proprement dite ils n'ont past de rapports directs."

23. This appears to me to be the crucial weakness of the classic attempt to derive most features of the cult of saints from pagan practice: Ernst Lucius, *Die Anfänge des Heiligenkultes in der christlichen Kirche* (Tübingen: Mohr, 1904): 14–48. When Christian writers speak of the martyrs as "heroes," this is a literary flourish with as little precise cultic associations as our own use of the word.

24. F. W. Deichmann, "Die Spolien in der spätantiken Architektur," *Sitzungsberichte der bayerischen Akademie der Wissenschaften: Philol.-hist. Klasse* 1975, no. 6.

25. Euripides *Hippolytus* 1437–38. Compare Paulinus of Nola on the priest Clarus, buried near an altar, *Ep.* 32. 25: "Divinis sacris animae iungentur odores."

26. Salvian *De gubernatione Dei* 2. 1. 3; Greg. Tur. *VJ* 1. 113.

27. Eunapius of Sardis *Lives of the Sophists* 472.

28. Julian *Contra Galilaeos* 335C.

29. Ibid., 339E, citing Isaiah 65. 4.

30. Julian, *Epistulae et leges,* ed. J. Bidez and F. Cumont (Paris: Les Belles Lettres, 1922): 194–95; see A. D. Nock, *Essays in Religion,* 2: 530: "He desired more than obedience, he wished to create a spirit." The inhabitants of Gaza attacked the bishop for having brought the corpse of a deacon "martyred" by being beaten up into the city; the "martyr" saved the situation by recovering and setting on the crowd with a cudgel! *Marc le Diacre: Vie de Porphyre* 25, ed. H. Grégoire and M. Kugener (Paris: Les Belles Lettres, 1930): 22.

31. Eunapius of Sardis 472.

32. Jürgen Christern, *Das frühchristliche Pilgerheiligtum von Tebessa* (Wiesbaden: F. Steiner, 1976): 221–60.

33. Paulinus *Carm.* 28. 177; R. C. Goldschmidt, *Paulinus' Churches at Nola: Texts, Translation and Commentary* (Amsterdam: North Holland, 1940); A. Weis, "Die Verteilung der Bildzyklen des Paulins von Nola in den Kirchen von Cimitile (Campanien)," *Römische Quartalschrift* 52 (1957): 129–50.

34. Athanasius *Life of Anthony* 14: ἡ ἔρημος ἐπολίσθη ὑπὸ μοναχῶν; Heliodorus *Aethiopica* 1.5.3 for a similar deliberate sense of paradox surrounding a brigand's lair in the marshes: Ἐν δὴ τούτοις ὅσον Αἰγυπτίων ληστρικὸν πολιτεύεται.

35. As a monk, Paulinus actually lived with his community in the buildings of the shrine: Joseph T. Lienhard, *Paulinus of Nola*

and *Early Western Monasticism,* Theophaneia 28 (Cologne: Peter Hanstein, 1977): 65, 70–72.

36. Jerome *Contra Vigilantium* 8, *PL* 23. 346.

37. The priest who looked after the shrine of Saint Thecla at Meriamlik outside Seleucia (Selefke) constituted himself the spokesman of the saint and recorder of her miracles, and lived under constant threat of excommunication from one bishop, to whom he refers as a "guttersnipe," and he calls his successor "the arch-swine": G. Dagron, "L'auteur des 'Actes' et des 'Miracles' de Sainte Thècle," *Analecta Bollandiana* 92 (1974): 5–11, and the same author's edition *Vie et miracles de sainte Thècle,* no. 12, *Subsidia Hagiographica,* 62 (Brussels: Société des Bollandistes, 1978): 314–22, 410.

38. On the difficulty with which the bishops of Jerusalem created a separate patriarchate for themselves on the strength of their connection with the holy places see H. E. Chadwick, "Faith and Order at the Council of Nicaea," *Harvard Theological Review* 53 (1960): 180–86.

39. Joachim Jeremias, *Heiligengräber in Jesu Umwelt* (Göttingen: Vandenhoeck and Ruprecht, 1958).

40. I. Goldziher, "Veneration of Saints in Islam," *Muslim Studies,* ed. S. M. Stern, transl. C. R. Barker and S. M. Stern (London: Allen and Unwin, 1971): 255–341.

41. E. Gellner, *Saints of the Atlas* (London: Weidenfeld, 1969) and M. Gilsenan, *Saint and Sufi in Modern Egypt* (Oxford: Clarendon Press, 1973)—to both authors I owe a deep personal debt of gratitude for unstinting advice and unfailing inspiration; V. Crapanzano, *The Hamadsha: A Study in Moroccan Ethnopsychiatry* (Berkeley and Los Angeles: University of California Press, 1973); D. Eickelman, *Moroccan Islam: Tradition and Society in a Pilgrimage Center* (Austin: University of Texas Press, 1976). See also Victor Turner, "Pilgrimages as Social Processes," *Dramas, Fields and Metaphors* (Ithaca: Cornell University Press, 1978): 166–230, and Victor Turner and Edith Turner, *Image and Pilgrimage in Christian Culture* (New York: Columbia University Press, 1978). While owing much to the work of Victor Turner, I should point out that the material on which he bases his analyses concerns Marian pilgrimages to distant shrines. Though unfailingly illuminating in the author's hands, the material presents fewer analogies to late antiquity than do the shrines of Muslim North Africa.

42. H. Delehaye, "*Loca sanctorum,*" *Analecta Bollandiana* 48

(1930): 5–64. For a vivid, and disapproving, account of the "mushroom" growth of shrines in Egypt, see the sermon translated in L. Th. Lefort, "La chasse aux reliques des martyres en Egypte au iv$^e$ siècle," *La Nouvelle Clio* 6 (1954): 225–30.

43. Gregory of Nyssa *Encomium on Saint Theodore*, PG 46. 740B.

44. Jerome *Contra Vigilantium* 12, PL 23. 364C.

45. *Barsanuphe et Jean: Correspondance* 433, trans. L. Regnault and P. Lemaire (Solesmes: Abbaye de Solesmes, 1971): 297–98.

46. J. Drescher, "Apa Claudius and the Thieves," *Bulletin de la société d'archéologie copte* 8 (1942): 63–86.

47. J. Romilly Allen, *The Early Christian Monuments of Scotland* (Edinburgh: Society of Antiquaries of Scotland, 1903): 330, 351–53.

48. J. Sauvaget, "Les Ghassanides et Sergiopolis," *Byzantion* 14 (1939): 116–30; P. Peeters, "L'*ex voto* de Khusro Aparwez à Sergiopolis," *Analecta Bollandiana* 65 (1947): 5–56.

49. D. Oates, *Studies in the Ancient History of Northern Iraq* (London: British Academy, 1968): 106—17, on a Nestorian countershrine to that of Sergiopolis, at Qasr-Serīj.

50. For a sketch of the later development of the cult, see Nicole Hermann-Mascard, *Les reliques des saints: Formation coutumière d'un droit* (Paris: Klincksieck, 1975); Patrick J. Geary, *Furta Sacra: Thefts of Relics in the Central Middle Ages* (Princeton: Princeton University Press, 1978); Sofia Boesch Gajano, *Agiografia altomedioevale* (Bologna: il Mulino, 1976): 261–300, a magnificent bibliography.

51. *The Encyclopedia of Philosophy* (New York: Macmillan, 1967), 4: 89.

52. David Hume, "The Natural History of Religion," *Essays Moral, Political and Literary* (London: Longman, Green, 1875), 2: 334.

53. Hume, "Natural History of Religion," p. 334.

54. Edward Gibbon, *The Decline and Fall of the Roman Empire*, ed. J. B. Bury (London: Methuen, 1909), 3: 225.

55. Ibid., p. 225.

56. Duncan Forbes, *The Liberal Anglican Idea of History* (Cambridge: At the University Press, 1952): 81.

57. Gibbon, 4: 136.

58. H. Milman, *A History of Latin Christianity* (New York: Armstrong, 1903), 3: 417. The attitude has continued unmodified: Ronald C. Finucane, *Miracles and Pilgrims: Popular Beliefs in Medieval England* (London: Dent, 1977): 23–24.

59. J. H. Newman, *Difficulties of Anglicans* (Dublin: Duffy, 1857): 80–81.

60. H. Delehaye, *Les légendes hagiographiques* (Brussels: Société des Bollandistes, 1955): 16. This and similar views are carefully presented and criticized by F. Graus, *Volk, Herrscher und Heiliger im Reich de Merowinger* (Prague: Československá Akademia Věd, 1965): 31–32.

61. A. Mirgeler, *Mutations of Western Christianity* (London: Burns and Oates, 1964): 44–65.

62. Ramsay MacMullen, "Sfiducia nell'intelletto nel quarto secolo," *Rivista storica italiana* 84 (1972): 5–16.

63. E. Kitzinger, "The Cult of Images in the Age before Iconoclasm," *Dumbarton Oaks Papers* 7 (1954): 119–20, 146.

64. Patrick J. Geary, "L'humiliation des saints," *Annales* 34 (1979): 27–42 shows very elegantly how the same rite could have a different meaning for each different group of participants.

65. Tertullian *Adversus Praxean* 3. 1. But we must remember that, compared with Tertullian almost any other Christian would seem "unlettered," and that "unlettered"—*idiotae*—meant no more than to be ignorant of a specific language and the terms of art derived from it (in this case, the Greek term *oikonomia*): it did not necessarily carry with it the later connotation of a general lack of culture or intelligence; see H. Grundmann, "*Literatus—illiteratus*," *Archiv für Kulturgeschichte* 40 (1958): 1–65.

66. Josef Engemann, "Magische Übelabwehr in der Spätantike," *Jahrbuch für Antike und Christentum* 18 (1975): 22–48; Alexander Murray, *Reason and Society in the Middle Ages* (Oxford: Clarendon Press, 1978): 15–17; Geary, "L'humiliation des saints," p. 28.

67. P. Brown, *Making of Late Antiquity*, 9–10.

68. A. D. Momigliano, "Popular Religious Belifs and Late Roman Historians," *Studies in Church History*, vol. 8 (Cambridge: At the University Press, 1971): 18, in *Essays in Ancient and Modern Historiography* (Oxford: Blackwell, 1977): 156.

69. For shrewd presentation and criticism of this view, see Natalie Z. Davis, "Some Tasks and Themes in the Study of Popular Religion," *The Pursuit of Holiness in Late Medieval and Renaissance Religion*, ed. Charles Trinkaus and Heiko A. Oberman (Leiden: Brill, 1974): 307–36 and Dario Rei," Note sul concetto di 'religione popolare,'" *Lares* 40 (1974): 262–80. R. C. Trexler, *Speculum* 52 (1977): 1019–22 is a succinct and forceful statement.

70. As in M. P. Nilsson, *Geschichte der griechischen Religion* (Munich: C. H. Beck, 1950), 2: 498–516.

71. Gibbon, 3: 226.

72. E. O. James, "The influence of folklore on the history of religion," *Numen* 1 (1962): 3: "The peasant, like the primitive, is a plain, unsophisticated person."

73. Louis Ginzberg, *The Legends of the Jews* (Philalelphia: Jewish Publication Society of America, 1925), 5: viii: "One of the outstanding characteristics of the 'popular mind' is its conservatism and adherence to old forms." For a deeply humane and perceptive critique of such views in the history of religion in late antiquity, see P. A. Février, "Le culte des morts dans les communautés chrétiennes durant le iii$^e$ siècle," *Atti del ix° congresso internazionale di archeologia cristiana* (Rome, 1977), 1: 245: "Nous sommes devenus sensibles d'une part à la longue durée nécessaire d'une histoire des mentalités . . . mais aussi aux mutations qui peuvent s'accomplir parfois relativement brutalement."

74. On the beginnings of this vogue, A. D. Momigliano, "La riscoperta della Sicilia antica da T. Fazello a P. Orsi," *Studi Urbinati di storia filosofia e letteratura* 52 (1978): 16; J. C. Lawson, *Modern Greek Folklore and Ancient Greek Religion* (Cambridge: At the University Press, 1910): 63: "The peasant of today in his conception of the higher powers and in his whole attitude towards them remains a polytheist and a pagan." Recent studies of Greek folklore are noticeably more cautious: Richard and Eva Blum, *The Dangerous Hour: The Lore of Crisis and Mystery in Rural Greece* ((London: Chatto and Windus, 1970): 263–352, and Margaret Alexiou, *The Ritual Lament in Greek Tradition* (Cambridge: At the University Press, 1974).

75. A. D. Nock, "The Study of the History of Religion," *Essays in Religion*, p. 331: "In spite of all differences of race and land, the soul of man has many curiously recurrent characteristics."

76. F. Dölger, *Der Exorzismus im altchristlichen Taufritual* (Paderborn: Schöningh, 1909): vi: "Etwas Gutes haben alle diese Studien aber doch: sie lassen entgegen der früheren Auffassung auch die irdischen Erscheinungsform des Christentums mehr zur Geltung kommen und machen dadurch für den religiös gestimmten Menschen den göttlichen Gehalt nur um so liebenswürdiger. Den berechtigten Gedanken spricht A. Dufourcq aus: 'Il est vrai de dire que, en un sens, le christianisme est sorti de terre.'"

77. For a learned and balanced treatment of the problems of pagan-Christian syncretisms, it is difficult to surpass Johannes Geffcken, *The Last Days of Graeco-Roman Paganism*, trans. Sabine MacCormack (Amsterdam: North Holland, 1978): 281–304.

Chapter Two

1. *ILCV* 1570.
2. *ILCV* 2127.
3. Giovanni di Pagolo Morelli, *Ricordi*, ed. V. Branca (Florence: F. LeMonnier, 1956): 182–83.
4. E. F. Bruck, *Totenteil und Seelengerät* (Munich: C. H. Beck, 1926): 302–4.
5. L. Gernet, *Le génie grec dans la religion* (Paris: Aubin Michel, 1932): 160; O. C. Crawford, "Laudatio funebris," *Classical Journal* 37 (1941); 17–19.
6. L. Massignon, "La cité des morts au Caire," *Opera Minora* (Beirut: Dar al-Maaref, 1963), 3: 233–285.
7. Allan I. Ludwig, *Graven Images: New England Stonecarving and Its Symbols* (Middletown: Wesleyan University Press, 1966): 57–58.
8. For the severe control of funerals in Florence: Lauro Martines, *The Social World of the Florentine Humanists* (Princeton: Princeton University Press, 1963): 239–45; and the effects of fluctuations of control: J. Coolidge, "Further Observations on Masaccio's Trinity," *Art Bulletin* 48 (1966): 382–84; "During the 1420s acclaim of the recently deceased became a conspicuous feature of public life. This competitive, extravagant and socially disruptive means of expressing political feelings provided a succession of major opportunities for artistic patronage." I owe this reference to the kindness of Professor Gene Brucker.
9. Augustine *Confessions* 6. 2. 2.
10. Augustine *Ep.* 29. 9.
11. J. Quasten, "'Vetus superstitio et nova religio': The problem of refrigerium in the Ancient Church of North Africa," *Harvard Theological Review* 33 (1940): 253–66, and Bruck, *Totenteil and Seelengerät*, p. 290, accept this explanation.
12. J. N. D. Kelly, *Jerome* (London: Duckworth, 1975): 290.
13. Jerome *Contra Vigilantium* 4, *PL* 23. 357B.
14. Paulinus *Carm.* 31. 109–10:

Ut de vicino sanctorum sanguine ducat
quo nostras illo spargat in igne animas.

15. On the circumstances of the letter, see P. Courcelle, *Les Confessions de saint Augustin dans la tradition littéraire* (Paris: Etudes augustiniennes, 1963): 595–600.

16. Augustine *City of God* 22. 8.

17. A. H. M. Jones, *The Later Roman Empire* (Oxford: Blackwell, 1964), 2: 963.

18. David Hume, "A Natural History of Religion," *Essays Moral, Political and Literary* (London: Longman, Green, 1875), 2: 319: "What age or period of life is most addicted to superstition? The weakest and most timid. What sex? The same answer must be given."

19. Jerome *C. Vigilant.* 7. 361A and 9. 363B.

20. Especially Augustine when he was a Christian layman and priest in controversy with Manichees and educated pagans: *Ep.* 17 and *De moribus ecclesiae catholicae* 1. 34. 75: "Nolite consectari turbas imperitorum, qui vel in ipsa vera religione superstitiosi sunt." See P. Brown, *Augustine of Hippo* (Berkeley and Los Angeles: University of California Press, 1967): 415.

21. See now the penetrating and original survey of the evidence by P. A. Février, "Le culte des morts dans les communautés chrétiennes durant le iii^e siècle," *Atti del ix° congresso, internazionale di archeologia cristiana* (Rome, 1977), 1: 212–74.

22. For Africa, see P. Brown, "Christianity and Local Culture in Roman North Africa," *Journal of Roman Studies* 68 (1968), reprinted in *Religion and Society in the Age of Saint Augustine* (London: Faber, 1972): 288. Johannes Geffcken, *The Last Days of Greco-Roman Paganism*, trans. Sabine MacCormack: 225–39, is still the best study of what remains an obscure development.

23. E. Marec, *Les monuments chrétiens d'Hippone* (Paris: Arts et Métiers graphiques, 1958): 43; H. I. Marrou, "La basilique chrétienne d'Hippone," *Revue des études augustiniennes* 6 (1960): 125–28 in *Patristique et humanisme*, Patristica Sorbonensia 9 (Paris: Le Seuil, 1976): 200–204.

24. *The Sixth Book of the Select Letters of Severus* 1. 60 ed. and trans. E. W. Brooks (Oxford: Clarendon Press, 1903), 2: 187, on the reading of the names of the catechumens; Caesarius of Arles *Sermon* 204.3, ed. G. Morin, Corpus Christianorum 104 (Turnholt: Brepols, 1953): 821, on the washing of their feet.

25. F. W. Kent, *Household and Lineage in Renaissance Florence* (Princeton: Princeton University Press, 1977): viii.

26. Antoninus Placentinus 4, *Corpus Scriptorum Ecclesiasticorum Latinorum* 39. 161.

27. Sozomen *Historia Ecclesiastica* 5. 15.

28. P. Brown, *The Making of Late Antiquity* (Cambridge: Harvard University Press, 1978): 77–78.

29. J. Stuiber, "Heidnische und christliche Gedächtniskalendar," *Jahrbuch für Antike und Christentum* 3 (1960): 24–33.

30. Cyprian *Ad Demetrianum* 10; Eusebius *Historia ecclesiastica* 7. 22; Julian *Ep.* 22—but this last was a unique case: A. Harnack, *Mission und Ausbreitung des Christentums* (Leipzig: Hinrichs, 1906): 143–45. Paul Veyne, *Le pain et le cirque* (Paris: Le Seuil, 1976): 291–92, sees clearly the significance of the gesture of offering burial.

31. Cyprian *Ep.* 1. 2.

32. Cyprian *Ep.* 12. 2 and 39. 3.

33. In the mid-third century the Roman church had a staff of 155 members of the clergy and supported 1,500 widows and poor: Eusebius *Hist. Eccles.* 6. 43. If we remember that the largest associations of craftsmen in Rome had 1,200 to 1,500 members, while most were considerably smaller, the Christian community already appears to have become a dangerously unwieldy body: R. Duncan-Jones, *The Economy of the Roman Empire* (Cambridge: At the University Press, 1974): 283. For Alexandria: H. I. Marrou, "L'Arianisme comme phénomène alexandrin," *Comptes rendus de l'Academie des Inscriptions et Belles Lettres* (1973): 535–38 in *Patristique et Humanisme*, pp. 323–26.

34. Février, "Le cult des morts," p. 254: "On ne peut s'empêcher de retrouver une transposition, par delà de la mort, d'oppositions de classes"—referring to the late-third century catacombs.

35. G.Kretschmar, "Die Theologie der Heiligen in der frühen Kirche," *Aspekte frühchristlicher Heiligenverehrung*, Oikonomia: Quellen und Studien zur orthodoxen Theologie 6 (Erlangen: Zantner-Busch Stiftung, 1977): 111, makes this plain for the liturgy of Jerusalem itself: "Jedenfalls lösst sich bei diesem Wachstum des Heilegenkultes und mit ihrer immer stärkeren Umformung zu fürbittenden Patronen des einzelnen, einzelner Familien und anderer Sozialgebilde die ursprünglich für Jerusalem so charakteristische ekklesiologische Verankerung." It is precisely Vigilantius's concern.

36. Jerome *C. Vigilant.* 6. 359A.

37. Ibid. 13. 349C.

38. Ibid. 9. 347C.

39. On this environment, see J. Fontaine, "Société et culture chrétiennes sur l'aire circumpyrénéenne," *Bulletin de littérature ecclesiastique* 75 (1974): 241–82; J. F. Matthews, *Western Aristocracies and Imperial Court, A.D. 364–425* (Oxford: Clarendon Press, 1975): 146–153.

40. A. Goldberg, "Der Heilige und die Heiligen: Vorüberlegungen zur Theologie des heiligen Menschen im rabbinischen Judentum," *Aspekte frühchristlicher Heiligenverehrung,* p. 29 and Kretschmar, "Die Theologie der Heiligen," ibid., p. 89.

41. *Acta Maximiliani* 3, 4, ed. and trans. H. Musurillo, *The Acts of the Christian Martyrs* (Oxford: Clarendon Press, 1972): 248.

42. E. Dyggve, *History of Salonitan Christianity* (Oslo: Aschenhoug, 1951): 78.

43. Février, "Le culte des morts," p. 269, citing *ILCV* 2071, where it is the parents of African martyrs who make the inscription in A.D. 329.

44. *Gesta apud Zenophilum:* appendix to Optatus of Milevis *De schismate Donatistarum,* in *Corpus Scriptorum Ecclesiasticorum Latinorum* (Vienna: Tempsky, 1893), 7: 194; Augustine *Ad Catholicos epistula* 25. 73.

45. Optatus of Milevis *De schism. Don.* 1. 16.

46. *ILCV* 2148; some made great show of not wanting it, *ILCV* 1194.5: "Nil iuvat, immo gravat, tumulis haerere piorum sanctorum meritis optima vita prope est." Yet the inscription comes from just outside the shrine of Saint Laurence!

47. Ludwig, *Graven Images,* p. 57.

48. Augustine *De cura gerenda pro mortuis* 4. 6. Cynegius's inscription makes the issues plain, *ILCV* 3482. 6: Sic tutus erit iuvenis sub iudice Christo. On the family connections of Flora, see Matthews, *Western Aristocracies,* p. 144.

49. Augustine *De cura ger.* 18. 22; Courcelle, p. 699.

50. Augustine *Ep.* 22. 6.

51. Brown, *Augustine of Hippo,* pp. 226–27.

52. Ch. Pietri, *Roma christiana,* Bibliothèque de l'école française d'Athènes et Rome 224, 2 vols. (Paris: Boccard, 1976), 1: 581.

53. Paulinus *Ep.* 13. 15. Such feasting was intimately connected with papal propaganda: Ch. Pietri, "'Concordia apostolorum et renovatio urbis' (Culte des martyrs et propagande pontificale)," *Mélanges d'archéologie et d'histoire* 73 (1961): 275–322, slightly modified in the author's *Roma christiana,* p. 605

n.1. P. A. Février, "Natale Petri cathedra," Comptes rendus de l'Académie d'Inscriptions et Belles Lettres 1977: 514–31.

54. As Augustine was aware, Ep. 29. 10: characteristically he explained these practices by the difficulty of asserting episcopal control. If only he had read Professor Pietri!

55. For a brilliant discussion of the importance and ambivalence of the enormous cemetery basilica of Saint Lawrence and of the cemetery areas in general: R. Krautheimer, "Mensa, coemeterium, martyrium," Cahiers archéologiques 11 (1960): 15–40, in Studies in Early Christian, Medieval and Renaissance Art (New York: New York University Press, 1969): 35–58; note the extraordinary incident by which a heretical sect with aristocratic patronage could "appropriate" the shrine of a martyr: Praedestinatus De haeresibus 1. 86, PL 53. 616.

56. Collectio Avellana 1. 9, Corpus Scriptorum Ecclesiasticorum Latinorum (Vienna: Tempsky, 1895), 35: 4.

57. Jerome, Ep. 22. 28.

58. E. Dassmann, "Ambrosius und die Märtyrer," Jahrbuch für Antike und Christentum 18 (1975): 49–68.

59. Ambrose Ep. 22. 10; Dassmann, "Ambrosius," pp. 54–55.

60. Ambrose Ep. 22. 9.

61. Augustine Confessions 6. 2. 2.

62. ILCV 1700; P. Courcelle, "Quelques symboles funéraires du néo-platonisme latin," Revue des études anciennes 46 (1944): 65–73.

63. ILCV 1825. 6–9; 11–13.

64. Augustine City of God 22. 8: he was "greatly annoyed" when he heard that the recipeint of a cure, an influential lady in Carthage, had done nothing to publicize it in the city.

65. H. Delehaye, "Les premiers 'libelli miraculorum,'" Analecta Bollandiana 29 (1910): 427–34.

66. Miracula sancti Stephani 1. 14, 2. 1, PL 40. 841–42.

67. N. Himmelmann-Wildschütz, Typologische Untersuchungen an römischen Sarkophagreliefs des 3. und 4. Jahrhunderts (Mainz: Zabern, 1973): 24–28; Février, "Le culte des morts," pp. 245–51, and "À propos du culte funéraire: Culte et sociabilité," Cahiers archéologiques 26 (1977): 29–45.

68. Augustine Sermon 310. 2; John Chrysostom In sanctum martyrem Ignatium 1, PG 50: 587; Maximus of Turin Sermon 3. 2., ed. A. Mutzenbecher, Corpus Christianorum 23 (Turnholt: Brepols, 1962): 11. For the giving of a banquet by a patronus: S. Lancel, "Le populus Thuburbusitanus et les gymnases de

Quintus Flavius Lappianus," *Karthago* 6 (1958): 142–57. S. Mrozek, "Munificentia privata in den Städten Italiens der spätrömischen Zeit," *Historia* 27 (1978): 355–68.

69. Paulinus *Carm.* 27. 511–36.
70. Ibid. 542–67.
71. Greg. Tur. *VJ* 36. 129.
72. Pseudo-Athanasius *canon* 16, cited by E. Wipszicka, *Les ressources et les activités économiques des églises en Egypte,* Papyrologica Bruxellensia 10 (Brussels: Fondation égyptologique Reine Élizabeth, 1972): 110.
73. Aline Rousselle, "Aspects sociaux du recrutement ecclésiastique au iv^e siècle," *Mélanges d'archéologie et d'histoire: Antiquité* 89 (1977): 333–70. For a slightly later example, see the building activity of Bishop Rusticus and his supporters: *ILCV* 1806, with H. I. Marrou, "Le dossier épigraphique de l'évêque Rusticus de Narbonne," *Rivista di archeologia cristiana* 46 (1970): 331–49, and Matthews, *Western Aristocracies,* pp. 341–42.
74. Paulinus of Milan *Vita Ambrosii* 4; Augustine *Confessions* 6. 13. 22.75. N. Gussone, "Adventus-Zeremoniell und Translation von Reliquien: Victricius von Rouen 'De laude sanctorum," *Frühmittelalterliche Studien* 10 (1976): 126–27.
76. Sidonius Apollinaris *Ep.* 7. 1. 7.
77. Jones, *Later Roman Empire,* 2: 894–910; W. Zeisel, Jr., "An Economic Survey of the Early Byzantine Church" (Ph.D. diss., Rutgers University, 1975); R. M. Grant, *Early Christianity and Society* (New York: Harper and Row, 1977); R. Staats, "Deposita pietatis—Die Alte Kirche und ihr Geld," *Zeitschrift für Theologie und Kirche* 76 (1979): 1–29.
78. Ramsay MacMullen, *Roman Social Relations* (New Haven: Yale University Press, 1974): 101–2. Hence the extreme sensitivity of fourth-century observers to legacy-hunting by the clergy: Ammianus Marcellinus 27. 3. 14; *Collectio Avellana* 1. 9; *Codex Theodosianus* 16. 2. 20.
79. Augustine *Ep.* 126. 7.
80. Thus Augustine advised the rich clergyman Leporius to build a *xenodochium* and a shrine for the Eight Martyrs, whereas Heraclius, his successor, built the shrine of Saint Stephen: *Sermon* 356. 7 and 9.
81. J. Gaudemet, *L'eglise dans l'Empire romain* (Paris: Sirey, 1958): 311–15; Grant, *Early Christianity,* pp. 55–65. See Athanasius *Historia Arianorum* 78. 1: Men become bishops "for the ignoble motives of exemption from taxes and the opportu-

nity to exercise patronage"—no better motives for a late-Roman man, but none more productive of envy.

82. On episcopal public building as a form of self-protection in the Eastern Empire: Theodoret of Cyrrhus *Epp.* 68 and 81. Bishops, and even their sons, were forbidden to give games: *Breviarum hipponense* 11, ed. C. Munier, *Concilia Africae, A.345–A.525, Corpus Christianorum* 259 (Turnhout: Brepols, 1974): 37, and Innocent I *Ep.* 2. 2, *PL* 20. 478A.

83. E. Patlagean, *Pauvreté économique et pauvreté sociale à Byzance, 4ᵉ–7ᵉ siècles* (Paris: Mouton, 1977): 181–95; 426–27.

84. Palladius *Dialogus de vita Johannis* 6, *PG* 47. 22.

85. Pagan officials were only too happy to prosecute clergymen who built up against town walls or against temples: Symmachus *Relatio* 22 and the anonymous *Carmen adversus paganos* 39.

86. Even this did not happen without tension with the urban authorities: Paulinus *Carm.* 21. 655–717—a brush with the town of Nola over the water supply to Felix's shrine.

87. Prudentius *Peristephanon* 2. 137–84, on the scene in which the deacon Lawrence was supposed to have shown the prefect of Rome a crowd of beggars and cripples, saying that these were the only "wealth" of the church: the point would not have been lost on a fifth-century reader, who may have had his doubts. Augustine *Ep.* 126. 7 is at great pains to point out that, though the wealth of the church of Hippo was more than he could have dreamed of, he did not own it personally *ut dominus.*

88. The truly damning feature of Ammianus Marcellinus's account of the bishops of Rome is that he took rivalry for their office for granted, and the wealth and influence of the popes as merely one example among so many of the *ostentatio . . . rerum urbanarum:* Amm. Marc. 27. 3. 12. The prefect Praetextatus could joke with Pope Damasus, "Make me bishop of the city of Rome, and I will straightaway become a Christian!": Jerome *Contra Johannem Hierosolymitanum, PL* 23. 361. It now needed to be said of a Roman deacon, "non illum sublimis honor non extulit ordo": *ILCV* 1195. 7.

89. On the bishop as *patronus* in his capacity as successor to the patron saint: A. B. Orselli, *L'idea e il culto del santo patrono cittadino nella letteratura latina cristiana* (Bologna: Zanichelli, 1965): 97–119, reprinted in Sofia Boesch Gajano, *Agiografia altomedioevale* (Bologna: il Mulino, 1976): 85–104; Peter Brown, *Relics and Social Status in the Age of Gregory of Tours,* Stenton

Lecture (Reading: University of Reading Press, 1977): 15–19. For an account of the manner in which the *mizwar* of a Moroccan shrine creates a "role distance" between his everyday self and his position as the head of an "ideal exchange system" associated with gift giving at the shrine: V. Crapanzano, *The Hamadsha: A Study if Moroccan Ethnopsychiatry* (Berkeley and Los Angeles: University of California Press, 1973): 117–23.

90. *ILCV* 1825. 1–4.

91. See chap. 1 above, pp. 7–8, and Krautheimer, "*Mensa, coemeterium, martyrium,*" pp. 42–48.

92. Jerome, *Ep.* 107. 1.

93. Pietri, *Roma christiana,* pp. 127–29; the main vigils fell on the warm summer nights.

94. Victor Turner, "Pilgrimages as Social Processes," *Dramas, Fields and Metaphors* (Ithaca: Cornell University Press, 1974): 166–230.

95. William A. Christian, Jr., *Person and God in a Spanish Valley* (New York: Seminar Press, 1972): 70.

96. Prudentius *Peristephanon* 11. 191–92; 199–202. This aspect of the role of Christian festivals in Rome has been well seen by Matthews, *Western Aristocracies,* pp. 368–69.

97. Ibid. 11. 203–9. On the impact of hillsmen on the Mediterranean cities: F. Braudel, *The Mediterranean and the Mediterranean World in the Age of Philip II,* trans. S. Reynolds (London: Collins, 1972): 44–47, quoting Stendhal, *Promenades dans Rome:* "They come down from their mountains to celebrate the feast day at St. Peter's, and to attend *la funzione* (the Mass)... their wild eyes peer from behind disordered black hair.... These peasants are accompanied by their families, of equally wild aspect." Imperial laws controlled brigandage in the area: *Cod. Theod.* 9. 30. 1–5 and 31. 1; MacMullen *Roman Social Relations,* pp. 30–40 and notes on pp. 156–61 gives a comprehensive and depressingly circumstantial catalog of urban contempt for and exploitation of the peasant.

98. Paulinus *Carm.* 13. 25–59; 18. 105–8; 21. 655–711 and 816–18.

99. Upper-class women in Antioch only went out on muleback: John Chrysostom *De virginitate* 66. 1, *PG* 48. 583, and *Hom. 7 in Matth.* 5, *PG* 57. 80; as also in Rome: Jerome *Ep.* 66. 13.

100. Theodoret of Cyrrhus *Historia religiosa* 20, *PG* 82. 1429.

101. Jerome *C. Vigilant.* 9. 363B; *Ep.* 107. 9: a Christian girl

should not budge a nail's breadth from her mother's side at vigils of the saints; John Chrysostom *Homilia in Martyres, PG* 50. 663; Schenute of Atripe, in A. Zoega, *Catalogus Codicum Copticorum* (Leipzig: Hinrichs, 1903): 423; Augustine *Confessions* 3. 3. 5; *Miracula sanctae Theclae* 14, *PG* 85. 597AB, ed. G. Dagron, *Vie et miracles de Saint Thècle* no. 33. *Subsidia Hagiographica* 62 (Brussels: Société des Bollandistes, 1978): 378: a disastrous pick-up—the lady turned out to be a demon; Ḥamza b. Abī Salāma, *Masālik al-Ahṣar* 313–16 cited in H. Putman, *L'eglise et l'Islam sous Timothée I (780–823)* (Beirut: Dar el-Mashreq, 1975): 122; H. Idris, "Fêtes chrétiennes en Ifriqiya," *Revue africaine* 98 (1954): 273.

102. Characteristically, Jerome *Ep.* 54. 13 on a Roman lady on pilgrimage. The same reserves in Gregory of Nyssa, *Ep.* 2, *PG* 46. 1012B.

103. Turner, "Pilgrimages," p. 208: "Thus social and cultural distinctions are not abolished . . . but the sting of their divisiveness is removed." Cf. A. Dupront, "Pèlerinages et lieux sacrés," *Mélanges F. Braudel* (Toulouse: Privat, 1973), 2: 201: "La société de pèlerinage est une société confondue, donc éminement une société d'union, où âges, sexes, hiérarchies, et même clercs et laïcs participent dans une communion indistincte."

104. See especially M. Meslin, *La fête des kalendes de janvier dans l'empire romain* (Brussels: Collection Latomus, 1970). Libanius *Oration* 9. 10 says that if the mood of the kalends lasted all year men would no longer need to yearn for the Islands of the Blessed. The secular urban ceremonies of late antiquity have not yet received a study worthy of their importance and sociological interest. See the sensible remarks of James W. Halporn, "Saint Augustine 'Sermon 104' and the Epulae Venerales" *Jahrbuch für Antike und Christentum* 19 (1976): 82–108. See also O. Pasquati, *Gli spettacoli in Giovanni Crisostomo: Paganesimo e cristianesimo ad Antiochia e Costantinopoli* (Rome: Pontificium Institutum Orientalium Studiorum, 1976) and Y. M. Duval, "Des Lupercales de Constantinople aux Lupercales de Rome," *Revue des études grecques* 55 (1977): 222–70.

105. Hence the universal suspicion with which women's visits to the cemeteries were regarded: Synod of Elvira (A.D. 306) *canon* 35: "Placuit prohibere, ne foeminae in coemeterio pervigilent, eo quod saepe sub obtentu orationis latenter scelera committunt"; the Calif al-Hakim of Cairo (A.D. 1101) was of the

same opinion: "Women were forbidden to visit graves and not a single woman was henceforth seen in the cemeteries on public holidays." Bernard Lewis, *Islam* (New York: Harper Torchbooks, 1974), 1: 55.

106. *Mirac. Theclae* 8. 577B and 10. 581B: *Vie* nos. 24 and 26, ed. Dagron, pp. 350 and 356; young men hoped to pick up girls at picnics under the trees: 19. 600B: *Vie* no. 34, ed. Dagron, p. 380. Cf. Procopius *The Buildings* 1. 3. 6 on the shrine of the Virgin at Pégé: "In that place is a dense grove of cypresses and a meadow abounding in flowers in the midst of soft glebe, a park abounding in beautiful shrubs and a stream bubbling silently forth with a gentle stream of sweet water—and especially suitable to a sanctuary." Fatima Mernissi, "Women, Saints and Sanctuaries," *Signs* 3 (1977): 101–12, gives a vivid and perceptive account of women at a north African Muslim shrine.

107. *Miracula sancti Stephani* 2. 2. 1, *PL* 40: 843.

108. Ibid. 2. 2. 1. 844.

109. Ibid. 2. 2. 5. 846.

110. Ibid. 2. 2. 7. 847.

111. Ibid. 2. 2. 5. 846; 2. 2. 6. 847; 2. 2. 9. 848.

112. Ibid. 2. 2. 6. 847.

113. Ibid. 2. 2. 6. 846–47.

114. Patlagean, *Pauvreté*, pp. 114–28.

115. Ambrose *De viduis* 11. 54, *PL* 16. 250.

116. Turner, "Pilgrimages," p. 177: "Pilgrimages represent, so to speak, an amplified symbol of the dilemma of choice versus obligation in the midst of a social order where status prevails."

117. Greg. Tur. *VJ* 9. 118; 12. 119; *VM* 1. 31. 153; 1. 40. 154.

118. Jerome *Ep.* 66. 5 and 79. 2 and Brown *The Making of Late Antiquity*, p. 79 and p. 128 n.98.

119. Patlagean, *Pauvreté*, pp. 17–35; Veyne, *Le pain et le cirque*, pp. 45–66.

120. A. Chastagnol, *La préfecture urbaine à Rome sous le bas-empire* (Paris: Presses universitaires, 1960): 312–34; J. M. Carrié, "Les distributions alimentaires dans les cités de l'empire romain tardif," *Mélanges d'archéologie et d'histoire: Antiquité* 87 (1975): 995–1101.

121. A. Alföldi, *Die Kontorniaten* (Leipzig: Harrassowitz, 1943); H. Stern, *Le calendrier de 354* (Paris: Geuthner, 1953).

122. S. Mazzarino, *Aspetti sociali del quarto secolo* (Rome: Bretschneider, 1951): 217–69; L. Ruggini, *Economia e società nell'*

"*Italia annonaria*" (Milan: A. Giuffré, 1961): 116–76.
123. Ambrose *De officiis* 3. 45–51; Ammianus Marcellinus 14. 6. 17; H. P. Kohns, *Versorgungskrisen und Hungerrevolte im spätantiken Rom* (Bonn: Habelt, 1971); L. Cracco-Ruggini, "'Fame laborasse Italiam': Una nuova testimonianza della carestia del 383," *Athenaeum*, fascicolo speciale 1976 (Pavia: Tipografia del Libro, 1976): 83–98.
124. Matthews, *Western Aristocracies*, pp. 18–21.
125. Veyne, *Le pain et le cirque*, pp. 682–701.
126. Ammianus Marcellinus 27. 3. 5.
127. Harnack, *Mission und Ausbreitung*, pp. 59–67. The role of the women of Rome as almsgivers and as a behind-the-scenes "senate" of the church was already plain in the late third century to the pagan Porphyry: Porphyry, *Gegen die Christen*, no. 94, ed. A. Harnack, *Abhandlungen der preussischen Akademie der Wissenschaften. Philos.-Hist. kl.* 1916, 1: 104; J.-M. Demarolle, "Les femmes chrétiennes vues par Porphyre," *Jahrbuch für Antike und Christentum* 13 (1970): 42–47.
128. This is well documented for contemporary Constantinople: Kenneth G. Holum, "Pulcheria's Crusade A.D. 421–422 and the Ideology of Imperial Victory," *Greek, Roman and Byzantine Studies* 18 (1977): 153–72; it will form a major theme of his forthcoming book, "Theodosian Empresses: Women and Imperial Dominion in Late Antiquity."
129. S. Mazzarino, *The End of the Ancient World*, trans. G. Holmes (London: Faber, 1966): 131–32.
130. *Cod. Theod.* 6. 4. 17.
131. See the diptych of the Lampadii: R. Delbrueck, *Die Consulardiptychen* (Berlin: de Gruyter, 1929): 218–21.
132. Peter Brown, "Pelagius and his Supporters," *Journal of Theological Studies* n.s. 19 (1968): 98–100, reprinted in *Religion and Society*, pp. 189–92; Matthews, *Imperial Aristocracies*, pp. 289–91. A. Demandt and G. Brummer, "Der Prozess gegen Serena im Jahre 408 n. Chr.," *Historia* 26 (1977): 479–503.
133. Matthews, *Imperial Aristocracies*, p. 365.
134. A. H. M. Jones, J. R. Martindale and J. Morris, *The Prosopography of the Later Roman Empire* (Cambridge: At the University Press, 1971): stemma no. 7, p. 1133.
135. Augustine *Ep.* 150; Pelagius *Ep. ad Demetriadem* 14, *PL* 30. 30B; Jerome *Ep.* 130. 3. All represent the gesture as outstripping the prestige of the men of the family.
136. Zosimus *Historia nova* 6. 7.

137. Jerome *Ep.* 130. 6.

138. *Liber pontificalis,* ed. L. Duchesne (Paris: de Boccard, 1886), 1: 238 and 531.

139. Katherine M. D. Dunbabin, *The Mosaics of Roman North Africa: Studies in Iconography and Patronage* (Oxford: Clarendon Press, 1978): 70.

140. Ramsay MacMullen, *Enemies of the Roman Order* (Cambridge: Harvard University Press, 1967): 170–79; Alan Cameron, *Circus Factions* (Oxford: Clarendon Press, 1976): 157–192; Veyne, *Le pain et le cirque,* pp. 682–701.

Chapter Three

1. Theodoret *Curatio affectionum graecarum* 8. 67, PG 83. 1033A.

2. Gregory of Nyssa *Encomium on Saint Theodore,* PG 46. 745D.

3. *Miracula sancti Demetrii* 1. 14, PG 116. 1213A.

4. Plutarch *De facie lunae* 28, 943A; Peter Brown, *The Making of Late Antiquity* (Cambridge: Harvard University Press, 1978): 68–72.

5. Plotinus *Ennead* 3. 4. 3 makes this plain.

6. Brown, *The Making of Late Antiquity,* p. 72 and p. 121 n.64.

7. Ammianus Marcellinus 21. 14. 3; M. Riley, "The Purpose and Unity of Plutarch's *De genio Socratis,*" *Greek, Roman and Byzantine Studies* 18 (1977): 257: "Plutarch wishes to show how guidance works and how the gap between thinker and doer can be bridged."

8. A. Henrichs and L. Koenen, "Der Kölner Mani-Kodex," *Zeitschrift für Papyrologie und Epigraphik* 19 (1975): 23; *The Cologne Mani Codex. "Concerning the Origin of his Body".* ed. and trans. Ron Cameron and Arthur J. Dewey (Missoula, Mont.: Scholars Press, 1979): 20–21.

9. *Panegyrici Latini* 7. 21. 4. Compare *Cologne Mani Codex,* pp. 18–19.

10. Origen *Contra Celsum* 7. 34.

11. Gregory Thaumaturgus *In Origenem* 4, PG 10. 1064A. The identity of Gregory has been subdivided: P. Nautin, *Origène: Sa vie et son oeuvre* (Paris: Beauchesne, 1977): 82–86. I owe this correction to the kindness of Raymond Van Dam.

12. Synesius *Hymn* 4. 264, trans. A. Fitzgerald, *The Essays and Hymns of Synesius of Cyrene* (Oxford: Clarendon Press, 1930), 2: 386.

13. W. H. C. Frend, "Paulinus of Nola and the Last Century of the Western Empire," *Journal of Roman Studies* 59 (1969): 1–11; Joseph T. Lienhard, *Paulinus of Nola and Early Western Monasticism*, Theophaneia 28 (Cologne: Peter Hanstein, 1977): 24–29.

14. J. F. Matthews, *Western Aristocracies and Imperial Court* A.D. 364–425 (Oxford: Clarendon Press, 1975): 77–87.

15. Augustine *City of God* 1. 10; Sulpicius Severus *Vita Martini* 25: "Praestantissimum exemplum"; Ambrose *Ep.* 58. 1–3; Lienhard, *Paulinus of Nola*, p. 29.

16. Paulinus *Carm.* 21. 344–46.

17. E. Lucius, *Die Anfänge des Heiligenkultes in der christlichen Kirche* (Tübingen: Mohr, 1904): 302.

18. Helen Waddell, *Wandering Scholars* (London: Constable, 1927): 12.

19. Lienhard, *Paulinus of Nola*, p. 141: "His writings suggest, far better than Augustine's or Jerome's, the relative simplicity, almost naïvety, of the earliest Western monks." Though the author is right to emphasize the specifically monastic commitment of Paulinus, *l'oeuil naïf* is not what we have learned to expect in western monks: see now the fine study of Philip Rousseau, *Ascetics, Authority and the Church in the Age of Jerome and Cassian* (Oxford: Clarendon Press, 1978), cf. A. Michel, *In hymnis et canticis: Culture et beauté dans l'hymnique chrétienne latine* (Louvain: Publications universitaires, 1976): 50: "Dans les *Psaumes*, les chrétiens de ce temps trouvent le langage d'une conversion radicale, en même temps que l'accomplissement très simple d'une culture très subtile."

20. J. Fontaine, "Valeurs antiques et valeurs chrétiennes dans la spiritualité des grands propriétaires terriens du ive siècle occidental," *Epektasis: Mélanges patristiques offerts au cardinal Jean Daniélou* (Paris: Beauchesne, 1972): 571–95.

21. Lienhard, *Paulinus of Nola*, p. 151: "He innocently and joyously accepts the growing cult of saints." G. Boissier, *La fin du paganisme* (Paris: Hachette, 1891), 2: 105–17.

22. A. Michel, *In hymnis et canticis*, p. 50: "Pour le doux Paulin, ce n'est pas le désert qui se trouve au bout de la route, mais la campagne, la nature, et encore Vergile."

23. Aline Rousselle, "Deux exemples d'évangélisation en Gaule à la fin du ive siècle: Paulin de Nole et Sulpice Severe," *Béziers et le Biterrois, 43e Congrès de la Fedération historique du Languedoc méditerranéen et du Rousillon* (Montpellier, 1971): 91–98; Rousseau, *Ascetics, Authority and the Church*, pp. 143–65.

Paulinus had met Martin at Vienne: Paulinus, *Ep.* 8. 9; he had been cured of an eye illness by Martin: Sulpicius Severus *Vita Martini* 19. 3; and he knew Sulpicius as *Martini beatissimi frequentator* Paulinus *Ep.* 11. 13. When Melania the Elder visited Paulinus, it is Sulpicius's *Vita* that he reads to her: Paulinus, *Ep.* 29. 14: "Martinum illum nostrum illi studiosissimae talium historiarum recitavi."

24. Rousseau, ibid., p. 94: "What must be stressed is that both the need for models, and the literature in which models were displayed, were features of the ascetic life proper to the West."

25. F. Nietzsche, *Die fröhliche Wissenschaft* 3. 261 (Stuttgart: Alfred Kröner, 1956): 175–76.

26. Plotinus *Enneads* 3. 4. 3.

27. Porphyry *Life of Plotinus* 10; Brown, *The Making of Late Antiquity*, p. 69 and p. 120 n.54.

28. Marcus Aurelius *Meditations* 5. 27.

29. Horace *Ep.* 2. 2. 183; Firmicus Maternus *Mathesis* 2. 19. 12.

30. Paulinus *Carm.* 15. 188: "Cui iam sociatus in omnia Christus."

31. It is possible, therefore, for Christ to appear in a vision with the features of Saint Felix: Paulinus *Ep.* 49. 3.

32. Paulinus *Carm.* 21. 355–57; cf. *Carm.* 15. 5–6.

33. Paulinus *Ep.* 5. 4.

34. Paulinus *Carm.* 22. 80.

35. Ibid. 23. 214: "Ergo veni, Felix animaeque perenne patronus." Even before his conversion, Paulinus chose to perform the traditional Roman ceremony of the *depositio barbae* at the shrine: *Carm.* 21. 377–78; Lienhard, *Paulinus of Nola*, p. 26, n.56. See in general E. Cesareo, *Il Carme Natalizio nella poesia latina* (Palermo: Società tipografica "Orfani di Guerra," 1929): 169–79.

36. Paulinus *Carm.* 21. 175–77; 183–86; 448–59, and *Carm.* 27. 146–47: "Cui privato specialius astro ista dies tantum peperit sine fine patronum."

37. Paulinus *Ep.* 30. 2: "Pauper ego et dolens, qui adhuc terrenae imaginis squalore concretus sum, et plus de primo quam de secundo Adam carnis sensibus et terrenis actibus refero, quomodo tibi audebo me pingere." Cf. Prophyry *Life of Plotinus* 1: "He showed too an unconquerable reluctance to sit for a painter or a sculptor: ... 'Is it not enough to carry about this

image in which nature has enclosed us? Do you really think that
I must also consent to leave, as a desirable spectacle to posterity,
an image of the image?';" and the *Acts of John* 29, trans. M. R.
James, *The Apocryphal New Testament* (Oxford: Clarendon
Press, 1924): 234: "Thou hast drawn a dead likeness of the
dead."

38. Gregory of Nyssa *Vita Macrinae, PG* 46. 961B; see *Grégoire
de Nysse: Vie de sainte Macrine*, Sources chrétiennes 178, ed. and
trans. P. Maraval (Paris: Le Cerf, 1971): 146–47. The re-
semblance is so close that a woman recognizes Saint Thecla
because she looked like her daughter, named Thecla! *Vie et
Miracles de Sainte Thècle* 11. ed. G. Dagron, Subsidia Hagiographica 62 (Brussels: Société des Bollandistes, 1978): 314.

39. Gregory of Nyssa *Vita Macrinae:* 964D.

40. Ibid.: 969CD.

41. Brown, *The Making of Late Antiquity*, pp. 73–76. Cf. the
new identity independent of the stars achieved by the emperor
on his accession, thought of as a *natalis:* H. Stern, *Le calendrier
de 354* (Paris: Geuthner, 1953): 74; Sabine MacCormack, "Roma,
Constantinopolis, the Emperor and His Genius," *Classical
Quarterly* 25 (1975): 137–38.

42. A. Poidebard and R. Mouterde, "A propos de saint Serge,"
*Analecta Bollandiana* 67 (1949): 114.

43. J. Wilpert, *Die Malereien der Katakomben Roms* (Freiburg
in Breisgau: Herder, 1903): 392, pl. 132,2; F. Cumont, *Recherches
sur le symbolisme funéraire des romains* (Paris: Geuthner, 1942):
29; B. Andreae, *Studien zur römischen Grabkunst* (Heidelberg:
F. H. Kerle, 1963): 30–39.

44. P. Styger, *Römische Märtyrergrüfte* (Berlin: Verlag für
Kunstwissenschaft, 1935), 1: 168.

45. Matthews, *Western Aristocracies*, p. 5; P. Fabre, *Saint Paulin
de Nole et l'amitié chrétienne* (Paris: de Boccard, 1949).

46. Paulinus *Carm.* 27. 346–48.

47. Uranius *De obitu sancti Paulini* 2, *PL* 53. 860A.

48. Paulinus *Carm.* 10. 21–22 and 29; C. Witke, *Numen Litterarum* (Leiden: Brill, 1971): 44–46 and 80–83.

49. Paulinus *Carm.* 10. 148–152.

50. Ibid. 11. 47–48.

51. Ibid. 10. 54–56, trans. Waddell, *Wandering Scholars*, p. 11.

52. Uranius *De obitu* 3. 861A.

53. G. N. Knauer, *Psalmenzitate in Augustins Konfessionen*
(Göttingen: Vandenhouck and Ruprecht, 1955). Though the

language of the Pslams is pervasive in Paulinus, it is not used in the same way: P. G. Walsh, *The Poems of Paulinus of Nola*, Ancient Christian Writers 40 (New York: Newman Press, 1975): 18–19 and Lienhard, *Paulinus of Nola*, pp. 129–30.

54. Augustine *City of God* 10.1, 3, 7, and 20.

55. Ibid. 8. 27.

56. Ibid. 10. 16.

57. Augustine *Sermon* 319. 8. 7.

58. G. Dix, *The Shape of the Liturgy* (London: Dacre Press; A. and C. Black, 1945): 380–82; E. Nordström, *Ravennastudien* (Uppsala: Almqvist and Wiksell, 1953): 21–24. G. E. M. de Ste Croix "Suffragium: From Vote to Patronage," *British Journal of Sociology* 5 (1954): 46; G. Gagov, "Il culto delle reliquie nell'antichità riflesso nei due termini 'patrocinia' e 'pignora,'" *Miscellanea Franciscana* 58 (1958): 484–512; A. B. Orselli, *L'idea e il culto del santo patrono cittadino nella letteratura latina* (Bologna: Zanichelli, 1945): 40–61.

59. On the final draining of significance from the archangels in medieval Italian art, as these are replaced by human intercessors such as the Virgin: C. Lamy-Lassalle, "Les archanges en costume impérial dans la peinture murale italienne," *Synthronon: Art et archéologie, de la fin de l'antiquité et du moyen âge: Recueil d'etudes par André Grabar et un groupe de ses disciples* (Paris: Klincksieck, 1968): 189–98. Angels carried with them associations of the absolute monarchy of God, surrounded by his servants and not open to manipulation by patronage: E. Peterson, *The Angels and the Liturgy* (New York: Herder and Herder, 1964): 25. Their continued importance in the Byzantine world is due, in part, to the fact that the surviving Eastern Empire was a society in which patronage, though current, never emerged as unambiguousy as in the West as the only viable alternative to absolute government through a bureaucratic hierarchy of stable ranks. In a Coptic legend, the archangel Michael even recieves his commander-in-chief's diploma from God, in correct Byzantine court style: C. Detlef and G. Müller, *Die Engellehre der koptischen Kirche* (Wiesbaden: Harrassowitz, 1959): 16. See. R. Rémondon, "Les contradictions de la société égyptienne à l'époque byzantine," *Journal of Juristic Papyrology* 13 (1974): 17–22.

60. Maximus of Turin *Sermon* 12.1, ed. A. Mutzenbecher, *Corpus Christianorum* 23 (Turnholt: Brepols, 1962): 41.

61. Ibid., 12. 2. 41–42.

62. Ibid. 36. 2. 141.
63. Ibid. 83. 2. 336.
64. R. C. Trexler, "Ritual Behavior in Renaissance Florence," *Medievalia et Humanistica* n.s. 4 (1973): n.59: "The creative formality of personal rituals calls for a formalized behavior of the patron as well as the client."
65. Origen *In Num. hom.* 10. 2; W. Rordorf, "La 'diaconie' des martyrs selon Origène," *Epektasis,* p. 395–402.
66. E. Dassmann, *Sündenvergebung durch Taufe, Busse und Märtyrerfürbitte in den Zeugnissen frühchristlicher Frömmigkeit und Kunst* (Münster in Westfalen: Aschendorff, 1973): 438, is puzzled that in earlier centuries a belief in the intercession of saints would not be reflected in the art of the catacombs. In fact, such a hiatus between what a group believes and what it has developed visual modes to express is always possible.
67. Clifford Geertz, "Art as a cultural system," *Modern Language Notes* 91 (1976): 1478, on art forms: "They materialize a way of experiencing; bring a particular cast of mind into the world of objects, where men can look at it."
68. E. Josi, "Il 'coemeterium maius,'" *Rivista di archeologia cristiana* 10 (1933): 11–13, fig. 6.
69. Nordström, *Ravennastudien,* pp. 42–45; 80–81, and 83–87. A. Grabar, *Christian Iconography: A Study of its Origins* (Princeton: Princeton University Press, 1968): 31–54; Ch. Pietri, *Roma Christiana* Bibliothèque de l'Ecole française d'Athènes et Rome, 224 (Paris: de Boccard, 1976), 2: 1413–1654.
70. Gibbon, *The Decline and Fall of the Roman Empire,* ed. J. B. Bury (London: Methuen, 1909), 3: 164. He adds: "So natural is the alliance between good taste and good sense that I am always astonished by the contrast." He is not the last commentator on the *Vita Martini* to be thus astonished.
71. R. Rémondon, *La crise de l'empire romain* (Paris: Presses universitaires de France, 1964): 304: "Ils opposent les patronages aux patronages en jouant sur les conflits entre catégories sociales (militaires, curiales, clercs, par exemple);" P. Brown, "The Rise and Functon of the Holy Man in Late Antiquity," *Journal of Roman Studies* 61 (1971): 85–87; and on the relation of women to saints, see chap. 2, above, p. 44.
72. The identification was appropriately intimate. As Paulinus portrays him, Saint Felix was an outsider; he had come, like Abraham, to make his grave in a strange land: *Carm.* 15. 61ff. This is precisely what a contemporary writer said of

Paulinus: Ps.-Jerome, *Ep.* 2: *Ad Geruntii filias* 7, PL 30. 50A. Having lost his inheritance to his brother—*Carm.* 15. 76—Felix was a model for the abandonment of wealth: *Carm.* 21. 530: "Homo quondam ex divite pauper." The identification with Felix, propertyless and tortured by the persecutors, explains Paulinus's exemplary courage and detachment during the Gothic invasion of 410–11: Augustine *City of God* 1. 10.

73. See chap. 2, above, p. 43.

74. Frend, "Paulinus of Nola," pp. 6–8.

75. P. Brown, *Augustine of Hippo* (Berkeley and Los Angeles: University of California Press, 1967): 146–57 and *The Making of Late Antiquity*, pp. 98–99.

76. P. Brown, *The World of Late Antiquity* (New York: Harcourt Brace, 1972): 107–8 and *Relics and Social Status in the Age of Gregory of Tours*, Stenton Lecture (Reading: University of Reading Press, 1977): 10; Averil Cameron, *Agathias* (Oxford: Clarendon Press, 1970): 53–56; L. Cracco-Ruggini, "The Ecclesiastical History and the Pagan Historiography: Providence and Miracles," *Athenaeum* 55 (1977): 107–26.

77. W. Liebeschuetz, "Did the Pelagian Movement have Social Aims?" *Historia* 12 (1963): 228–32; Matthews, *Western Aristocracies*, pp. 7–31; F. Pedersen, "On Professional Qualifications for Public Posts in Late Antiquity," *Classica et Medievalia* 31 (1975): 180.

78. Rousselle, "Deux exemples d'évangélisation en Gaule," p. 96.

79. Sulpicius Severus *Vita Martini* 7. 7.

80. Sulpicius Severus *Ep.* 2, PL 20. 178–79.

81. Ibid.: 179C.

82. Ambrose *De excessu Satyri* 1. 29; R. I. Frank, "*Commendabilis* in Ammianus Marcellinus," *American Journal of Philology* 88 (1967): 309–18.

83. J. Wilpert, *Die Malereien der Katakomben Roms*, p. 394, pl. 247.

84. Brown, *The Making of Late Antiquity*, pp. 99–100; G. M. H. Hanfmann, *The Season Sarcophagus in Dumbarton Oaks* (Cambridge: Harvard University Press, 1951), 1: 237–38: "The new note which is sounded in the third century is the deep preoccupation with the individual soul and the consciousness of its connection with the eternal cosmic order." By the fourth century, this consciousness is replaced, on Christian sarcophagi, by images of personal dependence: the soul, previously shown as already alone in paradise, is now flanked by

rows of imposing protectors: F. Gerke, *Die christlichen Sar-kophage der vorkonstantinischen Zeit* Berlin: de Gruyter, 1940): 60.

85. Tertullian *De anima* 53. 6.

86. P. Nautin, "L'évolution des ministères au ii^e et au iii^e siècle," *Revue de droit canonique* 23 (1973): 57: "La conversion de Constantin et l'entrée des évêques à la cour impériale n'ont pas modifié la vie de l'église aussi profondément que l'on l'a cru. On entend souvent dire, lorsqu'on trouve dans l'église des manières d'être et d'agir qui heurtent les aspirations modernes, qu'elles sont la conséquence de ce qu'on appelle le 'césaro-papisme,'.... Il faut savoir que c'est là une vue apologetique qui ne correspond pas à l'histoire. Non, la faute n'est pas à Constantin. Les structures, les mentalités et les comportements que nous avons évoqués sont tous antérieures au iv^e siècle." This clear warning cannot be repeated too often to students of late antiquity and the early church.

87. C. Andresen, *Die Kirchen der alten Christenheit* (Stuttgart: Kohlhammer, 1971): 401.

88. See chap. 2, above, pp. 26-28.

89. Brown, *Augustine of Hippo*, pp. 177–79 and *The Making of Late Antiquity*, pp. 89–94.

90. Gregory of Nyssa *Vita Macrinae*: 984B; see *Grégoire de Nysse: Vie de sainte Macrine*, ed. P. Maraval, pp. 74–77. J. Ntedika, *L'évocation de l'au delà dans la prière pour les morts* (Louvain: Nauwelaerts, 1971): 259, notes a growing anxiety that the Devil will snatch the soul at the moment of death.

91. Brown, *Augustine of Hippo*, pp. 29–30.

92. Augustine *Confessions* 9. 13. 36.

93. I. Guidi, "Vita di Daniele," *Revue de l'Orient chrétien* 5 (1900): 563.

94. E. Le Blant, *Les inscriptions chrétiennes de la Gaule* (Paris: Imprimerie Impériale, 1856), 2: no. 708.

## Chapter Four

1. *ILCV* 1549.

2. Prudentius *Cathemerinon* 10. 161–62.

3. Ibid. 10. 45. Cf. Augustine *Confessions* 9. 12. 29–33 on the numbing effect of grief held under control by the whole group of Christians at the funeral of his mother. We need only compare Ambrose on Mary at the Cross—*De obitu Valentiniani* 39: "Stantem illam lego, flentem non lego"—with the late medieval

image of the *Mater Dolorosa,* to measure the distance between ourselves and the early Christian world: Millard Meiss, *Painting in Florence and Siena after the Black Death* (Princeton: Princeton University Press, 1951): 128–30. On the strict suppression of mourning at Christian funerals: Ernesto de Martino, *Morte e pianto rituale nel mondo antico* (Turin: Einaudi, 1958): 334–36; *Grégoire de Nysse: Vie de sainte Macrine,* Sources chrétiennes 178, ed. and trans. P. Maraval (Paris: Le Cerf, 1971): 77–89.

4. Prudentius *Cathemerinon* 10. 158: "Quibus atra e morte triumphans."

5. A. Moćsy, *Pannonia and Upper Moesia* (London: Routledge, 1974): 334–35, pl. 40c.

6. A. Mossay, *La mort et l'au delà dans saint Grégoire de Nazianze* (Louvain: Publications universitaires, 1960); Robert C. Gregg, *Consolation Philosophy* (Cambridge, Mass.: Philadelphia Patristic Foundation, 1975). Apart from the beautifully written study of Jaroslav Pelikan, *The Shape of Death: Life, Death and Immortality in the Early Fathers* (New York: Abingdon Press, 1962) we lack a study of the meaning of death in the early Christian world, and its expression in burial practices and attitudes to mourning: P. A. Février, "Le culte des morts dans les communautés chrétiennes durant le iiie siècle," *Atti del ixo congresso internazionale di archeologia cristiana* (Rome, 1977), 1: 265: "Il est curieux, en effet, que l'on ne dispose d'aucune étude récente sur là mort, ni sur l'idée de mort."

7. Gregory of Nyssa *Vita Macrinae, PG* 46. 996A.

8. Gregory of Nyssa *Encomium on saint Theodore, PG* 46. 737C.

9. Greg. Tur. *GC* 72: 341.

10. Greg. Tur. *VP* 1. praef.: 213.

11. P. Brown, *Augustine of Hippo* (Berkeley and Los Angeles: University of California Press, 1967): 403–7.

12. J. Chéné, "Le origines de la controverse semipélagienne," *Année théologique augustinienne* 13 (1953): 90.

13. Brown, *Augustine of Hippo,* p. 407.

14. Augustine *De corruptione et gratia* 12. 35.

15. Augustine *De dono perseverantiae* 7. 14.

16. R. Bernard, *La prédestination du Christ total chez saint Augustin* (Paris: Etudes augustiniennes, 1965).

17. J. Gagé, "*Membra Christi* et la déposition des reliques sous l'autel," *Revue archéologique* 5. ser. 29 (1929): 137–53.

18. A. Grabar, *Martyrium* (Paris: Collège de France, 1946), 2: 57, pl. 56, 2: "On ne saurait imaginer une association plus complète de l'iconographie du Christ et du martyr."

19. H. J. W. Drijvers, "Spätantike Parallelen zur altchristlichen Heiligenverehrung unter besonderer Berücksichtigung
des syrischen Stylitenkultes," *Aspekte frühchristlicher Heiligenverehrung,* Oikonomia: Quellen und Studien zur orthodoxen
Theologie (Erlangen: Zantner-Busch Stiftung, 1977): 71–72.
20. Augustine *Sermon* 344. 4.
21. P. Brown, "Pelagius and His Supporters," *Journal of
Theological Studies* n.s. 19 (1968): 108–14 in *Religion and Society in
the Age of Saint Augustine* (London: Faber, 1972): 193–207.
22. Paulinus *Carm.* 19. 18.
23. Ibid. 15: Martyr stella loci simul et medecina colentum.
24. Greg. Tur. *LH* 2. 6. 47.
25. Ibid. 8. 33. 402–3. He reveals, but omits to emphasize,
that all the other houses were of wood!
26. Genesis 3. 19 and Psalm 103. 16 cited by the priest; Greg.
Tur. *LH* 10. 13. 496.
27. Allan I. Ludwig, *Graven Images: New England Stone Carving and Its Symbols* (Middletown: Wesleyan University Press,
1966): 17.
28. Grabar, *Martyrium,* 2: 39.
29. Greg. Tur. *LH* 10. 13.
30. Edward Gibbon, *The Decline and Fall of the Roman Empire,*
ed. J. B. Bury (London: Methuen, 1909), 3: 223.
31. Maximus of Turin, *Sermon* 14. 2, ed. A. Mutzenbecher,
*Corpus Christianorum* 23 (Turnholt: Brepols, 1962): 55.
32. Greg. Tur. *LH* 2. 16. 64; 2. 31. 77; *GC* 94. 359.
33. Robert Murray, *Symbols of Church and Kingdom: A Study in
the Early Syriac Tradition* (Cambridge: At the University Press,
1975): 261.
34. Sulpicius Severus *Vita Martini* 13. 1–2; but see *Sulpice
Sévère: Vie de saint Martin,* Sources chrétiennes 134, ed. and trans.
J. Fontaine (Paris: Le cerf, 1968), 2: 741. E. Mâle, *La fin du
paganisme en Gaule* (Paris: Flammarion, 1950). F. Graus, *Volk,
Herrscher und Heiliger im Reich der Merowinger* (Prague: Ces-
koslovenská Akademie Věd, 1965): 186–88.
35. Greg. Tur. *GM* 90: 98.
36. Greg. Tur. *GC* 50: 328. It would be fitting if this grave of a
"Severus" were the grave of Sulpicius Severus.
37. Greg. Tur. *GC* 40. 323.
38. Greg. Tur. *LH* 4. 12. 143.
39. Paulinus *Carm.* 21. 633–35: unde piis stat gratia viva
sepulchris/quae probat in Christo functos sine morte
sepultos / ad tempus placido sopiri corpora somno.

40. Prudentius *Cathemerinon* 10. 97–100.
41. Greg. Tur. *VP* 7. 3. 328.
42. A. H. M. Jones, *The Later Roman Empire* (Oxford: Blackwell, 1964), 2: 963–64.
43. Augustine *City of God* 22. 9.
44. Brown, *Augustine of Hippo*, pp. 415–18.
45. Augustine *Sermon* 344. 4.
46. H. I. Marrou, *The Resurrection and Saint Augustine's Theology of Human Values* (Villanova, Pa.: Villanova University Press, 1966); in a French version, "Le dogme de la résurrection des corps et la théologie des valeurs humains selon l'enseignement de saint Augustin," *Revue des études augustiniennes* 12 (1966): 111–36 in *Patristique et Humanisme*, Patristica Sorbonensia 9 (Paris: Le Seuil, 1976): 429–55—the work of a master. M. R. Miles, *Augustine on the Body*, American Academy of Religion Dissertation Series 31 (Missoula, Mont.: Scholars Press, 1979).
47. Victricius of Rouen *De laude sanctorum* 11, *PL* 20. 454 B.
48. Ibid. 10. 453A.
49. H. Buschhausen, *Die spätrömischen Metallscrinia und frühchristlichen Reliquiare* (Veinna: Böhlau, 1971).
50. Paulinus *Ep.* 31. 1.
51. Paulinus *Carm.* 19. 358–62; Greg. Tur. *GM* 12. 46. Compare Gregory Nazianzenus, *Oratio* IV. 664; *PG* 35. 589C.
52. Victricius of Rouen *De laude sanctorum* 10. 452B.
53. Ibid. 12. 456CD.
54. *Decretum Gelasianum, PL* 59. 171; M. Férotin, *Le Liber Mozarabicus Sacramentorum* (Paris: Firmin-Didot, 1912): 394, on the martyrdom of Saint Laurence: "Nam quis crederet corpus fragile compage glutinatum tantis sine te sufficere conflictibus potuisse?
55. *Passio Perpetuae et Felicitatis* 15. 5–6, ed. and trans. H. Musurillo. *The Acts of the Christian Martyrs* (Oxford: Clarendon Press, 1972); 123–25.
56. Augustine *Gesta cum Felice* 1. 12.
57. Grabar, *Martyrium,* 2. 14: a simple medal juxtaposes the martyrdom of saint Lawrence on the gridiron, his soul in paradise and, on the reverse, his shrine.
58. Aelius Aristides *Sacred Tales* 3. 15, trans. C. A. Behr (Amsterdam: Hakkert, 1968): 244.
59. H. Delehaye, *Les Passions et les genres littéraires* (Brussels: Société des Bollandistes, 1921): 313.
60. B. de Gaiffier, "La lecture des Actes des martyrs dans la

prière liturgique en Occident," *Analecta Bollandiana* 72 (1954): 134–66.

61. Greg. Tur. *VM* 2. 43. 174.

62. Joseph Engemann, "Zu der Apsis-Tituli des Paulinus von Nola," *Jahrbuch für Antike und Christentum* 17 (1974): 33.

63. Paulinus *Carm.* 20. 28–32. C. Witke, *Numen Litterarum* (Leiden: Brill, 1971): 80–90.

64. Eusebius, *Vita Constantini* 1. 10; *Scriptores Historiae Augustae: Quadriga Tyrranorum* 1. 2, the author will be no Marius Maximus, "qui et mythistoricis se volumnibus implicavit." We now know better than to take him at his word: R. Syme, *Ammianus and the Historia Augusta* (Oxford: Clarendon Press, 1968): 2–3.

65. G. Rodenwaldt, "Eine spätantike Kunstströmung in Rom," *Römische Mitteilungen* 36/37 (1921/1922): 67–83.

66. Greg. Tur. *GM* 75. 89.

67. Greg. Tur. *LH* 5. 4. 200.

68. Greg. Tur. *GM* 79. 92. This quality is well seen by Emil H. Walter, "Hagiographisches in Gregors Frankengeschichte," *Archiv für Kulturgeschichte* 48 (1966): 298–303.

69. Greg. Tur. *VM* 1 praef.: 135; *GC* 6. 302.

70. Greg. Tur. *GC* 94: 359.

71. Greg. Tur. *VM* 2. 14. 163; 2. 29. 170; 2. 49. 176.

72. Greg. Tur. *VJ* 16. 121.

73. Sabine G. MacCormack, "Latin Prose Panegyrics," *Revue des études augustiniennes* 22 (1976): 41–54.

74. Greg. Tur. *GM* 63. 81.

75. T. Baumeister, *Martyr Invictus* (Münster: Regensberg, 1972): 169.

76. R. W. Gaston, "Prudentius and Sixteenth-Century Antiquarian Scholarship," *Medievalia et Humanistica*, n.s. 4 (1973): 169: "visceral, almost obscene realism."

77. Prudentius *Peristephanon* 1. 26.

78. Ibid. 3. 91–93.

79. Ibid. 3. 144.

80. Angel Fábrega Grau, *Pasionario hispánico* (Barcelona: Instituto P. Enrique Florez, 1955), 2: 76–77. The participation of the congretation is assumed in the Spanish liturgy: M. Férotin, *Liber Mozarabicus* p. 482: "Ut in conversatione gestorum populi fidelis intentio, dum admonetur celebrare quod creditur, videatur sibi exspectare quod legitur," and 484: "Hanc plebem Martyrum agonibus congaudentem intende clemens; et da sin-

gulis quod poscunt, qui sanctis tribuisti de hoste triumphare."
81. Venantius Fortunatus *Carm.* 5. 3. 11.
82. Greg. Tur. *VJ* 25. 125.
83. Greg. Tur. *GM* 50. 73.
84. Venantius Fortunatus *Carm.* 2. 7. 38 and 41–42.
85. Helen Waddell, *Wandering Scholars* (London: Constable, 1927): 30.

## Chapter Five

1. G. W. F. Hegel, *The Philosophy of History*, trans. J. Shibree (New York: Wiley Book Co., 1944): 377.
2. *ILCV* 1831; Y. M. Duval and Ch. Pietri, "*Membra Christi:* Culte des martyrs et théologie de l'Eucharistie," *Revue des études augustiniennes* 21 (1975): 289–301.
3. A. Dupront, "Pèlerinages et lieux sacrés," *Mélanges F. Braudel* (Toulouse: Privat, 1973), 2: 190.
4. Victor Turner and Edith Turner, *Image and Pilgrimage in Christian Culture* (New York: Columbia University Press, 1978): 15: "A pilgrim is one who divests himself of the mundane concomitants of religion—which become entangled with its practice in the local situation—to confront in a special "far" milieu, the basic elements and structures of his faith in their unshielded, virgin radiance."
5. Dupront, "Pèlerinages," p. 191. Hence the constant toying with the theme in letters of edification: is it better to go to Jerusalem or to find true religion at home? In favor of going: *Epistola "Honorificentiae tuae"* 2, ed. C. P. Caspari, *Briefe, Abhandlungen und Predigten* (Christiania: Mallingsche Buchdruck, 1890): 8: "Et ego me, cum in patria consisterem, Dei aestimabam esse cultorem et placebam mihi." Against: Gregory of Nyssa, *Ep.* 2 *PG* 46. 1012C; Jerome *Ep.* 58. 3—yet written from the Holy Land. The debate continued: G. Constable, "Opposition to Pilgrimage in the Middle Ages," *Studia Gratiana* 19 (1976): 123–46.
6. Urs Peschow, "Fragmente eines Heiligensarkophags in Myra," *Istanbuler Mitteilungen* 24 (1974): 225–31: the plain marble side is pierced with peepholes or with holes to allow healing myrrh to flow out.
7. J. Christern, *Das frühchristliche Pilgerheiligtum von Tebessa* (Wiesbaden: F. Steiner, 1976): 245–46; Dupront, "Pèlerinages," p. 204: "Au terme du voyage, de marcher encore."
8. Charles Pietri, *Roma Christiana* (Paris: de Boccard, 1976): 39–40.

9. Greg. Tur. *GM* 27. 54.

10. Ibid. 27. 54.

11. Ibid. 27. 54.

12. *Collectio Avellana* 218, *Corpus Scriptorum Ecclesiasticorum Latinorum* (Vienna: Tempsky, 1895), 36: 678–79.

13. See chap. 2, above, p. 44.

14. *Miracula sancti Stephani* 2. 6, *PL* 41. 847.

15. *ILCV* 2129: a grave bought "ad domnu Laurentium."

16. See chap. 4, above, pp. 78–79; J. M. McCulloh, "The Cult of Relics in the Letters and Dialogues of Pope Gregory the Great: A lexicographical study," *Traditio* 32 (1975): 158–61.

17. F. Prinz, "Stadtrömisch-italische Märtyrer und fränkische Reichsadel im Maas-Mosel-Raum," *Historische Jahrbuch* 87 (1967): 1–25 is a good example of how a previously peripheral region came to do justice to its growing political importance by the importation of Italian relics. The story is the same for Anglo-Saxon England and for central Europe.

18. F. Pfister, *Der Reliquienkult im Altertum* (Giessen: Töpelmann, 1912), 2: 614, makes plain that this is an aspect of the cult of relics largely absent in the ancient pagan world.

19. Patrick J. Geary, *Furta Sacra: Thefts of Relics in the Central Middle Ages* (Princeton: Princeton University Press, 1978).

20. W. Liebeschuetz, "Did the Pelagian Movement have Social Aims?" *Historia* 12 (1963): 228–38; J. F. Matthews, *Western Aristocracies and Imperial Court, A.D. 364–425* (Oxford: Clarendon Press, 1974): 7–31; Paulinus *Ep.* 31. 1: "Sed quia non habuimus huius muneris copiam et ille se spem eiusdem gratiae habere dixit a sancta Silvia," on the promise of a relic; Greg. Tur. *GM* 5. 41: "Unde ei tanta ibidem fuisset gratia, ut meruisset," the first question of a suspicious bishop to the bearer of a relic; the response was reassuring: "Quando, inquit, Hierosolymis abii, Futen abbatem repperi, qui magnam cum Sophia augusta gratiam habuit."

21. Santo Mazzarino, *Stilicone e la crisi imperiale dopo Teodosio* (Rome: Signorelli, 1942): 78–91; G. Dagron, *La naissance d'une capitale: Constantinople et ses institutions de 330 à 451* (Paris: Presses universitaires de France, 1974): 72; S. G. MacCormack, 'Roma, Constantinopolis, the Emperor and his Genius," *Classical Quarterly* 25 (1975): 148.

22. *ILCV* 2068.

23. Helen Waddell, *Wandering Scholars* (London: Constable, 1927): 28.

24. Paulinus *Ep.* 32. 3.

25. E. D. Hunt, "Saint Silvia of Aquitaine: The Role of a Theodosian Pilgrim in the Society of East and West," *Journal of Theological Studies* n.s. 23 (1972): 357–73; Kenneth G. Holum, "Pulcheria's Crusade A.D. 421–22 and the Ideology of Imperial Victory," *Greek, Roman and Byzantine Studies* 18 (1977): 153–72; Kenneth G. Holum and Gary Vikan, "The Trier Ivory, Adventus Ceremonial and the Relics of S. Stephen," *Dumbarton Oaks Papers* 33, in press.

26. Victor Turner and Edith Turner, *Image and Pilgrimage*, p. 233.

27. Augustine *Sermon* 319. 6. 6.

28. P. Peeters, *Le tréfonds oriental de l'hagiographie byzantine* (Brussels: Société des Bollandistes, 1950): 56, on Aramaic fragments of the letter of Lucianus.

29. *Epistula Luciani* 2, *PL* 41. 809.

30. Ibid. 8: 815.

31. Ibid. 9: 815.

32. Sozomen *Historia ecclesiastica* 9. 17; Glenn F. Chesnut, *The First Christian Historians* (Paris: Beauchesne, 1977): 167–200.

33. N. H. Baynes, "The Supernatural Defenders of Constantinople," *Byzantine Studies and Other Essays* (London: Athlone Press, 1960): 248–60; P. J. Alexander, "The Strength of the Empire and Capital as Seen through Byzantine Eyes," *Speculum* 37 1962): 349–57.

34. For the extraordinary mood revealed in an incident reported by Augustine *Sermo de urbis excidio* 9.

35. Dagron, *Formation d'une capitale*, p. 102 n.7; Holum and Vikan, "The Trier Ivory" (in press) on the commemorative quality of the ivory portraying the arrival of the relics of Saint Stephen. We must never forget the resilience of secular, sub-pagan rituals for the salvation of the city: citizens would gather at the base of the porphyry statue of Constantine, "with sacrifices, the burning of lights and incense and supplications to ward off catastrophe": Philostorgius *Historia ecclesiastica* 2. 7; Dagron, *Formation d'une capitale*, pp. 307–9, for further examples of a totally non-Christian myth of the city and its protection.

36. G. W. Bowersock, *Greek Sophists in the Roman Empire* (Oxford: Clarendon Press, 1969): 58.

37. Gregory of Nyssa *Vita Macrinae*, *PG* 46: 981B.

38. See chap. 3, above, p. 64.

39. Paulinus, *Ep.* 31. 1: "Accipite ergo ab unanimis fratribus

in omni bono vestrum sibi consortium cupientibus.

40. See the letter of the notables of Hermoupolis Magna to a philosopher representing their interests at the court of Gallienus; they pray that "Hermes, the god of our hometown, may ever be beside you": G. Méautis, *Hermoupolis la Grande* (Lausanne: Université de Neuchâtel, 1918), p. 175. Paulinus always experienced the protection of Felix on his journeys: *Carm.* 12. 25 and 13; he expected that Sulpicius Severus would keep a fragment of the Holy Cross to carry on his person, "ad cotidianam tutelam atque medecinam": *Ep.* 32. 7; when deported to the north as a hostage, Gregory of Tours's father took with him a golden locket of relics whose names were unknown to him: Greg. Tur. *GM* 83. 94; these relics offered him the same protection as other amulets: e.g., *Codex Bonnensis* 218 (66a) in J. Tambornino, *De Antiquorum Daemonismo* (Giessen: Töpelmann, 1909): 26; Gregory himself traveled with relics of saint Martin round his neck, "licet temerario ordine": Greg. Tur. *VM* 3. 17. 187; J. Engemann, "Magische Übelabwehr in der Spätantike," *Jahrbuch für Antike und Christentum* 18 (1975): 22–48.

41. Ambrose *Ep.* 22. 12; Pope Damasus, also, was personally implicated as discoverer and validator of the tombs of the martyrs in the Roman catacombs, in a manner that stressed his personal relationship to them: *ILCV* 1981. 7; 1993. 9–10.

42. Sidonius Apollinaris *Ep.* 7. 1. 7.

43. P. Brown, *Relics and Social Status in the Age of Gregory of Tours*, Stenton Lecture (Reading: University of Reading Press, 1977): 15.

44. Gaudentius of Brescia *Sermon* 17, *PL* 20. 965A.

45. Ibid.: 964A.

46. Ibid.: 965A: "Idoneos veneratores tanti nos esse muneris approbantes."

47. Ibid.: 971A.

48. Ibid.: 960A.

49. Paulinus *Ep.* 18.9.

50. Ibid. 18. 4.

51. E. Demougeot, "La Gaul nord-orientale à la veille de l'invasion germanique," *Revue historique* 236 (1966): 17–46.

52. The wife of a prefect of Gaul was taken back from Trier to Pavia to be buried: E. Gabba and G. Tibiletti, "Una signora di Treveri sepolta a Pavia," *Athenaeum* n.s. 38 (1960): 253–62.

53. Paulinus *Ep.* 18. 5.

54. Innocent *Ep.* 2, *PL* 20. 469B.

55. Victricius of Rouen *De laude sanctorum* 1, *P/L* 20. 443B.
56. H. Delehaye, *Les origines du culte des martyrs* (Brussels: Société des Bollandistes, 1912): 65.
57. Victricius *De laude* 1: 444B.
58. Ibid. 2: 445A.
59. Ibid. 6: 448B; cf. Paulinus *Ep.* 32. 17: "Hic simul unum pium complectitur arca coetum et capit exiguo nomina tanta sinu."
60. Ibid. 7: 449E.
61. Ibid. 1: 444A; J. Gagé, "*Membra Christi* et la déposition des reliques sous l'autel," *Revue archéologique* 5 ser. 9 (1929): 137–53.
62. The relics of the Forty Martyrs of Sebaste, being ashes, were literally indistinguishable, and so the perfect image of a group indissolubly fused together: Gaudentius *Sermon* 17. 971A.
63. A. P. Billanovich, "Appunti di agiografia aquileiense," *Rivista di storia della chiesa in Italia* 30 (1976): 5–24.
64. Ch. Pietri, "*Concordia Apostolorum et Renovatio Urbis* (Culte des martyrs et propagande pontificale)," *Mélanges d'archéologie et d'histoire* 73 (1961): 275–322 and *Roma Christiana*, Bibliothèque de l'Ecole française d'Athènes et Rome, 224 (Paris: De Boccard, 1976), 1: 350–51: Peter as Moses, also, is a symbol of concord in a rebellious community. P. A. Février, "Natale Petri de cathedra," *Comptes rendus de l'Académie d'Inscriptions et Belles-Lettres*, 1977: 514–31.
65. *Chromace d'Aquilée: Sermons*, Sources chrétiennes 154, ed. J. Lemarié (Paris: Le Cerf, 1969): 182.
66. See chap. 2, above, pp. 000–00.
67. I. N. Wood, "Early Merovingian Devotion in Town and Country," *The Church in Town and Countryside*, Studies in Church History 16, ed. D. Baker (Oxford: Blackwell, 1979): 72.
68. Greg. Tur. *VJ* 30. 126–27; on Brioude as a joining point of separate cities, Wood, "Early Merovingina Devotion," p. 74; cf. Victor Turner and Edith Turner, *Image and Pilgrimage*, pp. 200–201, for an analogous role in modern times for Le Puy: "set apart from major administrative centers."
69. Greg. Tur. *LH* 9. 20. 438: at the treaty of Andelot, A.D. 588, the kings promise each other "pura et simplex . . . in Dei nomine concordia." The concord of the Franks was a myth passed on to Byzantium, possibly by ambassadors: Agathias *Historiae* 1. 2. Need for concord may have influenced the attitudes of the Gallo-Roman episcopate and aristocracy, and ensured that the divisions of power among the Merovingian kings were territo-

rially based: I. N. Wood, "Kings, Kingdoms and Consent," *Early Medieval Kingship*, ed. P. H. Sawyer and I. N. Wood (Leeds: The School of History, University of Leeds, 1977): 6–29—a new departure on a threadbare topic. For Gregory's own heartfelt wishes: Greg. Tur. *LH* 5 praef. On ecclesiastical solidarity shown in frequent councils: Council of Orléans (A.D. 541), canon 38, ed. C. de Clercq, *Concilia Galliae*, Corpus Christianorum 148A (Turnholt: Brepols, 1963): 142: "Ut per unitatem antestitum ecclesiastica fulgeat disciplina et inconvulsa maneat constitutio sacerdotum."

70. Greg. Tur. *VJ* 50. 133.

71. Sabine G. MacCormack, "Change and Continuity in Late Antiquity: The ceremony of *Adventus*, " *Historia* 21 (1972): 721–52; N. Gussone, "Adventus-Zeremoniell und Translation von Reliquien: Victricius von Rouen *De laude sanctorum*," *Frühmittelalterliche studien* 10 (1976): 125–33; for a sixth-century carving of a translation in Vienne: *Bulletin de la société des amis de Vienne* 67 (1971): 31, fig. 2; the ceremonial survived in its secular forms in Gaul: Greg. Tur. *LH* 6. 11. 281; 8. 1. 370.

72. Sabine G. MacCormack, *Art and Ceremonial in the Later Roman Empire* (Los Angeles and Berkeley: University of California Press, 1980), in press.

73. Victricius *De laude* 12: 454D–455A; Venantius Fortunatus *Carm.* 5. 3. 3; Greg. Tur. *LH* 8. 1. 370: The parade to greet the king included Jews and Syrians, chanting in Hebrew and Syriac. Compare Gregory Nazianzenus *Oratio* XXI, 29; *PG* 35. 1116B.

74. Victricius *De laude* 2. 446B: "Hinc denique totius populi circa maiestatem vestram unus affectus."

75. P. Andrieu-Guitrancourt, "La vie ascétique à Rouen au temps de saint Victrice," *Recherches de science religieuse* 40 (1952): 90–106.

76. Victricius *De laude* 3. 445C.

77. Count Becco came to the shrine of Saint Julina at Brioude in full dress with his retinue. No good came of that occasion; but it was intended to be an annual presence at the festival: Greg. Tur. *VJ* 16. 121.

78. I find it hard not to connect this with the puzzling forms of the ceremony of Clovis's reception of the insignia of a consul in Tours in A.D. 507. The ceremonial is connected at every point with the processional route associated with the cult of Saint Martin: Greg. Tur. *LH* 2. 38. 89.

79. Venantius Fortunatus *Carm.* 4. 26. 14–17; cf. *Carm.* 2. 8.

23–37, on Launebodis and his wife Bercthruda, who built the church of Saint Severinus, which no Roman had done, while Bercthruda distributed alms in person: on the integration of women through almsgiving, see chap. 2, above, pp. 46–47.

80. Greg. Tur. *VM* 2. 28. 169. This was at the approach of Easter, where leading members of the community were commanded not to stay in their villas, but to come to the ceremonies to receive the blessing of the bishop: Counci of Orleans, cannon 25, *Concilia Galliae*, p. 11; *Concilium Epaonense* 35: 33; Clermont 15: 109.

81. Greg. Tur. *VM* 2. 14. 163.

82. Greg. Tur. *VM* 1. 11. 145.

83. Greg. Tur. *VJ* 9. 118: "Visum est ei quasi multitudo catenarum ab eis membris solo decidere"; Greg. Tur. *GC* 86. 354; 93. 357.

84. Brown, *Relics and Social Status*, pp. 19–21 for the effect of this ceremony on the position of the bishop. His election was a result of a *consensus* of the community in his favor, so that the *consensus* of the saint's festival was a reenactment and revalidation of this election. See. V. Crapanzano, *The Ḥamadsha: A Study in Moroccan Ethnopsychiatry* (Los Angeles and Berkeley: University of California Press, 1973): 116–17, for an analogous demonstration of consensus at the "arrival" of the *mizwar* at the shrine of the saint. The ideal bishop was one who maintained a high level of concord: Venantius Fortunatus *Carm.* 3. 4. 25–26, on Leontius of Bordeaux: "Nam suos cives placida sic voce monebat, / confiteris ut hunc ad sua membra loqui" It remained a distant ideal: Brown, *Relics and Social Status*, pp. 17–20.

85. On the associations of the violently executed: A. D. Nock, *Sallustius: Concerning the Gods and the Universe* (Cambridge: At the University Press, 1926): xcii n.219, and "Tertullian and the Ahori," *Vigiliae Christianae* 4 (1950): 129–41 in *Essays in Religion and the Ancient World*, ed. Z. Stewart (Oxford: Clarendon Press, 1972), 2: 712–19. Saint Martin had to determine whether a tomb in a shrine was that of a martyr or an executed brigand: Sulpicius Severus *Vita Martini* 11.

86. Sulpicius Severus *Vita Martini* 20; *Dialogi* 2. 3; 2. 5; 3. 4; 3. 8; 3. 11–13.

87. Victricius *De laude* 1. 443A.

88. This was a tendency far more widespread than we might think. The Christian communities were prepared to venerate as

martyrs anyone they considered unjustly executed by the Roman secular authorities. See the extraordinary *Letter 1* of Jerome: *De muliere septies percussa* on a contemporary incident at Vercelli. The emperor Valentinian I was deterred from executing the town councils of three Pannonian cities for fear that they would be worshiped as martyrs, as were courtiers whom he had executed in Milan: Ammianus Marcellinus 27. 7. 5–6; H. I. Marrou, "Ammien Marcellin et les 'Innocents' de Milan," *Recherches de science religieuse* 40 (1952): 179–90.

89. See Prudentius *Peristephanon* 2. 313–488 on the lively and talkative martyrdom of Saint Lawrence. Yet at a time when the wealth of the Roman church was notorious, and when priests were only recently believed to have been subjected to judicial torture by a pagan prefect of the city, there is a topicality about the whole poem: Symmachus *Relatio* 21.

90. *Miracula sancti Stephani* 2. 5. 851.

91. Ibid. 2. 5. 852.

92. Ibid. 2. 5. 852.

93. The activities of the proconsuls of Carthage were subject to popular judgment, in the form of acclaim or hissing when their names were read out from a list: pseudo-Prosper of Aquitaine (Quodvultdeus) *Liber de promissionibus et praedictionibus Dei* 5. 14–15, *PL* 51. 855.

94. P. Brown, *Augustine of Hippo* (Los Angeles and Berkeley: University of California Press, 1967): 336–37.

95. As in the relations between the Frankish counts of the Auvergne and the shrine of Saint Julian at Brioude: Greg. Tur. *VJ* 16. 121, the case of count Becco; ibid. 43. 131, the power of a silk hanging from the shrine effects cures "et potestas iudicum, quotienscumque in eo loco superflue egit, confusa discessit."

96. *Epistula Severi ad omnem ecclesiam*, *PL* 41. 821–32.

97. Ibid. 2. 822.

98. Ibid. 4. 823.

99. Ibid. 10. 825. They even tell each other their dreams at this time of crisis: ibid. 8. 824.

100. Ibid. 4. 823: "Christiani autem ut corde, ita etiam et viribus humiles . . . patroni Stephani patrocinium deprecabantur."

101. Ibid. 5–6. 823, both sides are spoken of as "armies"; ibid. 9. 824: they are armed with sticks, stones, and slings, making a show of force which Roman law only permitted against brigands; some Jewish converts were brutally frank: ibid. 14.

170   Notes to Pages 104–8

829: "Ego igitur vitae meae periculo consulens ad ecclesiam iam pergam, ut necem quae mihi paratur effugiam."
102. Ibid. 3.823.
103. Ibid. 10. 825.
104. Ibid. 11. 826; 13. 827–28.
105. Though Severus is pleased that there were no Jews settled in Jammona, there is no evidence that he or his supporters intended to drive the Jews from the island, or that they were in a position to do so: ibid. 2. 822.
106. Ibid. 12. 826; 14. 829; 17. 831; 18. 832: remarkable vignettes of the status and interrelations of the Jewish families. As a junior member of one family said to Theodore: "Quid times, domine Theodore? Si vis certe securus et honoratus et dives esse, in Christum crede, sicut et ego credidi. Modo tu stas, et ego cum episcopis sedeo." On the significance of lay patrons sitting beside the bishop as the joint heads of the community, see Julian Ep. 18, 450C.
107. Ibid. 15: 830. They first thought it was an angel.
108. Ibid. 15: 830.
109. Ibid. 17: 831.
110. Miracula sancti Stephani 2. 1. 843.

Chapter Six

1. Jerome Ep. 103. 13.
2. J. D. Mansi, Sacrorum conciliorum nova et amplissima collectio (Venice, 1776), 9: 771B.
   Greg. Tur. VP 15. 3. 272.
4. Augustine Ep. 78. 3: "Ubi mirabiliter et terribiliter daemones confitentur."
5. J. Stuiber, "Heidnische und christliche Gedächtniskalender," Jahrbuch für Antike und Christentum 3 (1960): 30.
6. N. Z. Davis, "The Reasons of Misrule," and "The Rites of Violence," Society and Culture in Early Modern France (Stanford: Stanford University Pres, 1975): 97–123; 152–87.
7. I have found most help from S. M. Shirokogoroff, The Psycho-Mental Complex of the Tungus (Peking and London: Routledge, 1935); M. Leiris, La possession et ses aspects théâtraux chez les Ethiopiens de Gondar (Paris: Plon, 1958); Spirit Mediumship and Society in Africa, ed. J. Beattie and J. Middleton (London: Routledge, 1969); I. Lewis, Ecstatic Religion (Harmondsworth: Penguin, 1971).

8. "Exorzismus," *Reallexikon für Antike und Christentum* (Stuttgart: Hiersemann, 1969), 7: 44–117; "Geister," ibid. 1975), 9: 546–797.

9. P. Brown, "The Rise and Function of the Holy Man in Late Antiquity," *Journal of Roman Studies* 61 (1971): 88–89.

10. Greg. Tur. *VJ* 30. 127.

11. Paulinus *Carm.* 14. 35: "... latet ultor, poena videtur."

12. Victricius of Rouen *De laude sanctorum* 11, *PL* 20. 453D–454A.

13. T. Mommsen, *Römischer Strafrecht* (Leipzig: Dunckner and Humboldt, 1899): 405–8.

14. Sulpicius Severus *Dialogi* 3. 6, *PL* 20: 215C: "Videres sine interrogatione vexatos et sua crimina confitentes."

15. Ibid.

16. *Vita sancti Severi Viennensis presbyteri, Analecta Bollandiana* 5 (1886): 422: "Cum se daemonia nullis fantasiae figmentis ab eo possent ullatenus expedire, qui nulla quiverit locali visibilitate conspicari, sed negotium magis perambulans in tenebris."

17. Sulpicius Severus *Vita Martini* 21. 1.

18. Sulpicius Severus *Dialogi* 2(3). 15. 220–21.

19. Sulpicius Severus *Vita Martini* 18. 2.

20. K. K. Kirk, *The Vision of God* (London: Longman, 1931): 275–79.

21. *Vita Rusticulae* 13, *Monumenta Germaniae Historica, Scriptores Rerum Merovingicarum* (Hanover: Hahn, 1892), 4: 346.

22. Possessions came to happen more frequently at the shrine of Saint Felix as his festival approached: Paulinus *Carm.* 23. 58. Paulinus was well aware of the similarity between the behavior of the possessed and Bacchanalian trance states: *Carm.* 19. 276: "sacrorum memores veterum. ...." But he perceived the onset and resolution of the possession as a judicial enquiry by the saint.

23. *Statuta ecclesiae antiqua* 62 and 64, ed. G. Morin, *Sancti Caesarii Arelatensis Opera Varia* (Maredsous, 1942), 2: 94–95.

24. Greg. Tur. *LH* 8. 29. 349.

25. Ibid. 4. 11. 142.

26. Greg. Tur. *VP* 17. 2. 279.

27. Paulinus *Carm.* 14. 34.

28. Paulinus *Carm.* 26. 307–318.

29. Jerome *Ep.* 108. 13.

30. Paulinus *Carm.* 23. 66–68; 88–94.

31. Paulinus *Carm.* 26. 352.

32. F. Dölger, *Exorzismus im altchristlichen Taufritual* (Paderborn: F. Schöningh, 1909): 56–62; 75–76.

33. Paulinus *Carm.* 23. 124–125; Venantius Fortunatus *Carm.* 1. 1. 1: emicat aula potens solido perfecta metallo / quo sine nocte manet continuata dies / invitat locus ipse deum sub luce perenni.

34. *ILCV* 1769A.

35. Augustine *Ep.* 78. 3.

36. Venantius Fortunatus *Carm.* 2. 16. 30, on a thief of the vineyards of Saint Medardus: Te praesente tamen non licet esse reum.

37. Greg. Tur. *VM* 2. 4. 161; 2. 57. 178; 2. 58. 178; 2. 59. 179; 3. 46. 193; 4. 46. 211; *GC* 67. 338.

38. W. C. Till, "Die koptischen Rechtsurkunden aus Theben," *Sitzungsberichte der österreichischen Akademie der Wissenschaften* 244, 3 (Vienna, 1964): 173; L. S. B. Mac Coull, "Child Donations and Child Saints in Coptic Egypt," *East European Quarterly* 13 (1979): 409–415.

39. Greg. Tur. *VJ* 31. 127. The mingling of a potentially dangerous animal with the crowd at a festival is an ancient motif: L. Robert, *Hellenica* 11–12 (1960): 543, on an ox in the procession of Zeus Panamaros at Stratoniceia. (The miracle, of course, is that the ox got away without being sacrificed and eaten: "Ce brave boeuf sociable a d'ailleurs eu de la chance.") But in this case the good behavior of the ox was not considered to reflect the judicial "presence" of the god, but to mirror the impeccable religious decorum of the officiating priest.

40. Marcellus Burdigalensis, *De medicamentis*, ed. M. Niedermann, trans. J. Kollesch and D. Niebel, Corpus Medicorum Latinorum 5, 2 vols. (Berlin: Akademie Verlag, 1968); Aline Rousselle, "Du sanctuaire au thaumaturge: La guérison en Gaule au iv<sup>e</sup> siècle," *Annales* 31 (1976): 1085–1107.

41. J. F. Matthews, *Western Aristocracies and Imperial Court* (Oxford: Clarendon Press, 1974): 155–56; 159–60.

42. Marcellus *De medicamentis*, praef. 2. 2.

43. J. Grimm, "Über Marcellus Burdigalensis," *Kleinere Schriften* (Berlin: F. Dümmler, 1865): 121–25.

44. [H. J. Rose], "Superstition," *The Oxford Classical Dictionary*, 2d. ed. (Oxford: Clarendon Press, 1970): 1024: "The extraordinary mixture of traditional remedies and conjuring that has come down to us from Marcellus of Bordeaux."

45. V. Crapanzano, *The Ḥamadsha: A Study in Moroccan Eth-*

*nopsychiatry* (Berkeley and Los Angeles: University of California Press, 1973): 133. Loring M. Danforth, "The Role of Dance in the Ritual Therapy of the Anastenaria," *Byzantine and Modern Greek Studies* 5 (1979): 144–48.

46. *Miracula sanctae Theclae* 2, PG 85: 568C, ed. G. Dagron, *Vie et Miracles de Sainte Thècle* no. 18, Subsidia Hagiographica 62 (Brussels: Société des Bollandistes, 1978): 338. "The woman Ava was still a pagan. But she did not abominate Jews or keep away from Christians. She wandered around to all persons and rites." A girl cured at Saint Martin's shrine in Tours reverted to paganism on returnng to her village: Greg. Tur. *VM* 1. 2. 137.

47. Crapanzano, *The Ḥamadsha*, p. 179.

48. Rousselle, "Du sanctuaire au thaumaturge," p. 1095.

49. On the horrors of surgery, see Augustine *City of God* 22. 8. 106–19 on the terror of a man awaiting an operation.

50. Marcellus *De medicamentis*, praef. 3. 2.

51. Pliny the Younger *Ad amicos de medicina* cited by Marcellus, ibid., p. 34; Oribasius, *Liber ad Eunapium*, Corpus Medicorum Graecorum 6, 3 (Leipzig: Teubner, 1926): 317–18.

52. *Every Man His Own Doctor; or, The Poor Planter's Physician* (1734); Williamsburg, Va.: Printing and Post Office, 1971). I owe this reference, and a copy of this delightful manual, to the kindness of Guy Lytle.

53. Ibid., p. 45.

54. Rousselle, "Du sanctuaire au thaumaturge," p. 1092.

55. Marcellus ibid. *Carmen de speciebus* 1–4. 624.

56. Ibid. 20–21. 624: Quae quis natura bonis terraque marique / Edidit, illa suis altrix simul atque creatrix.

57. On doctors as the "sons of Asclepius": Glen Bowersock, *Greek Sophists in the Roman Empire* (Oxford: Clarendon Press, 1969): 69–70.

58. J. Grimm, "Über die marcellischen Formeln," *Kleinere Schriften*, pp. 152–72.

59. J. F. Matthews, "Gallic Supporters of Theodosius," *Latomus* 30 (1971): 1083–87.

60. Hence the wide range of material excerpted from books, from which a fifth-century reader might learn, for instance, the formula for toothpaste used by Octavia, sister of Augustus: Marcellus *De medicamentis* 13. 1: 2, and the remedies for pimples and hypertension of Livia Augusta: ibid. 15. 6: 248; 35. 6: 588. The ingredients are assumed to come from all over the known world: Marcellus *Carmen de speciebus* 41–67.

61. Marcellus *De medicamentis, praef.* 2: 2.

62. Ibid. 4: 2.

63. Hence the extreme reluctance with which many pagans accepted exorcism as a form of cure. What repelled them was not the belief in demons or the possibility of possession as such, as the *psychodrame* of authority and dependence implied in the cure: Plotinus *Enneads* 2. 9. 14: "This pretension may enhance their importance with the crowd gaping upon the powers of magicians." This was precisely what the crowd was supposed to do at a Christian shrine: Paulinus *Carm.* 14. 40: "... concurrit hiantum turba tremens hominum."

64. Marcellus *De medicamentis* 8. 30: 122.

65. Greg. Tur. *GM* 50: 73; see chap. 4, above, p. 000.

66. Rousselle, "Du sanctuaire au thaumaturge," p. 1095.

67. Incubation does not appear to have been practiced in Christian shrines in Gaul, with all that this implies: P. Brown, "Eastern and Western Christendom in Late Antiquity: A Parting of the Ways," *The Orthodox Churches and the West,* Studies in Church History 13, ed. D. Baker (Oxford: Blackwell, 1976): 18–19.

68. Greg. Tur. *VJ* 46: 132.

69. P. Brown, *Relics and Social Status in the Age of Gregory of Tours.* Stenton Lecture 1976 (Reading: University of Reading Press, 1977): 8–9.

70. Caesarius of Arles *Sermon* 44. 7, ed. G. Morin, *Corpus Christianorum* 103 (Turnholt: Brepols, 1953): 199.

71. Greg. Tur. *VM* 1. 26: 151: a huntsman suffering from panic fear in the woods of Francia is first treated by his kinsmen: "Ut mos rusticorum habet, sortilegis et hariolis ligamenta ei potiones deferebant.

72. Greg. Tur. *VJ* 46: 132.

73. Greg. Tur. *GM* 100: 105.

74. *Memoirs of the Baron de Tott on the Turks and Tartars,* vol. 1 (London: 1785) cited in F. Braudel, *The Mediterranean and the Mediterranean World in the Age of Philip II,* trans. S. Reynolds (London: Collins, 1972): 40.

75. Theodoret of Cyrrhus *Historia religiosa,* PG 82. 1444BC. Here the saints are called quite explicitly, "protectors of cities."

76. Sebastian Mariner, "La difusión del cristianismo como factor de latinizición," in *Assimilation et résistance à la culture gréco-romaine dans le monde ancien,* Travaux du VIᵉ Congrès International d'Etudes classiques, Madrid 1974 (Bucharest:

Editura Academiei; Paris: Les Belles Lettres, 1976): 271–82; J. Whatmough, *The Dialects of Ancient Gaul* (Cambridge: Harvard University Press, 1970): P. Brown, "Christianity and Local Culture in Late Roman Africa," *Journal of Roman Studies* 58 (1968), reprinted in *Religion and Society in the Age of Saint Augustine* (London: Faber, 1972): 289–90. J. Ropert, "Mentalité religieuse et régression culturelle dans la Gaule du iv$^e$ au viii$^e$ siècle," *Les cahiers de Tunisie* 24 (1976): 45–68.

77. J. Geffcken, *The Last Days of Greco-Roman Paganism*, trans. Sabine MacCormack (Amsterdam: North Holland, 1978): 25–29, with updated bibliographical references by the translator in the footnotes: 85–87. E. Wightman, "Il y avait en Gaule deux sortes de Gaulois," *Assimilation et résistance*, pp. 407–20, rightly stresses the role of preexisting divisions in Celtic society, rather than the impact of the Romans, in bringing about the breach with the past in Gaul.

78. F. Dölger, "Christliche Grundbesitzer und heidnische Landarbeiter," *Antike und Christentum* 6 (1958): 297–320.

79. Greg. Tur. *VM* 1. 27: 151; C. E. Stancliffe. "From Town to Country: The Christianisation of the Touraine," in *The Church in Town and Countryside,* Studies in Church History 16, ed. D. Baker (Oxford: Blackwell, 1979): 43–51, is a thoughtful survey.

80. I. N. Wood, "Early Merovingian Devotion in Town and Country," *The Church in Town and Countryside,* p. 72.

81. Greg. Tur. *VP* 80: 349: a peasant refuses to stop work for the festival of a saint: "Melius est enim opus necessarium in domo exercere, quam talem sanctum excolere."

82. In the wild country of Estremadura, the peasants simply murdered a newly installed holy man: "Melius est nobis mori quam tali domino servire": *The Vitas Patrum Emeritensium* 3. 8, ed. and trans. J. N. Garvin (Washington, D.C.: Catholic University of America, 1940): 158.

83. Greg. Tur. *VP* 80: 349: "O cruda rusticitas, quae semper in Deum et eius amicos murmuras."

84. For a possible analogy in the rise of healing cults among populations along the fringes of Greek influence in Thrace in the fourth and third centuries B.C.: I. Chirassi-Colombo, "Acculturation et cultes thérapeutiques," in *Les syncrétismes dans les religions de l'antiquité,* ed. F. Dunand and P. Lévêque (Leiden: Brill, 1975): 96–111: Apollo, the Greek god, by bringing both disease and healing also brings acculturation.

85. Greg. Tur. *VJ* 27: 127.

86. M. Renard, "Technique et agriculture en pays trévire et rémois." *Latomus* 18 (1959): 321–33; J. Kolendo, "La moisson-neuse antique," *Annales* 15 (1960): 1099–1114.

87. Greg. Tur. *VM* 1. 40: 150: "Ut putaris eum denuo fuisse renatum."

88. Greg. Tur. *VM* 1. 25: 151: "Oblitisque parentibus, in eo loco usque hodie pro beneficio accepto deservit."

89. Greg. Tur. *VM* 3. 46: 193: a woman from the countryside of Poitiers became paralyzed again when her masters sought her back; *VM* 2. 59: 179: a woman who had gained her freedom but was in danger of being sold off as a slave to the barbarians by her master's sons became paralyzed, "virtute sancti, quo facilius defensaretur." On the manner in which shrines offered protection to women, see chap. 2, above, p. 44.

90. Greg. Tur. *VJ* 45: 131.

91. J. Biraben, *Les hommes et la peste en France et dans les pays européens et méditerranéens* (Paris: Mouton, 1976), 1: 25–48.

92. Greg. Tur. *VP* 11. 2: 254: vision of Saint Martin to the womam Leubella laying down *oblationes* during the plague of 571.

93. Greg. Tur. *LH* 7. 44: 365, at a time of famine.

94. Greg. Tur. *LH* 9. 6: 418.

95. Ibid.: 417: "Ut iuniorem sibi beatum Martinum esse diceret, se vero apostolis coaequaret."

96. Ibid.: 420: "Multi enim sunt qui has seductiones exercentes populum rusticum in errore ponere non desistunt."

97. When Saint Boniface attempted to suppress the wandering preacher Aldebertus. the people complaimed, "quod eis sanctissimum apostolum abstulerim, patronum et oratorem virtutumque factorem et signorum ostensorem abstraxerim": *Concilium romanum ab annum 745, Monumenta Germaniae Historica: Concilia* (Hanover: Hahn, 1908), 2: 39–43. Aldebertus had had oratories dedicated and prayers offered in his mame. He had asked why men needed to go on pilgrimage to Rome. He had placed crosses and oratories in fields and at fountains. He forgave sins, which he could see without the need of confession. He distributed his own hair and nail clippings along with relics of Saint Peter.

98. Severus Endelechius *Carmen bucolicum de virtute signi Crucis* 105, *PL* 19. 798: Signum quod perhibent esse Crucis Dei / magnis qui colitur solus in urbibus.

99. Leo *Sermon* 82. 1, *PL* 54. 422–23; the anonymous *De vocatione ommium gentium* 2. 16, *PL* 51. 704A; Patrick *Confessio* 16,

*PL* 53. 809; Martin of Braga *In Basilica,* ed. C. W. Barlow, *Martini Bracarensis opera omnia* (New Haven, Conn.: American Academy at Rome. 1950): 282, which copies faithfully Sidonius Apollinaris *Carm.* 5, 7ff. on the tribes gathered to serve the emperor Majorian.

100. The impression given by the Touraine is that the greater Celtic holy sites had not been in occupation in Roman times and had not been replaced by any Romanized cult or building: J. Boussard, "Le peuplement de la Touraine du i$^{er}$ au viii$^e$ siècle," *Le Moyen Age* 60 (1954): 261–91; population was further dispersed from its previous centers in the course of the fifth and sixth centuries: Stancliffe, "From Town to Country," pp. 45–46.

101. J. Fontaine, "Séance de clôture," *Assimilation et résistance,* p. 549: "Mais le modèle devant lequel nous nous trouvons aux temps de la *pax Romana,* c'est celui de la coéxistance." On the hardening of attitudes, by which non-Christians and heretics were treated as "barbarians": P. Brown, "Approaches to the Religious Crisis of the Third Century," *English Historical Review* 83 (1968), reprinted in *Religion and Society,* pp. 90–91.

102. For an awareness of the imtimate interdependence between a sense of the binding quality of ritual and a specific form of social structure, I am deeply indebted to the work of Mary Douglas, *Natural Symbols* (New York: Vintage Books, 1973).

103. J. Le Goff, "Paysans et monde rural dans la litérature du haut moyen-âge." *Settimane di Studi del Centro Italiano di Studi sull'Alto Medio Evo* 13 (Spoleto: Centro di Studi sull'Alto Medio Evo. 1966): 723–41 and "Culture cléricale et tradition folklorique dans la civilisation mérovingienne," *Annales* 26 (1971): 587–603 in *Pour un autre moyen-âge* (Paris: Gallimard, 1977): 131–44. A repenetration of the (lay) upper classes by folklore occurs only in the twelfth century: J. Le Goff, "Mélusine maternelle et défricheuse," *Annales* 26 (1971): 587–603, *Pour un autre moyen-âge,* pp. 307–34; a similar "revival" took place in late medieval central Europe: F. Graus, *Volk, Herrscher und Heiliger im Reich der Merowinger,* Prague: Československa Akádemie Věd, 1965): 195–96.

104. I. N. Wood, "Early Merovingian Devotion in Town and Country," *The Church in Town and Countryside.* p. 76: "Heresy or *rusticitas* could emerge all too easily and against these the city was a bastion of true religion." The situation in late antiquity is analogous to that of Islam in Morocco: Ernest Gellner, *Saints of the Atlas* (London: Weibenfeld, 1969): 1–8, with the

vital difference that, in Morocco, it is the cult of the saints that is tinged with *rusticitas*.

105. William A. Christian, Jr.. *Person and God in a Spanish Valley* (New York: Seminar Press. 1972): 181: "The older set of divinities are not so much intercessors with God as they are intercessors with nature. . . . They mark off boundaries between village and village and boundaries between cultivated and uncultivated land. Throughout Spain they mark critical points in the ecosystem—contact points with other worlds."

106. Sulpicius Severus *Vita Martini* 13.

107. Ibid. 12: characteristically, as a former military man and town dweller, Martin mistook a funeral procession for such a ceremony.

108. Martin of Braga *De correctione rusticorum* 8, 10, 12, 16, ed. C. W. Barlow, p. 198; S. MacKenna, *Paganism and Pagan Survivals in Spain up to the Fall of the Visigothic Kingdom* (Washington, D.C.: Catholic University of America, 1938); M. Meslim, *La fête des kalendes de Janvier dans l'empire romain* (Brussels: Collection Latomus. 1970): 119–23.

109. Graus, *Volk, Herrscher und Heiliger*, pp. 481–84.

110. A. Dupront, "Pèlerinage et lieux sacrés," *Mélanges F. Braudel* (Toulouse: Privat, 1973), 2: 190–91; Rousselle, "Du sanctuaire au thaumaturge," p. 1104: "Mais ce qui fait la grande différence . . . c'est la substitution de l'homme au lieu."

111. Greg. Tur. *VP* 2: 300.

112. This, in itself, is not surprising, in that its function as a joining point for the region did not change: Victor Turner and Edith Turner, *Image and Pilgrimage in Christian Culture* (New York: Columbia University Press. 1978): 33: "Wherever communitas has manifested itself often and on a large scale the possibility of its revival exists, even when linked to a different religious system."

113. Greg. Tur. *VP* 2: 300. The foundation legend of the shrine of Saint Julian at Brioude tells the same story: the shrine competed for *ex voto*s with an adjacent pagan temple, at which a regular festival took place; but the *communitas* of which Brioude remained the center was linked to a network of aristocratic patronage relations which, in the foundation story, already stretched from Spain to Trier. Greg. Tur. *VJ* 4–7: 116–17.

114. P. Brown, *The Making of Late Antiquity* (Cambridge: Harvard University Press. 1978): 99–100.

115. Sir James George Frazer, *The Golden Bough,* pt. 2 (New York: MacMillan, 1935), 3: 218.

# Index